Joomla!® 3 Boot Camp: 30-Minute Lessons to Joomla!® 3 Mastery

Robin D. Turner and Herb Boeckenhaupt

Cengage Learning PTR

CENGAGE
Learning®

Australia • Brazil • Japan • Korea • Mexico • Singapore • Spain • United Kingdom • United States

Joomla!® 3 Boot Camp:
30-Minute Lessons to
Joomla!® 3 Mastery
Herb Boeckenhaupt and
Robin D. Turner

Publisher and General Manager,
Cengage Learning PTR:
Stacy L. Hiquet

Associate Director of Marketing:
Sarah Panella

Manager of Editorial Services:
Heather Talbot

Senior Acquisitions Editor:
Heather Hurley

Senior Marketing Manager:
Mark Hughes

Project/Copy Editor: Kezia Endsley

Technical Editor: Ryan Fidler

Interior Layout: Jill Flores

Cover Designer: Mike Tanamachi

Proofreader: Sue Boshers

Indexer: Larry Sweazy

Library of Congress Control Number: 2014932075

ISBN-13: 978-1-285-76467-2

ISBN-10: 1-285-76467-6

Cengage Learning PTR
20 Channel Center Street
Boston, MA 02210
USA

Cengage Learning is a leading provider of customized learning solutions with office locations around the globe, including Singapore, the United Kingdom, Australia, Mexico, Brazil, and Japan. Locate your local office at: **international.cengage.com/region**

Cengage Learning products are represented in Canada by Nelson Education, Ltd. For your lifelong learning solutions, visit **cengageptr.com**

Visit our corporate website at **cengage.com**

Printed in the United States of America
1 2 3 4 5 6 7 16 15 14

...to "Mummy"

We dedicate this book to the person we affectionately call "Mummy."
Doris Colgin is Robin's mom and encourages and supports our
book-writing and website-building efforts. She lives in Richmond,
Virginia, and hopefully very soon, will be a resident of
North Carolina, joining us here in Salisbury.

Doris is a kind and generous person and grew up "old school,"
when people planted gardens and harvested them to keep food on
the table. She has done her share of planting and harvesting.
Now, her life is at a more leisurely and relaxed pace.
We look forward to her becoming part of our household.

Doris, it is with great love and
affection that we dedicate this book to "Mummy."

...to Richmond Gage and his family

We also dedicate this book to a good friend and an excellent
instructor in his craft. We lost Richmond Gage just before Christmas
of 2013. He was the motorsports instructor at the Rowan-Cabarrus
Community College, a program he started. Hundreds of his graduates
found jobs in motorsports, NASCAR in particular.

We used to travel with a NASCAR race team and maintained
several motorsports websites and shopping carts for race teams.
We had much contact with Richmond at the race tracks and enjoyed
his great sense of humor. We also respected his seriousness and
approach to his job while at the track.

Richmond, we miss you, as do many of your
associates and staff at the college.

Acknowledgments

After getting our book-writing "sea legs" with Joomla! 1.6, which then changed to 1.7, and then changed to 2.5, we got smarter with this version. Our drafts were all done using Joomla! 3.0, and when the chapters were edited, we checked them against version 3.2.x and made changes as necessary late in the manuscript-editing process.

Because of all that, we would especially like to acknowledge our book editor, Kezia Endsley. She kept us crossing the T's and dotting the I's in the right places. Thanks for your sage advice on things and helping us produce the final product according to all the style manuals that applied. We enjoyed working with you.

To get a book published, you need to have the full support of the acquisitions editor at the publisher, and we had a good one. Thanks to Heather Hurley for helping us push this book up the mountain.

On the technical side of things, Ryan Fidler—who was also the technical editor on our first Joomla! book—came through with flying colors on this one. If we missed it, he found it. If we omitted it, he called it to our attention. His attention to the details of the exercises and the screenshots was a tremendous asset to the final product.

We also appreciate the layout staff, especially Jill Flores, for putting the book pages together and sticking the screenshot graphics into place and fitting the copy. Thanks so much for your efforts. As a former owner of a printing and graphics business in the Washington D.C. area, we've set our share of type and did thousands upon thousands of page layout over the years. We recognize and appreciate your efforts also.

Finally, our cats were an asset again to this book effort. One in particular shared in the writing duties by spending time in our laps and allowed us to use her as a hand rest in front of the keyboard. This cat is appropriately named "Laptop" because that's where she spends a lot of time. The purring and claw flexing was welcome.

We also thank the programmers and managers at iJoomla.com. The online companion for the book is using their GURU LMS for online courses and lessons, along with their Help Desk (MaQma) extension. Thanks guys, for helping us out in that direction. A lot of website users will benefit from your great extensions.

So, as *Joomla! 3 Boot Camp* goes to print, and the companion website at joomla3boot camp.com is assembled (using Joomla! 3.2, of course), we thank everyone involved and acknowledge your contributions, input, and assistance.

About the Authors

Robin Turner is a program head and instructor of accounting and economics at Rowan-Cabarrus Community College. She has 27 years of teaching experience at both the university and community college levels of higher education. She has authored print and digital educational support materials for over 25 college accounting texts and has reviewed an extensive number of business and economic college-level texts.

Robin has received a number of teaching excellence awards—she was a nominee for the R. J. Reynolds - NC Excellence in Teaching Award and a five-time winner of Who's Who Among American Teachers. She has distinguished herself and provided training in 21st Century Learning: Hybrid & Blended Courses - Bringing Web 2.0 to your classroom.

Robin is also the recipient of the 2009 Distinguished eLearning Educator by the Instructional Technology Council (ITC), among others. Additionally, Robin received awards for Phi Theta Kappa Outstanding Advisor, Phi Theta Kappa Horizon Advisor, State Council of Higher Education of Virginia Outstanding Faculty Award nominee, and Outstanding Faculty Among Students.

In her spare time, she loves to cook, makes candy to die for, reads mystery novels, gardens, and spends time golfing with her spouse, Herb Boeckenhaupt.

Herb Boeckenhaupt has an extensive background in the printing and graphics business for some 35 years in Maryland, serving clients in the Washington D.C. area. He retired from that business in the late '90s, just as the Internet was emerging. Following the sale of his business, he became a full-time website designer and developer and has helped hundreds of clients over the past 15 years.

His Joomla! involvement began shortly after Joomla! was "forked" from the Mambo platform. Shortly after that, he narrowed his focus and began building websites exclusively on the Joomla! platform. His expert knowledge of Joomla! 1.0, then Joomla! 1.5 was channeled into the Joomla! 1.6 version as soon as it was released in early beta form. He mastered Joomla! 2.5 and grabbed version 3.x by the horns and worked with Cengage Learning PTR to bring this book about.

About the Authors

During 2010, he brought this expertise to the North Carolina Phi Beta Lambda organization and developed a website for the chapter at Rowan-Cabarrus Community College and the State organization's Professional Division. He also was instrumental in moving the NC PBL State website from hard-coded to the Joomla! platform, where it now operates and functions with high efficiency.

He was recognized as the North Carolina Businessman of the Year by the NC PBL organization. He was then selected as the Phi Beta Lambda National Business Person of the Year, receiving the award in Orlando, Florida.

He also volunteers as a member of the Information Technologies and Web Technologies Advisory Committees at Rowan-Cabarrus Community College. Herb also builds Moodle courses. He recently completed a number of Moodle courses in Emergency Action Planning for 45 high-rise buildings in New York City, a project that now includes mobile apps, which he also constructs for corporations. He recently launched an online mobile app service for small businesses.

Contents

Contents

Chapter 7
Adding and Managing Extensions 99

Contents

Chapter 12
Components: Newsfeeds 173

Chapter 13
Components: Redirects 185

Chapter 14
Components: Search and Smart Search 195

Contents

Chapter 19
Modules. 259

Chapter 20
Plug-Ins 275

Contents

Chapter 24
Using the Menu System **317**

Chapter 25
Joomla! 3 Websites on Mobile Devices **325**

Chapter 26
Using Forms **337**

Contents

Chapter 27
Using Fonts with Joomla! 3 357

Chapter 28
Website Backups 373

Appendix A
Installing Joomla! 3 via cPanel 379

Exercises

Exercises

Chapter 19 – Modules
EXERCISE 19-1: DOWNLOADING THE GLOBAL NEWS EXTENSION MODULE
EXERCISE 19-2: INSTALLING THE GLOBAL NEWS EXTENSION MODULE
EXERCISE 19-3: CONFIGURING THE GLOBAL NEWS EXTENSION MODULE
EXERCISE 19-4: USING {LOADPOSITION} FOR INSERTING MODULES INTO ARTICLES

Chapter 20 – Plug-Ins
EXERCISE 20-1: EXPLORING PLUG-IN PARAMETERS

Chapter 21 – Templates
EXERCISE 21-1: OBTAINING AND DOWNLOADING THE DEMOTEMPLATEA
EXERCISE 21-2: OBTAINING AND DOWNLOADING THE DEMOTEMPLATEB
EXERCISE 21-3: INSTALLING THE TEMPLATES
EXERCISE 21-4: DESIGNATING THE DEFAULT TEMPLATE
EXERCISE 21-5: CHECKING MENU ASSIGNMENTS FOR TEMPLATES
EXERCISE 21-6: ASSIGNING A TEMPLATE TO A MENU LINK ITEM

Chapter 22 – Images and Media
EXERCISE 22-1: EXAMINING THE MEDIA MANAGER

Chapter 23 – Access Control List and Permissions
EXERCISE 23-1: VIEWING THE GROUP PERMISSIONS
EXERCISE 23-2: CREATING A USER GROUP
EXERCISE 23-3: SET VIEWING ACCESS LEVELS FOR A GROUP
EXERCISE 23-4: SETTING ACTION PERMISSIONS FOR A GROUP
EXERCISE 23-5: CREATING USERS AND ASSIGNING THEM TO A GROUP
EXERCISE 23-6: SETTING PERMISSIONS FOR THE CONTACTS COMPONENT
EXERCISE 23-7: SETTING PERMISSIONS FOR A CONTACT ITEM

Chapter 24 – Using the Menu System
EXERCISE 24-1: CREATING A MENU
EXERCISE 24-2: CREATING THE MENU MODULE AND ASSIGNING IT TO MODULE POSITION
EXERCISE 24-3: ADDING A MENU LINK ITEM FOR AN ARTICLE
EXERCISE 24-4: ADDING A MENU LINK ITEM FOR A CATEGORY
EXERCISE 24-5: ADDING A MENU LINK ITEM FOR A LIST OF CATEGORIES
EXERCISE 24-6: ADDING A MENU LINK ITEM FOR A LIST OF WEBLINKS
EXERCISE 24-7: HIDING THE MODULE FOR ONE MENU LINK ITEM

Chapter 26 – Using Forms
EXERCISE 26-1: USING PROFORMS BASIC
EXERCISE 26-2: USING FORM MAKER LITE
EXERCISE 26-3: ADDING A CAPTCHA ELEMENT

Chapter 27 – Using Fonts with Joomla! 3
EXERCISE 27-1: USING THE HD GFONTS PLUG-IN
EXERCISE 27-2: USING THE PHOCA FONT COMPONENT

Appendix A – Installing Joomla! 3 via cPanel

EXERCISE A-1: DOWNLOADING THE JOOMLA! 3 INSTALLATION FILES FROM THE JOOMLA.ORG WEBSITE

EXERCISE A-2: CREATING A DIRECTORY LOCATION FOR THE JOOMLA! 3 WEBSITE FILES

EXERCISE A-3: UPLOADING THE JOOMLA! 3 INSTALLATION FILES TO THE WEBSERVER

EXERCISE A-4: EXTRACTING THE FILES FROM THE JOOMLA! 3 INSTALLATION FILE

EXERCISE A-5: CREATING A MYSQL DATABASE

EXERCISE A-6: ASSIGNING A USER TO THE MYSQL DATABASE

Appendix B– Installing Joomla! 3 via the Parallels Plesk Control Panel

EXERCISE B-1: DOWNLOADING THE JOOMLA! 3 INSTALLATION FILES FROM THE JOOMLA.ORG WEBSITE

EXERCISE B-2: CREATING A DIRECTORY LOCATION FOR THE JOOMLA! 3 WEBSITE FILES

EXERCISE B-3: UPLOADING THE JOOMLA! 3 INSTALLATION FILES TO THE WEBSERVER

EXERCISE B-4: EXTRACTING THE FILES FROM THE JOOMLA! 3 INSTALLATION FILE

EXERCISE B-5: CREATING A MYSQL DATABASE

EXERCISE B-6: ASSIGNING A USER TO THE MYSQL DATABASE

Introduction

When the Internet started to catch on fire a while back, all website pages were hand-coded and a limited number of folks built them. Then a few programs came along that helped you put a website together with, of all things, a way to navigate from one web page to another. The earth shifted on its axis just a tad when that happened.

After a few years, this thing called a CMS (Content Management System) started showing up here and there, and plenty of people scratched their heads for a while about it. Then, the Internet ramped itself up to reach every household via those screeching modem thingies.

Joomla! was born right around that time. Since its inception, it has been downloaded over 35 million times and it is estimated that almost eight percent of the world's websites are built using one version of Joomla! or another.

Sure, there are other CMS programs available, but Joomla! is taking the lead in building an expandable platform and a highly functional website-building tool.

Extensions

The basic Joomla! website can be expanded by the use of *extensions*, which are mini-programs that run on top of and within the Joomla! core program. There are thousands upon thousands of extensions available.

If you want to build a dynamic site with many features and varying content, you don't need to learn programming to do it. You simply need to access the Joomla! Extensions Directory (JED) and pick what you need, do a quick install, and off you go.

The Joomla! framework to allow extensions is ever evolving, and the better it gets, the better the extensions that independent developers produce. Many of them distribute these extensions free of charge, or ask for a few dollars in exchange for their efforts. That's a fair enough situation.

Templates

Of course, websites built on the Joomla! platform would all look pretty much alike if it weren't for those wonderful extensions called *templates*. They give websites the look and feel and visual impact they need.

We can't even guess at the number of sources for templates, but there are a good bunch. Among the template sources, there are hundreds of them available from each one.

Building templates takes skill involving the visual aspects and the coding components, especially in understanding Cascading Style Sheets and how everything fits together.

Some templates are available for free, whereas others you'll have to pay for. That too is a fair enough situation. Spending a few dollars on a high-quality and highly functional template is well worth the cost.

Our attitude about extensions, which includes templates, is "if you are going to have a dance, rent the hall; don't buy the building." Which means that if you need a template of a certain type, instead of trying to do it yourself, spending umpteen hours coding one, give a template developer a few dollars and "rent the hall" to meet your needs.

The Book's Organization

This book is split into 28 chapters and two appendixes. The summary of the content is as follows:

◆ Chapter 1, "Introduction to Joomla! 3," gives you an introduction and overview of Joomla!, the CMS that has been downloaded more than 35 million times and is used worldwide to build websites in many different languages.

◆ Chapter 2, "Installing Joomla! 3," guides you through the installation process on a webserver.

◆ Chapter 3, "Joomla! 3 Default Installation," explains what is installed and what parts of a website are available immediately after the program is installed. This gives you the foundation by explaining the tools that Joomla! 3 puts at your disposal.

◆ Chapter 4, "How Joomla! 3 Works," explains how everything works. Once you understand what was installed and what is available, this chapter explains how everything works together.

◆ Chapter 5, "Fast Track Start," avoids chapter after chapter of theory and explanations and gets right into "how to…" activities. You'll learn to create a category into which an article is assigned, and then create a menu link item to display the article. This is basic Joomla! 3, and once you understand how the content-creation process works, you're ready to learn about Joomla! 3 administration one chapter at a time.

◆ Chapter 6, "Front Page Content and Layout," helps you understand how content is laid out on a Joomla! 3 website and then how to manage the layout that comprises the typical front page of a website. This chapter, as do the other chapters that follow, builds on what you learned in the previous chapter and exercises.

◆ Chapter 7, "Adding and Managing Extensions," explains how Joomla! 3 is operationally enlarged beyond the default installation. It not only explains what extensions are and what they can do, but also shows you how to add extensions and implement them.

◆ Chapter 8, "Components: Banners," is one of nine chapters that deals with the individual components that are added during the default installation process. In this chapter, banners are covered and exercises are included on how to include a banner on your website.

◆ Chapter 9, "Components: Contacts," shows you how to create and manage contacts on your website that are administrated through the Contact Manager component.

◆ Chapter 10, "Components: Joomla! Update," gives you a brief glimpse of how a Joomla! 3 installation can be updated and some of the things to be aware of when you modify the installation and then allow it to update.

◆ Chapter 11, "Components: Messaging," explains how to use the messaging feature to communicate with other website administrators, should you manage a website that has a number of content editors and managers along with yourself.

◆ Chapter 12, "Components: Newsfeeds," provides specific instructions on how to include newsfeeds from other websites into your Joomla! 3 website. This chapter also shows you how to create an "outbound newsfeed," whereby other websites can pull and display content from your website.

◆ Chapter 13, "Components: Redirects," covers an often overlooked component that allows you to redirect website visitors who are using a bookmark to access content that is no longer available. This chapter takes you through the steps needed to create the redirect to prevent visitors from seeing an error page when they attempt to access content that has been removed.

◆ Chapter 14, "Components: Search and Smart Search," are two components that allow you to add a simple and an advanced search feature to your website if you have a lot of content on your website.

◆ Chapter 15, "Components: Tags," includes exercises that demonstrate how to tag content to help users find articles easier and to group articles and content. This is done in a manner similar to how "categories" function, and supplements them by using tagging to group and relate content to other parts of the website.

◆ Chapter 16, "Components: Weblinks," is a component that works like the Contact Manager, by creating categories and links to other websites that might have content that relates to your website, or has reference material of interest to your visitors.

◆ Chapter 17, "Categories," deals with the major way content is organized on a Joomla! 3 website, be it articles, contacts, weblinks, or content generated by extensions. All of the "category" management activities are covered.

◆ Chapter 18, "Articles," covers the next phase of content management by creating articles that are assigned to categories created in the previous chapter. Then, menu link items are created to allow one-click easy access to the articles, or categories of articles in different display formats.

◆ Chapter 19, "Modules," explains modules, which are movable blocks of content of many different types. Module content is not placed in the same location as the main content area, but are located where there are "module positions" on the templates used to display the web pages.

◆ Chapter 20, "Plug-Ins," covers plug-ins, which are often overlooked but play an important part in many areas of content display. Plug-ins kick into action when something "triggers" them to do this or that on a website. Components and modules are often associated with plug-ins to perform certain types of content-display events.

◆ Chapter 21, "Templates," covers templates. They are the visual side of a Joomla! 3 website, and while they are extensions, they have certain characteristics and administrative functions that all website administrators should know about.

◆ Chapter 22, "Images and Media," deals with how images and other visual content is managed on a Joomla! website. Images can be added to articles, along with videos or links to other media content, and these all need to be managed by the administrator. You'll learn how to do so in this chapter.

◆ Chapter 23, "Access Control List and Permissions," is the part of a Joomla! 3 website that offers administrators the ability to control who sees what and who can manage and edit what content. This is a powerful feature of Joomla! 3 that is used primarily on larger websites that have more than one administrator, or have many managers responsible for different parts of the website content.

◆ Chapter 24, "Using the Menu System," covers how to create a menu, place the menu module into a module position on the template, and then create individual menu link items to open any kind of content to be displayed. Content cannot be accessed without the use of menus. This chapter explains the fundamentals an administrator must know to create and manage menus effectively.

◆ Chapter 25, "Joomla! 3 Websites on Mobile Devices," covers all the issues related to preparing your website so it can be viewed properly on mobile devices, including the problems with viewing websites on mobile devices, creating responsive templates, testing templates for responsiveness, and more.

◆ Chapter 26, "Using Forms," explains how to use forms effectively on your website, where you can obtain form extensions, how to determine the form requirements of your website, how to use two different form extensions on the same website, and how to add spam prevention to your forms.

◆ Chapter 27, "Using Fonts with Joomla! 3," explains the fundamentals of using fonts on your Joomla! 3 website. This chapter includes topics such as using CSS, using the HD Gfonts plug-in extension, and using the Phoca Font component. It also discusses why it's best to avoid using font replacement, and why it's better to use fonts in moderation.

◆ Chapter 28, "Website Backups," explains why it's critical to back up your website consistently and often. You'll learn about some of the best extensions for managing backups and for adding website security, as well as learn how to find backup extensions in the JED.

- ◆ Appendix A, "Installing Joomla! 3 via cPanel," explains how to prepare your webserver using cPanel in order to install Joomla! 3.
- ◆ Appendix B, "Installing Joomla! 3 via the Parallels Plesk Control Panel," explains how to prepare your webserver using Plesk to install Joomla! 3.

Who Should Read This Book?

This book is written for anyone who wants to learn how to use Joomla! 3 to build and manage a personal or corporate website.

This book is specifically written with the Joomla! beginner in mind, with practical exercises on how to do things and build a website. If you have never created a Joomla! 3 website, this book covers installation and administration of your first Joomla! website.

Advanced users will be able to learn about the new features and methods used to administer a Joomla! 3 website.

If you are assigned to the task of administering a Joomla! 3 website after it has been installed, this book will serve as a reference to manage all the different components, extensions, and other content areas of the website.

Software and Versions

This book was written based upon Joomla! Version 3.2, which may have been updated since the book was published. Because Joomla! 3 is dynamically evolving with updates, there is a companion website at **joomla3bootcamp.com**, which covers updates through Version 3.5.x.

The website will be maintained for book users to stay on top of the many changes that may come about before the next major version of Joomla! is released, which might be 4.0, depending on what the programming team decides to release.

It is suggested that Joomla! 3.x.x users always update their installations with the latest incremental update within the "3.2" versions.

Conventions Used in This Book

Throughout this book, certain conventions are used to call attention to special actions in exercises, or other references, such as:

Things that the users should type appear in **boldface**.

Monospace font is used for database and filenames.

Websites appear in a **special font** as well.

Notes and sidebar text are included for important topics or to point out special items that a website administrator should be aware of while managing the website.

The exercise steps should be followed sequentially. You should complete the exercises sequentially in each chapter, because exercises in later chapters may rely on content you created previously.

USE YOUR DOMAIN NAME

On some screenshots, you will see the domain name of **joomla3bootcamp.com**. This is the domain being used for examples, exercises, and other tutorials associated with the explanations and exercises in this book. Substitute your domain name for **joomla 3bootcamp.com** whenever you see it on screenshots throughout this book.

The joomla3bootcamp.com Website

What you make of your experience with Joomla! is up to you. But one thing is for sure; there's no lack of resources if you want to find out anything about how the program operates. There are tons of videos, if you search for them. There is also an abundance of books that profess to offer this or that with respect to learning Joomla!

Because of these variances, we have taken a new approach to book-writing about Joomla! We recognized that during the time a book was being prepared, the Joomla! code folks will be making changes, doing updates, and issuing a new version.

This is why this book covers version 3.2 and has an online companion website that adds not only additional learning information, but is also a good reference point for upgrades. The website, at joomla3bootcamp.com, is committed to updating until Joomla! 4.0 is released, which might be late in 2014 or early 2015. The book and the website provide you, the website builder or administrator, with a treasure trove of additional information about using Joomla! 3.x.x.

On the website, you will find updates about Joomla! and, if we messed up in the book, we will post the corrected information in a special section on the website. There will also be online courses. A "Master Course" will give you a learning platform upon which to apply exercises. If you don't want to take the full course, which will issue a certificate upon completion, you can just pick and choose individual lessons about how to do things in Joomla! 3.

There is also a Help Desk that will be a resource for getting help and assistance if you are stuck somewhere in the website-building process. An open forum is also on the website to give all users a platform to exchange information and help each other.

Please visit the website and see if it can help you be a better Joomla! administrator.

joomla3bootcamp.com

- Book Updates
- Joomla! 3.x.x Updates
- More Appendices
- Topic Resources
- Exercise Resources
- "How to..." Lessons
- Help Desk
- FAQ Resources
- Extension Reviews

Joomla! 3 Boot Camp Online Companion

INSTANT ACCESS

JOOMLA! 3 BOOT CAMP: ACADEMY

JOOMLA! 3 BOOT CAMP: HELP DESK!

JOOMLA! 3 BOOT CAMP: FORUM

JOOMLA! 3 RESOURCES

Chapter 1

Introduction to Joomla! 3

Learning Objectives

What's included in this chapter:

- ◆ Understanding where Joomla! came from.

- ◆ Understanding what Joomla! is used for.

- ◆ Understanding Joomla!'s evolution to its current version.

- ◆ Understanding what a Content Management System (CMS) is.

- ◆ Understanding and using the improvements in Joomla! 3.

- ◆ Using the exercises in this book for best results.

Compared to other open source Content Management Systems (CMS), Joomla! hasn't been around that long. But, for the short time it's been available, Joomla! has made a huge impact in the world of CMS websites. There are millions of Joomla!-based websites on the Internet today and that number is growing by leaps and bounds as information about Joomla! circulates. Over 35 million copies of the Joomla! software have been downloaded and it is used on more than 2.7 percent of the world's websites.

Joomla! was not created from the ground up as someone's bright idea. Joomla! was derived from another program called *Mambo*, using the open source software *forking* method, which enables you to use the source code and build on it with your own code.

The history of Mambo and Joomla! has many versions, depending upon what you read and who wrote the information about the evolution of Joomla! from Mambo.

In a nutshell, Joomla! started as Mambo, which was created by an Australian group as far back as 2002. Without elaborating on all the details of how and why Joomla! spun off from Mambo, suffice to say that a good foundation was laid for what is now known as Joomla! You can visit the Mambo Wiki at http://en.wikipedia.org/wiki/Mambo_(software) for more about the history of Mambo.

How Joomla! Arrived on the Scene

As happens with many projects, the Mambo to Joomla! evolution not being the exception, the participants had a separation of thoughts on project direction. The result of this separation of minds was that Joomla!, which was a near mirror image of Mambo, found its first release as Joomla! 1.0 not long afterward.

The transition from Mambo to Joomla! was rather seamless. The Mambo license permitted others to take the code and start their own projects. In open source parlance, as stated earlier, Joomla! is a "fork" of Mambo and now runs as a completely separate project. There are an increasing number of code differences between the two, to the point where Joomla! 3 isn't a fork anymore, but a product standing in its own right.

As a result of this forking by Joomla! from Mambo in 2005, the headquarters of Joomla! shifted from Australia to Europe, resulting in a major ground swell of interest in Joomla! across Europe as a powerful website platform that was available at no cost. There are thousands upon thousands of websites built on the Joomla! 1.0 version of the platform, mostly for websites outside of the United States where Joomla! has been a little slow in catching on as a website development tool. More information is available on the Joomla! Wiki at http://en.wikipedia.org/wiki/Joomla. Successive versions of Joomla! caught on in the United States, where it is now the go-to CMS platform of choice for thousands upon thousands of personal, public, and commercial websites.

Joomla! 1.0 progressed through code improvements to version 1.0.15 and at that point, the Joomla! team discontinued support of that version and shifted emphasis to a completely reworked package for Joomla! They introduced version 1.5 in early 2008. The changes and enhancements were plentiful and resulted in a greatly improved CMS product. As a result, Joomla! now has a huge following in both Europe and the United States, and all other countries across the world are grabbing the platform for their websites in their respective languages.

Shortly after the Joomla! 1.5 release, it became obvious to the Joomla! core team that Joomla! needed some more major improvements in order to bring 1.5.x to a higher level. After examining the options, the team determined that a complete rework was necessary and proceeded to develop version 1.6, which was renamed 1.7, and then version 2.5.x, the last released version prior to Joomla! 3. The team determined that they needed to streamline the software's websites and, rather than patching up past code, they decided a new version was the better approach. We wholeheartedly agree, and the end-product is a greatly improved Joomla! 3 platform.

Who Runs Joomla?

It took a while to get fully organized, but the group, Open Source Matters, Inc. (OSM), "runs" the Joomla! project and manages all aspects of its programming, availability, and a bunch of other things. At first, the programmers who forked Joomla! from Mambo ran it, but since then, the leadership team has been more formally organized and structured, including all the various interest areas.

The programming group is comprised of folks who develop the code, streamline things, and make sure the platform at present, and that of the future, has good code and runs properly. One of their biggest challenges is to make sure the versions of Joomla! 3 are compatible with the extensions created by third-party developers, which is a challenge in itself.

The bottom line is that there are many, many people giving time and talent to the Joomla! project and many more who contribute little parts here and there. We thank all of them for their efforts.

OSM is internationally diverse, with leadership and involvement coming from all over the world. The ultimate authority for Joomla! is OSM and information about the group and its leadership can be found on the joomla.org website.

Joomla! Depends on Other Software

Joomla! is based on the PHP scripting language and the MySQL ("my see-quill") database system. Both of these are free and open source and almost every website server provides them for software developers and website builders who host websites.

Because of PHP/MySQL, which are also upgraded periodically, software based on them will likewise be upgraded. For example, Joomla! 3 requires PHP 5.3.1 or a later version to run properly (Figure 1-1). If your hosting server is configured with PHP versions prior to 5.3.1, you won't be able to install Joomla! 3.

More about all this in the next chapter–it's an important issue, so pay attention to that subject when you get to it.

These are the minimum versions of PHP and MySQL needed to run Joomla! 3 on a webserver.

Webservers operating with MSSQL or PostgreSQL databases can also run Joomla 3!

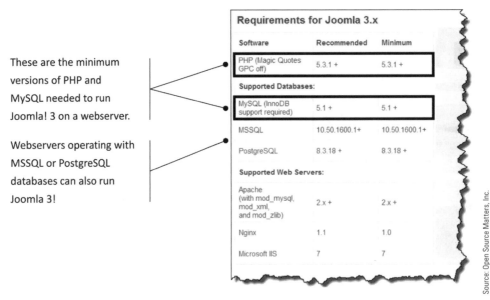

Figure 1-1 *When Joomla! 3 is installed in a typical leased server location, chances are that it will be configured for PHP and MySQL, although other databases may be used, as noted. Make sure that any server location on which you plan to host your website has the minimum requirements as shown.*

What Is a CMS Anyway?

The term "CMS" has been used to describe Joomla! as a product. But what is a CMS? It's an acronym for "Content Management System," which means that the website content can be managed, created, or edited, without having to know how to do website coding or how to design a website.

Typically, there are programmers, designers, and then content managers or editors who are involved in the overall management of a website. As an individual wanting to build your own website, and if you use a CMS, the programming and design tasks are not something that you need to learn. The content is what you are interested in managing. Joomla! 3 has accomplished that goal (Figure 1-2).

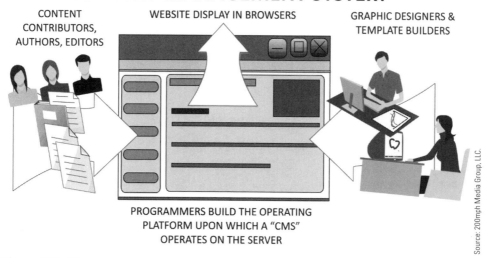

CONTENT MANAGEMENT SYSTEM

CONTENT CONTRIBUTORS, AUTHORS, EDITORS

WEBSITE DISPLAY IN BROWSERS

GRAPHIC DESIGNERS & TEMPLATE BUILDERS

PROGRAMMERS BUILD THE OPERATING PLATFORM UPON WHICH A "CMS" OPERATES ON THE SERVER

Source: 200mph Media Group, LLC.

Figure 1-2 *Three groups comprised of programmers, designers, and content managers are involved in a CMS website. You do not need the skills of all three to build and manage a website based on the Joomla! 3 platform.*

Extending Joomla! Beyond the Core Level

Joomla! in its basic form, "out-of-the-box" so-to-speak, has certain core functionalities built into it. The software operates in a certain way and has a limit to what it can do, given the method the developers initially chose to set it up for operation. This was done on purpose because the whole idea is to provide a platform with core features upon which other developers in the open source community can build upon. And they do, as evidenced by the thousands of extensions that are available for previous versions of Joomla!

What makes Joomla! such a great "CMS" is the manner in which its functionality can be enlarged. This is accomplished through Joomla! compatible *extensions*, which fall into six basic categories (Figure 1-3):

◆ Components
◆ Modules
◆ Plug-ins
◆ Templates
◆ Libraries
◆ Languages

Each of these is explained in greater detail in other chapters found later in this book, so don't worry about what they are or what they do at this point. Suffice it to say that after reading this book and following the tips and doing the exercises, you'll not only have a fundamental mastery of Joomla!, but also a working knowledge of the ways to extend its capabilities via extensions.

EXTENSIONS EXPAND THE PLATFORM

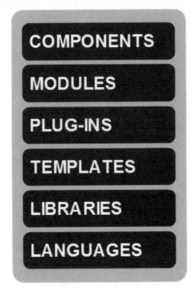

The Joomla! 3 "core" platform is built upon several different types of databases and most all standard website servers.

Once Joomla! 3 is installed, the content of the website is managed by the website Administrator. Other administrators may be added that manage content but do not manage the website at the same level as the Administrator.

COMPONENTS

MODULES

PLUG-INS

TEMPLATES

LIBRARIES

LANGUAGES

The operation of the Joomla! 3 platform along with the Extensions, provide the display, visual design and ability to manage the content of the website.

Extensions allow a wide range of content to be part of a Joomla! 3 website.

Additional Extensions may be added at any time to meet any content needs.

Source: 200mph Media Group, LLC.

Figure 1-3 *The Joomla! 3 "core" platform supports the use of extensions, which function to provide and display content in many different ways, resulting in how the website functions, looks and what content is displayed.*

Improvements in Version 3

Joomla! 3 has a number of distinct improvements over version 2.5.x. Probably the most significant areas are in content and user management areas of the backend in general. The Administrator backend was completely revamped in how things work and how Administrators "do things" and the method by which content is created. These changes were implemented after the Joomla! open source community at-large submitted a long wish list. The Joomla! core team selected the elements determined to be the best ones for the next release version and that meet the longer term goals of the developer team.

For example, many websites that started using Joomla! early had content provided by many different content authors. These early versions were severely limited in how these "users" or "editors" were managed with regard to what they could access and which part of a website they were allowed to edit. Joomla! 1.6 through 2.5 had a completely new system for user management, a great improvement with much flexibility for user or editor managing. Joomla! 3 solidified and retained those features, which is a major area of concern to large website managers and administrators.

Joomla! 3 also has an abundance of additional improvements that only developers and computer code geeks understand. This is technical stuff and you don't need to know it to install and run an efficient Joomla!-based website so we won't even delve into it. In a nutshell, Joomla! 3 is better than 2.5 and let's just leave it at that for the time being.

Another major improvement included in Joomla! 3 was the ability to set up the website to show content on desktops and laptops equally well, but also be able to display your site on mobile devices with the same content in an optimized configuration.

There were also many improvements added for developers, such as Twitter Bootstrap support and jQuery support, and this is the last time you will likely see those terms used in the remainder of this book, except maybe when you get to templates (covered in Chapter 21, "Templates").

There are a host of other "leap-forward" improvements in Joomla! 3, but rather than reviewing them all right now, this section shows you how to install, administer, and use Joomla! 3 to build your website project and start adding extensions. Installing extensions is relatively simple. The configuration of each might be complicated, depending upon the skills of the developer who created the extension and his or her ability to make them user friendly.

In many cases, computer science students doing a project for extra credit will create these extensions. Sometimes they come out of the Google Summer of Code Project, with which Joomla! has had a long association. Some of these have resulted in great add-ons to Joomla! Others–well, let's just say they missed the target.

> **BE SURE TO GET YOUR MONEY'S WORTH**
>
> Make sure the extension does what you want it to do before buying it. Do your due diligence and research before you put money on the table for extensions that may not do the job. And, above all, make sure you acquire extensions that are natively compatible with Joomla! 3. More on this subject in Chapter 7, "Adding and Managing Extensions."

Expanded Features in Joomla! 3

One of the major features of the Joomla! 3 CMS is its function as a solid platform upon which any number of website formats can be constructed. This is accomplished through the implementation of extensions and templates. Extensions add the functionality and content configuration for the website. Templates are used to change the "look." In fact, different templates can be assigned to different parts of the website to give each a distinct visual appearance. This neat trick is covered in detail later in Chapter 21.

Although the terms being used may not be exactly clear to you right now, templates typically represent different elements of a website than those features added through the extension process. Templates are actually extensions tried and true, but when discussed in this book, may appear to be separate website elements. They are, but they're not, so keep this ambiguity in mind when you run across what appears to be conflicting statements. Templates are extensions, but due to their special use, they are sometimes discussed without that distinction.

Building Your Website with Extensions

By using extensions, you can change the entire website's purpose. Let's say you install Joomla! as a general content site, but want to use it for blogging. This is accomplished by adding an extension to the basic install, and this can completely change the manner of how the content is displayed and its composition.

Extensions come in many forms, both free and paid. Some you don't pay for, some you must pay to obtain. Either way, the core Joomla! install instantly becomes a blogging site as soon as you install and activate the blogging extension. Or, you can make it a combination general content site *with* a blogging feature page. The possibilities are endless.

One point to keep in mind when looking for extensions is that there can be several extensions that do the same thing, or operate in a similar manner. Find out which one will work best for you, but don't expect the developers to tell you. These guys (and gals) are programmers and usually are not good at product support or help questions. After a while, you'll find out which companies or developers have the best extensions for Joomla! and you'll be looking at their products on a regular basis.

Not only can you add blogging, extensions come in many other forms and some 6,000-plus extensions are listed in the Joomla! Extensions Directory (JED), 2,000 of which are for Joomla! 3. Granted, not every one of them is going to be compatible with Joomla! 3. The big problem with extensions is that very few written for earlier versions of Joomla! will work in the current release. Only those extensions written specifically for Joomla! 3 should be installed, as previous versions don't work and may break the website when you attempt to install them. This topic is addressed in Chapter 7.

It's not a bad idea to make it a habit of visiting the JED daily to keep abreast of latest releases that have been added and updated.

Notes About How This Book Works

At many locations throughout this book, there will be times when certain information is presented in tip boxes and illustrations, both for emphasis and to call special attention to a topic or point of information. Pay attention to these bits of information as you will find them very helpful in the long run.

Also, during some of the practical exercises outlined in this book, some items on the figures are not discussed. This is done to streamline content in an effort to allow you to work the exercise without worrying about information that isn't relevant to the task. We might mention these control elements in the text or in graphics. But, if you don't see anything, it's because the controls do not apply to what you are doing to complete the steps of the current exercise.

Additionally, once the function of a button or action has been defined, and that action serves the same function in a different manager, it will not likely be explained again. An example is Save. It is Save in all the managers, and performs the same action. So, once such a function or action has been explained, it will not be explained every time the term or instruction appears in the book.

The 30-Minute Learning Concept

When starting out using the Joomla! 3 platform, you might find the tasks and content management actions somewhat confusing. Knowing that, we designed the exercises in this book to teach you any administrative task in 30 minutes or less.

An example of this 30-minute strategy is found in Chapter 5, "Fast Track Start." The exercises in Chapter 5 show you how to create a category, create an article and assign it to the category, and then create a menu link item, that when clicked, displays the article on the front page of the website. You can do it all in less than 30 minutes by just following the instructions, even if you don't know anything about Joomla! 3.

All other content, which the default Joomla! 3 installation can create, is taught in the same manner, whereby exercises take you step-by-step through the processes from start to finish, in 30 minutes or less.

Try consulting the "How Do I…" web reference by looking up what you want to do and then following the steps outlined to accomplish the task.

The "How Do I…" Reference Repository

As a new Joomla! 3 user, you will likely ask the question "How do I …" many times while you familiarize yourself with the administrator backend of the Joomla! 3 website.

Joomla! 3 admittedly has a steep learning curve on the backend. Learning how to accomplish content-development tasks and where to find the controls and manager screens can lead to frustration. This book will minimize the frustrations of learning how to use new, or unfamiliar, software.

Although this book covers all of the tasks and actions to accomplish them, and spells out step-by-step instructions, it's not an all-inclusive reference. Therefore, we've created a "How do I…" online reference, which serves as a virtual extension of this book.

Created in an FAQ-style format, the online reference located at **http://joomla3bootcamp .com** contains a lookup-style information repository. The instructions for the tasks have been categorized for easy searching and then broken down further into specific elements, which are accessible with only a few mouse clicks.

After the topic has been narrowed down to the task, the same exercise-format instructions as found in this book guide you with step-by-step instructions. These steps not only show you what to do, but also explain the "how and why" of the actions being taken to create or manage the content of the website.

Joomla! Version Updates

If Joomla! 3 has updates that change processes or modify how tasks are accomplished via the backend of the website, the online reference explains those items. Step-by-step instructions will also be added for the changes or revisions.

These updates will be accessible online until the next major release of Joomla! 3, which we understand will be version 3.5 sometime in late 2014. It is possible that a 4.0 version is on the horizon. Of course, the version numbering and release schedules can change at any time, and the online reference to the Joomla! 3.x.x will be maintained until the next major revision is released.

ANATOMY OF JOOMLA! 3

Joomla! 3 is actually a three-part software product and changes can be made in any part at any time with updates or upgrades. Here are the parts:

Joomla! Platform. This is the "core" of Joomla!, programming-wise, and an area that you will likely never venture into, nor have a need to do so. It's one of those things in a CMS that is transparent to the users, and usually remains that way.

Joomla! Framework. Joomla! operates under an MVC Framework, which means Model-View-Controller. This framework displays the different content items on the page, which the template interprets based on the HTML and CSS design. Just about every part of a Joomla! website that displays content uses the MVC Framework. This is an area that you will not likely need to explore as an administrator.

Joomla! CMS. This is the side of Joomla! 3 that you work with as a website administrator. Figure 1-2 illustrated the relationship among the different parts of Joomla!

If you do nothing else but master the content side of Joomla! 3, there won't be any limits to the types of websites you can build for yourself or others.

academy.joomla3bootcamp.com

Joomla! 3
Online Courses
& Mini-Lessons
with Certificates

Take the full course and obtain a certificate or individual Lessons to sharpen Admin skills

✔ **Learn Joomla! 3 FAST!**

✔ **Fully Understand Joomla! 3**

✔ **Courses for Administrators**

✔ **"How to..." Task Lessons**

✔ **Help Desk & Extensive FAQs**

Boot Camp Courses & Lessons are tailored to all skill levels and teach Joomla! 3 in detail

Joomla! 3 Boot Camp Courses & Lessons are powered by

Guru Award-winning Joomla! eLearning Software available from:

iJoomla.com

Chapter 2

Installing Joomla! 3

Learning Objectives

What's included in this chapter:

- ◆ Installing Joomla! 3 on a website.
- ◆ Entering the configuration information.
- ◆ Entering the database information.
- ◆ Entering sample data into the installation.
- ◆ Removing the installation folder.
- ◆ Logging in as the "super user" administrator.

Preparing the Webserver

At this point, depending upon which webserver is provided by the ISP to host your website, the Joomla! 3 installation files need to be hosted. This process involves several steps that include:

Step 1. Create a location for the Joomla! 3 files.

Step 2. Upload the Joomla! 3 installer file.

Step 3. Extract the working files from the installer file.

Step 4. Create a database that connects to Joomla! 3.

Step 5. Create a user who has privileges for the database.

Once you complete those steps, the actual Joomla! 3 installation can begin. It consists of configuring the program, connecting it to the database, and installing sample content.

Picking a Webserver Type

Joomla! 3 is a web-based program, which means that it must be installed on the webserver. Joomla! 3 does not run on a local computer. It must be located on a webserver that is set up to host a website with public access to it via a standard web browser.

If your ISP provides the standard cPanel, go to Appendix A, "Installing Joomla! 3 via cPanel," to configure the hosting. This version of control panel is probably the most frequently used by ISPs, although there are others, including custom control panels specific to the ISP. If your ISP provides the Parallels Plesk control panel, go to Appendix B, "Installing Joomla! 3 via the Parallels Plesk Control Panel," to configure the hosting for that type of control panel.

> ### WHICH CONTROL PANEL SHOULD YOU USE?
> If you do not know which control panel is provided with your hosting account with the ISP, ask them first, before you sign up and pay money. The cPanel sometimes has a small additional monthly cost above the hosting cost. It is worth the few dollars to have it available to manage your domain and website.

As far as Joomla! 3 goes, each type of control panel does essentially the same thing. They host the files, have database functions, and otherwise allow a website to be installed and accessed.

Of course, the control panels serve more functions, but they do not associate with Joomla! 3 per se. They have emails, FTP services, and a long list of other controls. But, for the most part, Joomla! 3 only needs an on-server location for installation and a database with which to connect and operate.

More than one instance of Joomla! 3 may be installed in any domain. For example, it can be installed in the "root" directory, and then additional instances can be installed within sub-directories. Separate instances generally should have their own database.

IS YOUR WEBSERVER CONFIGURED FOR JOOMLA!?

Joomla! 3 cannot be installed without configuring the respective webserver type using a control panel. If you have a standard cPanel, go to Appendix A. If you have a Parallels Plesk control panel, go to Appendix B. When your webserver has been configured as per these appendixes, return to this chapter and resume the Joomla! 3 installation at this point.

Installing the Website

Once the Joomla! 3 installation files are on the webserver, the next series of actions required is to install Joomla! 3 by connecting the program to the database created in the exercises in Appendix A or B, depending upon which type of webserver platform the ISP provided.

The installation of Joomla! 3 takes place using only five static screens. These screens are relatively straightforward and, if you entered the correct information for the database, this is a pretty simple process. Each screen is accessed by completing the information requested on the previous one and then by executing a Next or Install action.

Screen 1: Main Configuration—Adds the site name and the super user administrator information.

Screen 2: Database Configuration—Connects the installation to a specific database and identifies the assigned user.

Screen 3: Finalisation—Options to insert sample data into the installation. (Note the U.K. English spelling in the word "finalisation." You will find spelling differences like this throughout the Joomla! administrator screens.)

Screen 4: Multiple Information—Displays four information sections of the installation and identifies any issues. At this point, the installation starts and a progress bar indicates that the installation is in progress. This can take a few minutes based on the speed of your Internet connection.

Screen 5: Success and Finishing Up—Displays the "Congratulations! Joomla! 3 is now installed" message, indicating a successful installation. It also has the Remove Installation Folder button, which you should click to execute. When the removal is completed, the Site or Administrator link buttons are displayed.

Setting up a webserver to host a Joomla! 3 website is more complicated than actually installing it. Once the database/user is created, the rest of the install is a matter of entering the information on the installation screens.

Starting the Install

Here are the steps you need to take to perform a typical install of Joomla! 3 on a web-server:

Step 1. Complete the configuration information.

Step 2. Complete the database connection.

Step 3. Install the sample data into the website.

Step 4. Finish the installation tasks.

To start the installation process, open any web browser and type your website address (include the subfolder if you chose to locate the extracted Joomla! 3 files there) into the location bar (http://domainname.com/myfirstsite/).

When you start, if you typed the path correctly, your browser will automatically connect to the opening page of the install process (Figure 2-1).

There are only four screens involved in the installation process. Once you have completed the configuration of the webserver, the actual installation of Joomla! 3 is relatively easy; you simply follow the steps in the next section.

Installing Joomla!: Five Steps to a Successful Installation

Perform these steps as you read along:

Step 1. Enter the website and user information (Figure 2-1). This first part of the process requires information about the website and the administrator who, in Joomla! 3–speak, is called the *super user*. When the information is complete, click **[F]** Next to proceed.

Site Name—Enter the **[A]** website name, which will appear at the top of the backend after log in.

Description—Enter the **[B]** keywords to describe your website for search engines (optional).

Admin Email—Enter the **[C]** super user's email address, which might be different from your own if you are installing Joomla! 3 for a client. It is best to use your email address, and then set up an additional super user account for the client.

Admin Username—Enter the **[D]** super user's username for backend login. This is not the username for the database. It should be different.

Admin Password—Enter the **[E]** password for the super user. This can be changed by the super user once he logs in to the backend.

16

Site Offline—If you do not want the website to display immediately after Joomla! 3 is installed, select Yes. The default No makes the site accessible and visible immediately. For this installation, set this option to No, because the website is being installed into a subdirectory and isn't immediately visible at the website "root" level.

Figure 2-1 *This first screen of the installation process asks for essential information relative to the website and designates the super user, who will be the primary administrator.*

Step 2.   Connect Joomla! 3 to a database (Figure 2-2). Next comes the part where Joomla! 3 actually connects to the database that was created when the webserver was configured. During installation, Joomla! 3 creates tables in the database and enters data into them.

Database Type—Select **[G]** MySQL as the choice of database. MySQLi database type is another option, but MySQL is the preferred database choice.

Host Name—Use the default **[H]** localhost. Some ISPs often have different locations for accessing databases, and this information should have been provided to you. Enter that information if it is different. A different location may be something like 12345678.ourmysqlserver.com, which should be entered in place of localhost.

User Name—Enter the **[I]** username for the database (with the prefix if your website is hosted on a cPanel). Parallels Plesk does not require the prefix. This is the username you assigned to the database when it was created.

Password—Enter the database user's **[J]** password.

17

Database Name—Enter the **[K]** database name (with the prefix if your website is hosted on a cPanel). Parallels Plesk does not require the prefix.

Table Prefix—No need to change the **[L]** prefix used for the database tables, so leave this as is. It is randomly generated. You may, however, make your own prefix, but make sure it is followed by an underscore (_) character, such as **abc_** or something similar.

Click the **[M]** Next button at the top-right portion of the screen to execute this action.

Figure 2-2 *The most frequent failure during installation of Joomla! 3 websites happens here. If the database username, password, and database name are not entered correctly, the attempt to connect to it will fail.*

Step 3. Select the sample data (Figure 2-3). Ordinarily, for a regular website, you don't need to install any sample data. However, in this instance the sample data will be used for illustrations and exercises throughout the book. It is important that the "Learn Joomla! English" sample data be installed in this step.

Install Sample Data—For the purposes of the exercises in this book, select the **[N]** Learn Joomla! English option.

Review the Information—**[O]** The remainder of the information on the page is for informational purposes. If there are errors, they will be flagged and need to be corrected to complete a proper Joomla! 3 install.

Click the **[P]** Install button at the top-right portion of the screen to execute the addition of the sample data.

When the Install action is executed, Joomla! 3 will begin the installation progress and display the information (Figure 2-4). Allow the installation to complete. Do not close the browser window while this is happening.

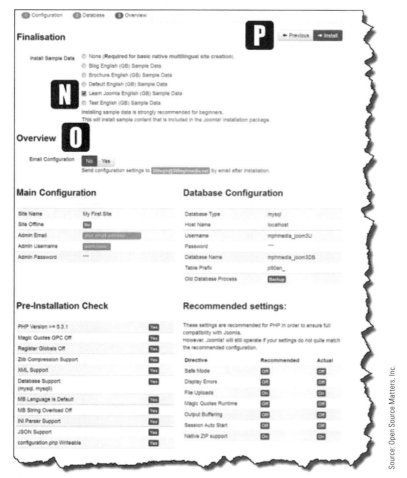

Figure 2-3 *This screen helps you select the sample data. It also displays information about the installation, indicating the status of all parts of the installation, and flagging anything needing attention.*

Step 4. Remove the installation folder (Figure 2-5, **[Q]**). If the Installation folder remains accessible, the actual installation process could be accidentally (or maliciously) started again. Therefore, the folder needs to be removed. The Joomla!

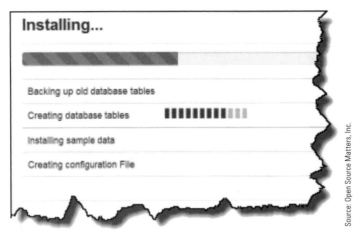

Source: Open Source Matters, Inc.

Figure 2-4 *Progress bars will display for each part of the installation. Allow them to complete and do not close the browser window during this time.*

3 installation process provides an automatic action for the removal. A "success" screen displays when the folder deletion has been accomplished.

Administration Login Details—This section verifies the super user's email address and login name.

Install Additional Languages—**[S]** Additional site languages can be added at this time, although this is not essential. Languages may also be added to Joomla! 3 at any time after Joomla! 3 has been installed, because languages are extensions, and extensions can be added at any time the website installation is completed.

Step 5. Access the Administrator backend (Figure 2-6). When the previous steps are completed, log in to the Administrator backend. Check the login to ensure that the installation is complete. Then, access the front-end to view the website and make sure the content is visible. If you can access both the backend and the front-end, the Joomla! 3 installation is finished.

Success Message—If the installation folder was removed, the **[T]** success message will display.

Access Site as Administrator—It is suggested that you test the **[U]** Administrator login at this point. Note the resulting URL in the browser location bar. Bookmark this page as the Administrator backend of the website. It's always **domainname/administrator/**. In this case, the Admin's URL is **domainname/myfirstsite/administrator**.

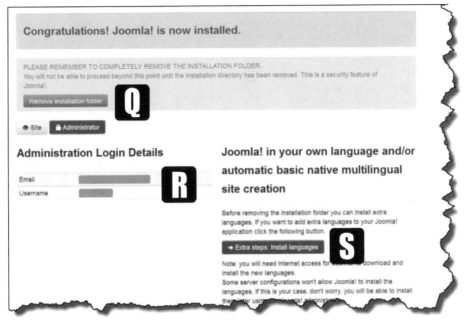

Figure 2-5 *This **[Q]** success message displays if all of the required information and actions have been executed as required by Joomla! 3. The Site and Administrator buttons now take you to the front-end or backend of the website from this screen.*

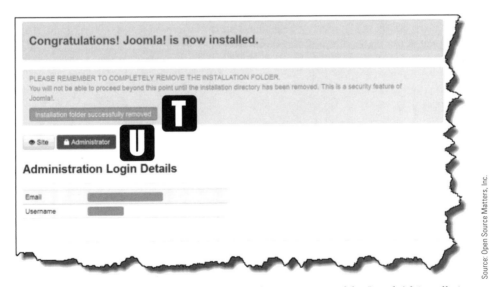

Figure 2-6 *The **[T]** success message indicates all requirements of the Joomla! 3 installation process have been completed correctly. The **[U]** Site and Administrator buttons also appear. This is the only screen that displays these buttons. The administrator accesses the backend using the regular login screen from this point on.*

Log in to the backend—Use the **[V]** super user login and password to access the backend of the website (Figure 2-7).

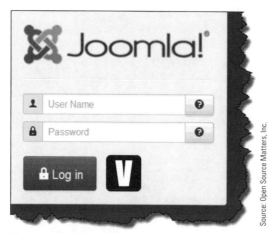

Source: Open Source Matters, Inc.

Figure 2-7 *This is the login screen that appears by default when accessing the /administrator/ directory of the website. After entering the super user name and the password, execute the* **[V]** *Log In action.*

Now that you've successfully installed Joomla! 3, the website is ready for content. This content will be added in Chapter 5, "Fast Track Start, " after you read two important chapters involved in managing Joomla! 3 content. You need to know the information provided in those chapters to get the full understanding of how Joomla! 3 works.

Summary

In this chapter, you learned:

◆ How to install Joomla! 3 on a website.

◆ How to enter the configuration information.

◆ How to enter the database information.

◆ How to include sample data and a language during the installation.

◆ How to remove the Installation folder after the installations were complete.

◆ How to log in to the Administrator backend.

Chapter 3

Joomla! 3 Default Installation

Learning Objectives

What's included in this chapter:

◆ Understanding the Joomla! 3 installation.

◆ Getting to know the Administrator control panel.

◆ Getting to know the drop-down menus.

◆ Navigating back to the control panel.

◆ Opening the website in a new browser tab.

◆ Using the Joomla! Help.

◆ Getting to know the Admin Left Menu.

What Happened During Installation

When you installed Joomla! 3, folders and files were created in the myfirstsite directory. Also, a database was populated with the MySQL tables and data.

By default, within those installation actions, Joomla! 3 configured its content. The installation process included these important elements:

◆ Created management areas in the backend to administer the website and the content.

◆ Created a super user, who is the main administrator of the website and, at this point, the only user who can log into the website backend.

◆ When the "Learn Joomla! English" content was installed, a collection of menus, categories, and articles was created.

◆ Installed a number of components and made them active for use.

◆ Added a series of extensions and provided the ability to add more.

All of the backend management features and their uses are discussed in chapters dedicated to each individual part. This chapter presents information regarding the backend, including and how and where to "do things" with content and website management.

Administrator Control Panel

All controls for the website are accessed via the Administrator control panel, which we refer to as "the backend" throughout this book. This control panel is different from the "ISP" hosting control panel. The ISP control panel hosts the website, whereas the Administrator backend control panel manages website content and determines how it displays on the browser screen.

The Administrator backend control panel is the hub of website management activity. Everything is started from this page after a proper login (Figure 3-1).

Mastery and knowledge of the Administrator backend is essential for all aspects of website management. Log in and spend some time looking over the control panel screens and familiarize yourself with the location of the different management areas and controls.

DON'T CHANGE THE BACKEND!

Do not make any changes to, or experiment with, anything in the backend at this point. The entire backend will be covered in various chapters of this book as the content and its administration are discussed. Right now, a "look, don't touch," rule is the best approach.

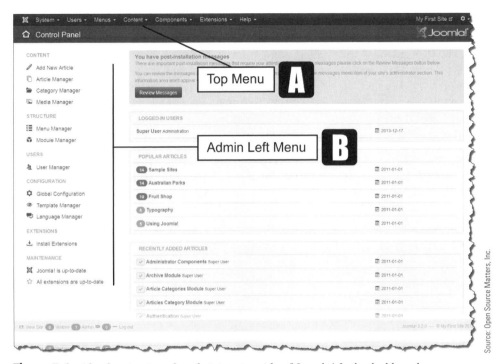

Figure 3-1 *After logging into the administrator side of Joomla! 3, the dashboard screen opens. All administrative functions are accessible from this screen. The* **[A]** *top menu accesses all admin areas. The Admin Left Menu* **[B]** *provides quick access to the most used admin managers in the backend.*

In Chapter 5, "Fast Track Start," there is a series of exercises that guide you through creation of content. After completing those exercises, you will be able to create and manage content with ease.

Additionally, the remaining chapters in this book address the different parts of Joomla! 3 administration in detail, including the use of each manager to affect, manage, and control content.

The Dashboard

By default, the super user's login displays the Joomla! 3 control panel dashboard, which is the starting point for all backend administration activities. The top menu accesses all of the admin managers, and the Admin Left Menu opens the most frequently used areas of the backend.

Admin Left Menu

On the left side, there is the Admin Left Menu, which opens most of the managers. The managers are used to control website content and appearance. In previous versions, these links were called Quick Icons and were located on the right side of the screen. They have now been moved to the left but perform the same function. Each manager is covered in detail, along with exercises, in their respective chapters.

Drop-Down Menus

Along the top of the screen, there is the website name and a series of drop-down menus that access six management areas and a link for Help if you need it (Figure 3-2). To help you understand the functions of the menus, each is explained next.

Source: Open Source Matters, Inc.

Figure 3-2 *This menu bar mirrors the Admin Left Menu area for access to the different content managers available to administrate the website. Less frequently used managers are available via the top menu.*

Top Menu Quick Navigation

There are two "quick" navigation links in the top menu that are not so obvious, but very handy.

Whichever screen you are viewing in the backend, you can go immediately back to the administrator's dashboard (Figure 3-1) by clicking on the **[C]** Joomla! logo above the Control Panel title, just to the left of the System link (Figure 3-3).

A quick way to view the website front-end is to click on the **[D]** website name in the top-right corner of the administrator's screen, above the color Joomla! logo and name. The website will open in a new browser tab, keeping the backend open in the original browser window. In this case, clicking My First Site opens the website in a new browser tab.

Source: Open Source Matters, Inc.

Figure 3-3 *Clicking on the **[C]** small Joomla! logo will take you immediately back to the administrator's dashboard. Clicking the **[D]** website name at the top right will open the website in a new browser window. These links appear on every admin screen.*

Using the Top Menu

This next section is a discussion of the individual drop-down menus found in the backend, within the dark blue top menu bar.

System Drop-Down Menu

The System drop-down gives you access to the information about the website and the configuration under which it is operating. In other chapters of this book, you'll learn about these different parts of the system and learn their functionality.

Users Drop-Down Menu

If you are the only person who will administer the website, you won't need the User Manager much. However, if you have a website with many users performing editing tasks, the User Manager enables you to add a near-unlimited number of users at different levels of access. This is covered in Chapter 23, "Access Control List and Permissions."

Menus Drop-Down Menu

The Menus Manager is the command post for creating menus and managing the Menu Link items that connect to articles, components, and modules, depending on what sort of content type assignment is given the item. Menus are discussed throughout most of the chapters as they relate to making content available for viewing.

Content Drop-Down Menu

The Content area typically accesses articles, categories, featured articles, and the Media Manager. These topics are covered in Chapter 17, "Categories," Chapter 18, "Articles," and Chapter 22, "Images and Media." Note that there are some fly-out menus that provide quick access to the Add screens within several content areas.

Components Drop-Down Menu

Components are "mini applications" that work inside of Joomla! 3. A comprehensive discussion of components is in Chapters 8 through 16. Each chapter deals with a separate component found in the default installation.

Some extensions that can be added to Joomla! 3 are, in fact, components. They will appear in this drop-down menu and their manager can be accessed from there. Note the fly-outs associated with some of the default components.

Extensions Drop-Down Menu

Extensions, which are discussed in Chapter 7, "Adding and Managing Extensions," are accessed from this menu. Extensions are classified as components, modules, plug-ins, templates, languages, and libraries. The Module Manager will likely be used frequently when developing the website and creating content that is not displayed via articles or components, which are opened with menu link items.

Help Drop-Down Menu

The Help drop-down menu opens a list of selections that direct you to a number of locations where Help is available. The Joomla! Help link opens a Help area that has plenty of information, if you know what you are looking for. It might be a good idea to spend an hour or so just surfing through the Help areas and doing some reading.

The Joomla! Help section is very useful for looking up information. The Help is classified by managers and breaks them down by task and function.

However, don't expect to find an abundance of detailed answers within the Documentation Wiki link. The Wiki tends to be incomplete in many informational areas. It is also somewhat difficult to find information specific to one version of Joomla!, as the content tends to get mixed among versions. Make sure when looking for help in the Wiki that you are seeing the Joomla! 3 screenshots or content. Otherwise, you will spend a lot of time chasing your tail and getting nowhere.

For more accurate information, you may access the Joomla! 3 Boot Camp reference site at http://joomla3bootcamp.com.

Super User Drop-Down Menu

This drop-down menu is to the far right of the top menu bar. In addition to managing the user name, password, and email address, there are other settings, such as selecting a different backend template style, which is covered in Chapter 21, "Templates."

Having the ability to configure Joomla! 3's backend for administrators is unique. If a website has, for example, four administrators, a couple of whom speak a language other than U.S. or U.K. English, their respective backends may be customized to their language needs.

Drop-Down Menus in Detail

The drop-downs in the top menu and the respective fly-outs are listed next. You can find the details about the menu and submenu items, as well as the functional screens, in the Joomla! Help section. Just look for the Manager part—such as Article Manager: Articles—to learn about the articles management in the backend (Figure 3-4).

Figure 3-4 *The major administration managers are accessed via the top menu. While the most frequently used managers are accessed via the Admin Left Menu, the top menu accesses all of the managers for the website.*

Each of the management and administration areas is covered in detail in other chapters, where their actual uses are explained and implemented.

[E] System: Controls that manage the website configurations and parameters.

> Control Panel
>
> Global Configuration
>
> Global Check-In
>
> Clear Cache
>
> Purge Expired Cache
>
> System Information

[F] Users: Contains the user manager and access control (ACL), configuration, and settings.

> User Manager
>> Add New User
>
> Groups
>> Add New Group
>
> Access Levels
>> Add New Access Level
>
> User Notes
>> Add User Note
>
> User Note Categories
>> Add New Category
>
> Mass Mail Users

[G] Menus: Manages the menus and menu link items needed to make content viewable on the website, and to establish a navigation system using menus contained in menu modules.

> Menu Manager
>> Add New Menu
>
> Main Menu
>> Add New Menu Item
>
> Author Menu
>> Add New Menu Item
>
> Bottom Menu
>> Add New Menu Item

[H] Content: This manager area deals primarily with categories and articles and how they are associated.

Article Manager

    Add New Article

Category Manager

    Add New Category

Featured Articles

Media Manager

[I] Components: This area contains mini-applications that control content and default components, along with those added as extensions to the website.

Banners

    Banners

    Categories

    Clients

    Tracks

Contacts

    Contacts

    Categories

Joomla! Update

Messaging

    New Private Message

    Read Private Messages

Newsfeeds

    Feeds

    Categories

Redirect

Search

Smart Search

Tags

Weblinks

    Links

    Categories

[J] Extensions: Provides a method to install/add extensions and manage them after being installed, including removing them from the website.

> Extension Manager
>
> Module Manager
>
> Plug-In Manager
>
> Template Manager
>
> Language Manager

[K] Help: Links to different Joomla! Help resources and areas of interest to Joomla! 3 users.

> Joomla! Help
>
> Official Support Forum
>
> Documentation Wiki
>
> Joomla! Extensions
>
> Joomla! Translations
>
> Joomla! Resources
>
> Community Portal
>
> Security Center
>
> Developer Resources
>
> Joomla! Shop

Bottom-Left Information Panel

There is an **[L]** information panel in the lower-left portion of the Backend screen that indicates how many visitors are viewing the website and how many admins are on the site. Also, an additional Logout link is located there (Figure 3-5). The other Logout link is in the upper-right corner of the screen via the **[M]** Super User link.

When you have completed working in the backend, always formally log out so that your checked-out items are checked in. This enables other administrators to access them.

Source: Open Source Matters, Inc.

Figure 3-5 *The information section at the bottom left of the screen* **[L]**, *has a Logout button, as does the* **[M]** *Super User drop-down located at the top right of all Admin Backend screens.*

BE SURE TO LOG OUT TO RELEASE CONTENT

When one administrator opens a content item on the backend, that item cannot be accessed by any other administrator or editor at any level. This prevents two administrators or editors from working on the same content item at the same time. If an administrator leaves the site without logging out, the content items that he/she checked out remain inaccessible. By formally logging out, it releases the content to other administrators.

Obviously, if you are the only administrator for the website, this isn't an important issue. However, when there are multiple administrators, the checked-out content needs to be released. Everyone needs to formally log out of the backend to prevent content from being inaccessible.

In their wisdom, the Joomla! 3 programmers have created a method of checking-in the content globally, and this method is explained later in this book.

Using the Admin Left Menu

The items in the Admin Left Menu on the dashboard screen are essentially duplications of the drop-down menus. These links are used to access the most frequently used management areas (Figure 3-6).

When a manager is open, the menus display additional items specific to that content area. They are described and discussed in their respective chapters.

One of the best ways to understand the complexities of the Joomla! 3 backend, which is a quantum leap forward from previous versions, is to actually do something with each manager.

Source: Open Source Matters, Inc.

Figure 3-6 *The Admin Left Menu has links that open the most frequently used managers. The top menu bar has more options via fly-out links. Most of the everyday tasks performed on a website can be accessed via the Admin Left Menu, and those not used so frequently, are accessed via the top menu.*

The Admin Left Menu is used in Chapter 5, which guides you with exercises that use backend managers to accomplish content creation and control how the content is displayed.

Summary

In this chapter, you learned:

- ◆ What's installed/created during the Joomla! 3 installation.
- ◆ What's contained in the Administrator backend.
- ◆ The functions and controls in the drop-down menus.
- ◆ How to navigate to the control panel.
- ◆ How to open the website in a new browser tab.
- ◆ Where to find Joomla! 3 Help.
- ◆ The function of the Admin Left Menu.

Chapter 4

How Joomla! 3 Works

Learning Objectives

What's included in this chapter:

◆ Learning about the Joomla! 3 platform.

◆ Learning about Joomla! 3 extensions.

◆ Learning about content sources.

◆ Learning about components, which display website content.

◆ Learning about modules, which display website content.

◆ Enabling the template preview feature of Joomla! 3.

◆ Finding the module positions of a template.

The Joomla! 3 Website Platform

The Joomla! 3 platform consists of the "core," which is the code that makes the website operate, and extensions, which enhance and enlarge the ability to add more content and display it in specific ways.

Joomla! 3, in addition to the core functions, has many administrative features built into it which allow the super user to manage all aspects of a website. Once a site is established on a webserver and a design (via a template) is selected, you can begin to work with content.

Content comes in many forms on Joomla! 3 websites, first through the features that are included in the installation process, and second by adding extensions to create content in many different configurations. The combination of all features and add-on extensions allows website administrators to create websites of all types with a wide range of content and determines how the content appears or displays on the front-end.

Because of these features, there is no need for administrators to modify or "hack" the core files to display content. Unless you have strong HTML, CSS, and PHP coding skills, modifying the core files isn't a good idea. There are "template overrides" that you can implement. This topic is covered in Chapter 21, "Templates," and explained in detail in the online supplement to this book.

ABOUT THOSE UPDATES

Joomla! 3 has an automatic updating system so that when a change is made to the core, the files can easily be uploaded to replace certain files and to update your installation. This is a major reason you don't want to change any coding/files in the core, because they will be automatically overwritten during subsequent updates. Even though the updating system is automatic, the super user has the option of installing the updates or not.

Types of Extensions

Extensions expand the function of Joomla! 3 in the areas of content and operation. In a nutshell, they are simply add-ons that can be installed by the super user to achieve certain content or display objectives of the website.

Joomla! 3 consists of six types of extensions (Figure 4-1). Each extension has unique characteristics regarding content or how the content is displayed, or accessed by website visitors.

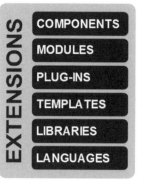

Source: 200mph Media Group, LLC

Figure 4-1 *With the exception of libraries and languages, website content is controlled by the super user and based on the parameters of each. You can display a wide and varied range of content on a Joomla! 3 based website.*

The extension types are summarized as follows:

Components–These are mini-applications that operate inside the Joomla! 3 framework. An example of a component is a photo gallery that displays images in an orderly way from photos that are located in a folder on the webserver. Another component that is often used is a contact form for website visitors to send messages to the website owner or administrator. Most of the "major lifting" of content in Joomla! 3 is done by components, supplemented with modules.

Modules–These are visible areas on the page that contain extensions that can be associated with a component. An example is a login form for users, or a module that displays the latest articles. Modules can be positioned anywhere on a page/screen that has designated "module positions." Modules can be relocated and also be set to appear on certain pages, or not, which allows a great deal of customization of content displays. They can also be "stacked," which is the process of adding several modules to the same module position and setting the order in which they appear.

Plug-Ins—Plug-ins are typically routines that are associated with "triggered events." When a triggered event occurs, it executes a function, if it associates with a plug-in. An example is having a plug-in that allows the display of a module within an article by specifying the module using special code inserted into the article. When the article is opened via a menu link item, the plug-in is "triggered" to display the designated module. Normally, other than installing and activating a plug-in, there isn't anything more needed to get them to function properly on a website. They are pretty much on auto-pilot when installed and require little or no intervention by the administrator.

Libraries–Libraries are packages of code that provide a related group of functions to the core Joomla! 3 framework, or to the extensions, and are installed, updated, and deleted like any other extension. Routine administrator functions normally do not require interaction with code libraries. The libraries are *not* locations to store data or images, so don't confuse the function with the name. They are code repositories that the Joomla! 3 core uses for itself.

Templates–These control the physical structure and visual layout of the website pages. A template displays the website in a certain layout, with module positions, cascading style sheets for colorization, and control over content and appearance. One or more templates, all different, may be used on a Joomla! 3 website, and can be highly customized.

Languages–If you want to add languages to a Joomla! 3 website, there are many language extensions to choose from. These can be configured to allow website visitors to select the language of their choice to view the website. Many language extensions can be available for viewer selection through a Language Switching extension. This feature is good if you want site visitors to choose between English and Spanish, as an example, or any other language for which there is a Language extension installed. There are many Joomla! 3 websites that have five or more language choice options.

Sources of Content

The content on Joomla! 3 websites is generated from four main sources (Figure 4-2).

Articles in Categories–Articles are the main content of most Joomla! 3 websites. Articles are assigned categories, which are discussed in depth in Chapter 17, "Categories." Articles are covered in Chapter 18, "Articles."

> **Module Content in Articles**–It is possible in Joomla! 3 to include or embed the content generated by modules into articles. This comes in handy for displaying content that is associated only with a specific article, or it provides a method for accessing more content.

Content in Modules–Much of the content in Joomla! 3 websites is generated and displayed by using modules, which are assigned to a fixed physical location on a web page template. Chapter 19, "Modules," offers complete information on modules, including what kind of information they can display, and how to use them for routine and creative content display.

Content from Components and Extensions–Components are the "mini-applications" that operate on the website. Extensions installed as components can enlarge the scope of content on a Joomla! 3 website. There are hundreds of components for Joomla! 3 available, both free and pay-to-use. Chapters 8 through 16 cover their installation and use.

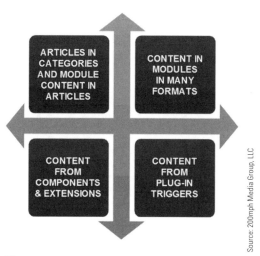

Source: 200mph Media Group, LLC

Figure 4-2 *There are four main methods used by Joomla! 3 to generate and display content, all of which are controlled by the super user via the Administrator backend.*

Content from Plug-In Triggers–Plug-ins generate content when something happens on the website that "triggers" them into action. Chapter 20, "Plug-Ins," covers their installation and configuration and includes examples of actual use.

Content Generated by Extensions

Many extensions are specialized as to what they do or how they function and as to the manner in which content is displayed. For example, when an extension displays a photo gallery, the content is controlled by the extension and not by an article or module, although you can use a module to control the position on the page where a gallery appears. Content extensions can be components, modules, or plug-ins. They are distinguished as being separate from the default installation. Extensions are thoroughly covered in Chapter 7, "Adding and Managing Extensions."

Extensions as Components

Some components generate content in their own format and display it in the center content area. Some of these built-in default components are described here (Figure 4-3):

Banners—Manages banners that you may want to place at various locations on your website. This component doesn't manage the page's top banner (the website header). The website header is usually controlled via the page's template. Banners are simply images that can be located in module positions on a web page.

Contacts—Create and display a list of contacts for your website. Typically not used on smaller websites, but are used on larger websites that have many people editing content, or a company that wants to list all its staff/employees and contact information, such as Sales, Customer Service, and Support, so that visitors can communicate to them directly.

Joomla! Update—This is a fast link to check if there are any updates to the Joomla! 3 core files. If there are, you have the option to update your website to the latest version.

Messaging—Allows sending and receiving of private messages among users who have accounts on the site; it's good for large sites, but not necessary for smaller, one-person websites.

Newsfeeds—Allows display of newsfeeds (RSS) from other websites on your site. You can also set up newsfeeds in categories to keep them organized or display them selectively or under specific conditions.

Redirect—Creates a redirect from one URL to another. This is usually used internally to direct visitors to another location on the site, but you can use it for external links also. It has limited value with respect to actual website administration. The Redirect function works when a user has a web page bookmarked, but that web page no longer appears on your website. The user can then be "redirected" to another location of your choosing.

Search—Displays the searches that were conducted on the website by the phrase that was used for the search event. Search features are helpful in larger sites. Smaller sites, however, usually don't need a Search module to be displayed.

Smart Search—Smart Search is enabled via a plug-in. It does not start by default; it must be enabled manually after installation is complete. It works off of an indexing system that must also run to invoke it.

Tags—Tagging is a nice way of organizing content, not by categories, but by using tags that can be applied to many different content items. Several tags may be assigned to the items. Tagging also allows you to see all the items that are tagged in a similar way with the same tag name. Tagging is a new and hot item with Joomla! 3, so learning how to use them will be very helpful, especially if your site has many content articles across a large number of categories.

Weblinks—Allows the creation of categorized weblinks for site visitors to view other websites you may want to reference. This is more or less a simple directory of links to other websites and is controlled by a site administrator.

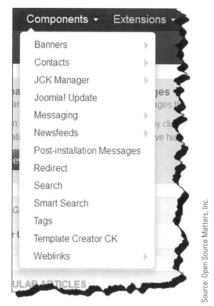

Source: Open Source Matters, Inc.

Figure 4-3 *Components are accessed via the drop-down menu available on the Control Panel page's top menu bar. Component managers are* not *available via the Admin Left Menu.*

Extensions as Modules

Modules give Joomla! 3 horsepower beyond the components and plug-ins. Modules fit into placeholders on a web page that have allocated space for them, usually called a "module position." In Joomla! 3, "positions" generally means a fixed location on a Joomla! 3 template.

By default, Joomla! 3 installed a number of modules (Figure 4-4) that have different, but specialized, uses on a website. Of course, not all of the modules must be used. The neat thing about Modules is that you can pick and choose which ones to use and which new ones to add via the Extensions Manager. Modules can also be easily removed from the backend.

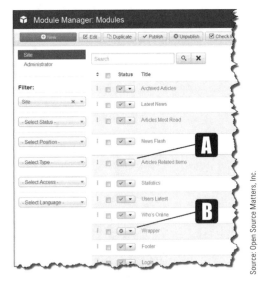

Figure 4-4 *When the Module Manager opens, the list of all modules installed as extensions will display, regardless if the module's status is active or inactive. The* **[A]** *green checkmark indicates the module is active; the* **[B]** *red "X" indicates that the module is inactive and not viewable on the website front-end.*

Types of Modules Available

A Joomla! 3 installation can have a number of modules that are installed but have not been included as functional content elements. This means that a module extension can be installed by the Extensions Manager, but not yet included to be part of a web page. A module must be selected for inclusion to appear on the Module Manager: Modules screen.

You include a module by executing a New action in the Module Manager, which will open a screen displaying all the module types available. The following list shows the default modules that come with a Joomla! 3 installation. When new module types are added, they will appear on the list.

Archived Articles—Shows a list of the articles that have been archived (stored and not visible on the site) and categorized historically.

Articles Categories—Displays a list of the categories that contain articles. This is referred to as the Category List view.

Articles Category—Displays a list of articles from one or more categories, and is referred to as the Category Article view.

Articles–Newsflash—Displays a fixed number of articles from one or more categories by designation.

Articles–Related Articles—This module displays other articles that are related to the one currently being viewed, and associated via keywords or tags.

Banners—The Banners module displays the active banners from the banners component.

Breadcrumbs—This module displays the viewing location information for the current web page, and the pathway of links clicked to get there. Generally referred to as a "pathway" or as "breadcrumbs" interchangeably.

Custom HTML—Allows content to be displayed in module positions that contain custom "HTML" code, which allows creation and placement of special coded content. This is a highly used module on most Joomla! 3 websites.

Feed Display—Can generate "RSS" feed display in module positions on the website with many controls on how/where the display is to appear.

Footer—This module appears in the footer position on the website and typically contains copyright and other information, such as how to contact the website manager.

Language Switcher—If multi-languages are included and invoked, changes the front-end display to another language.

Latest News—Displays the latest content published on the website by designation of Category and Order.

Latest Users—Shows which users have logged into the website recently.

Login—Standard user front-end login module. It's not usually needed on sites that only have one super user and no other content editors.

Menu—Can be a menu of any type or style and can be located in any module position desired. You can set it to hide or display based on which menu link item is associated with it.

Most Read Content—Shows which website content has been read the most. This is sometimes referred to as the "most popular" content on a website.

Popular Tags—Shows the tags most frequently used to find site content.

Random Image—Displays a random image array and is linked to an image folder that is controlled in the Media Manager.

Search—This is the basic site Search module you use to find website content. Helpful if there is a lot of tagged content on the website.

Similar Tags—Displays a list of links to other content items that have similar tags.

Smart Search Module—This is a search module for the Smart Search system, which allows highly specific or narrowed Search items to be used.

Statistics—The Statistics module shows information about your webserver installation together with statistics on the website users, number of articles in your database, and the number of weblinks.

Syndication Feeds—Smart Syndication module that creates a syndicated feed for the page where the Module is displayed.

Weblinks—This module displays weblinks from a category defined in the Weblinks component.

Who's Online—The Who's Online module displays the number of anonymous users (Guests) and registered users (ones logged in) who are currently accessing the website.

Wrapper—This module shows an iFrame window to specified location. The iFrame allows including a URL page from another website. Although it might appear to be a functioning module, it is rather quirky and often creates display issues on the website.

As you can see, there are a number of default modules, depending on what you want to present and where on the page. More can be added via the Extensions Manager, depending on what kind of additional content you want to display on the website. The Joomla! Extensions Directory (JED) is where all extensions are stored, whether you downloaded them from Joomla! or private parties.

More on Modules

Other than the main (center) content area, everything else on a Joomla! 3 web page is located within, or its position is controlled by, the location designation of the module. Modules, for example, can be assigned the left or the right position. You can also assign them as footers, banners, or anything else, provided there is a physical placeholder designated at that location on the template's page. Joomla! 3 calls many module positions simply "positions" with an assigned number and not an actual physical location ("position-7" rather than Left or Right, for example). This nomenclature does take some getting used to when you're adding modules here and there.

Modules may be set to show or not during certain types of events that result in clicking Menu Link items. For example, if you click a link to an article or a Category Blog layout, different modules can be set to appear only upon that link's execution. Likewise, you can set Modules to be hidden under the same set of conditions. This feature in Joomla! 3 allows some creative horsepower to be added to create many different page layouts.

This unique feature applies only to link items that are created in system-generated Menu modules. It does not work for hard-coded links within an article unless there is a Menu module inserted into the article. In that case, you can invoke the show/not show.

This all might sound confusing at this point, but once you have completed Chapter 5, "Fast Track Start" and Chapter 19, you'll find that managing modules is easy.

The Website Front Page

To better understand how Joomla! 3 structures visible content, let's look at how the front page is structured with the default installation templates (Figure 4-5). The actual layout of the front-end varies between templates and visual designs, and can even change dramatically from screen to screen, based on the configuration of modules and other content items. The anatomy of the page in Figure 4-5 is discussed in Chapter 6, "Front Page Content and Layout."

Figure 4-5 *If you installed the correct Learn Joomla! English Sample Data, the front-end of the website should look like this.*

Where Are the Module Positions

The first question asked when a template is installed is, "Where are the module positions and what are they called?" This question is easily answered, but it requires the super user to perform a couple of administrative tasks.

The template used for the Learn Joomla! English Sample Data layout is named Protostar.

To determine the module positions, follow the steps in Exercise 4-1.

EXERCISE 4-1: ENABLING THE VIEW MODULE POSITIONS FEATURE

Objective: This exercise illustrates how to determine the module positions for an installed template, whether being used or not, via a Joomla! 3 built-in feature. The Firefox web browser is used in all the exercises in this book.

This will be your first activity in the Admin backend, and it might seem confusing at first. Follow each step closely and take your time to make sure you are executing the actions required.

Step 1. Access the Administrator backend using the super user login.

Step 2. Open the Template Manager in the Admin Left Menu.

Step 3. When open, the screen should display the list of templates that are installed (Figure 4-6). Note the information that is displayed about each template. This is the Styles view of the Template Manager.

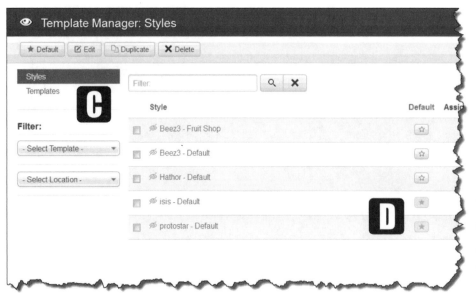

Figure 4-6 *The indicator and link on the left* **[C]** *display which part of the Template Manager is being viewed. The "gold stars"* **[D]** *indicate the currently active template for both the website and administrator.*

Step 4.   Click the **[E]** Options button above the Template Manager: Styles title bar, which is located to the far right under the Joomla! logo and name (Figure 4-7).

Figure 4-7 *The* **[E]** *Options area for the template styles opens a screen with additional parameters that can be globally set for templates.*

Step 5.   Under the Templates tab that opens is the setting for the Global Configuration for Templates, called **[F]** Preview Modules Positions (Figure 4-8). The default setting is Disabled.

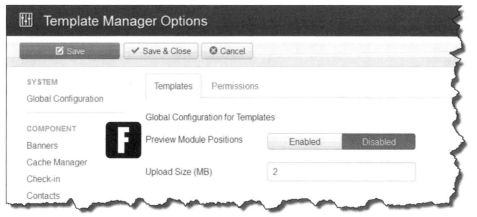

Figure 4-8 *By default, the* **[F]** *Preview Module Positions parameter is set to Disabled in the Template Options section.*

Step 6.   Change the setting to **[G]** Enabled (Figure 4-9).

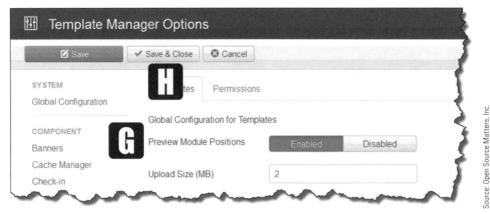

Figure 4-9 *Toggle the button to Enabled to allow viewing of module positions for templates. Anytime a parameter is changed, you must execute a Save action in order to implement the change.*

Step 7. With the button indicating Enabled, click **[H]** Save & Close to execute the action.

GOLD STARS

Within the Template Manager, when in the Styles view, there is a Default column that indicates which template is being used for the backend and front-end. A "gold star" indicates the template that will display when administrators log in or when visitors view the website.

This now enables module position viewing using the built-in template Preview feature in Exercise 4-2, or via a manual method, as outlined in Exercise 4-3.

EXERCISE 4-2: USING THE TEMPLATE PREVIEW FEATURE

Objective: This exercise explains the use of the templates Preview feature to determine module positions of a template. The procedure in this exercise is the built-in, internal feature to view module positions.

Step 1. Access the Template Manager again and click on the **[I]** Templates link at the top-left part of the screen (Figure 4-10).

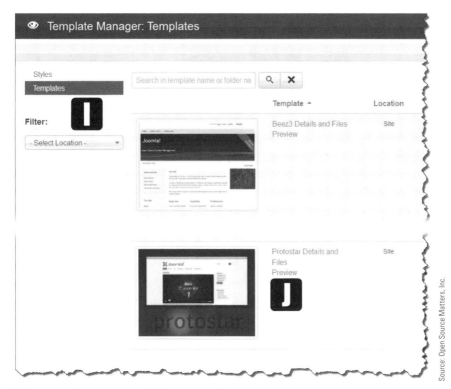

Figure 4-10 *Clicking on* **[I]** *Templates from the Styles page will display a list of the templates that are currently installed on the website. Note that the administrator templates do not have a* **[J]** *Preview feature, whereas those for the site do.*

Step 2. This screen displays the currently installed Templates. Click on **[J]** Preview for the Protostar template.

Step 3. The result is the front page of the website showing the available **[K]** module positions for this particular template (Figure 4-11).

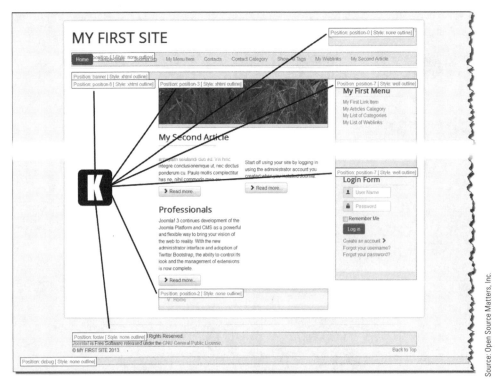

Figure 4-11 *When you're viewing the front-end as a preview of a template, the red-boxed captions indicate the name of the module position and shows its physical location.*

STACKING MODULE POSITIONS

When viewing Figure 4-11 showing the module positions, notice there is a "position-8" on the left and nothing is showing in that space. This means that a module position called "position-8" is in the Template page, but there are no modules assigned to it. The physical location is available but on this particular page view, no modules are designated to show in "position-8" when the Home page is the active screen.

Also note on the right side there are three modules in "position-7," which is quite proper because modules can be stacked in the same physical location. This stacking method is covered in Chapter 19.

EXERCISE 4-3: USING THE VIEW MODULE POSITIONS MANUAL FEATURE

Objective: This exercise guides the super user through the process of using an alternative method of viewing module positions on every web page generated from one or more different templates with different physical layouts. This exercise assumes that you've completed the elements of Exercise 4-1.

Step 1. Access the website's front-end home page (Figure 4-5).

Step 2. In the **[L]** URL location bar, at the end of the URL, add **?tp=1**, so that the URL looks like this:

http://yourdomainname/myfirstsite/?tp=1

Step 3. Press Return or Enter to invoke the new URL (Figure 4-12).

Figure 4-12 *The* **[L]** *URL ends with ?tp=1, which you can add after any Joomla! 3 website URL address to manually obtain the* **[M]** *module positions.*

Step 4. The screen should have **[M]** red text indicating the names of the module positions and their visual and physical location on the page. These are the available module positions for the particular web page. Note that this results in the same image as viewed in Figure 4-11. Either method will display the module positions for that website page.

> ### VIEWING THE MODULE POSITIONS
>
> Any template screen can be viewed for module positions by adding **?tp=1** at the very end of the URL. Use the feature when there are multiple templates on a Joomla! 3 website that have different physical page layouts and the module positions might be different between the web pages. This can also be done via the front-end without going into the Administrator backend to preview a template. It's more convenient and takes fewer steps to complete.

Module Positions May Be Different

When using templates other than those in the default installation, you may find that the names of the module positions are different. Some template developers use their own method of naming them, which are different than the method used by these exercises. In fact, most templates have an abundance of module positions, so you will certainly use the ?tp=1 feature with other templates.

Summary

In this chapter, you learned:

◆ About the Joomla! 3 platform and the core files.

◆ Which extensions are in the default installation.

◆ What type and sources of content there are on Joomla! 3 websites.

◆ That most content is generated via articles.

◆ That components are mini-applications that run inside Joomla! 3.

◆ That modules can contain and display content.

◆ That modules may be located on a web page only if there is a module position in the template.

◆ How to enable the template preview feature of the program.

◆ How to find the module positions of a template using two different methods.

Chapter 5

Fast Track Start

Learning Objectives

What's included in this chapter:

- ◆ How to access the Administrator backend.
- ◆ How to create and save a content category.
- ◆ How to create and save an article.
- ◆ How to assign an article to a content category.
- ◆ How to access an existing menu.
- ◆ How to link a menu item to an article.

Managing a Joomla! 3 website can seem daunting at first. This chapter leads you through content creation on a "fast track" step-by-step process. After you create a category, add an article, and then add a menu link item, you will understand how those three elements work together. After that, the rest of Joomla! 3's content creation will make a lot more sense.

Everything in the backend functions in a similar manner and the exercises in this book guide you through each of those areas in detail. They provide expanded information on the entire Joomla! 3 platform. When you are done, there won't be much about Joomla! 3 that you don't understand. There won't be much you won't be able to do.

Start Right Now

For the purposes of this "fast track" set of instructions, the assumption is that you are the site's super user and the only person permitted to edit content. As the super user, you must log into the Joomla! 3 backend, or administrator side of the website, to access the various managers for content creation and management.

EXERCISE 5-1: ACCESSING THE ADMINISTRATOR BACKEND

Objective: This exercise shows you how to access the administration area of the website. Unless the website is set up with front-end access options, this is the way the super user will always access the backend to administer all management areas.

Step 1. Go to this link: http://www.yourdomainname.com/myfirstsite/administrator/.

Step 2. The Admin Login page will appear (Figure 5-1).

Source: Open Source Matters, Inc.

Figure 5-1 *When any designated administrator accesses the website backend, he/she will be required to log in using this screen. Only super user administrators have all privileges available after login.*

Step 3. Log in using the username and the password that you assigned to the super user when you installed Joomla! 3.

If your username/password (U/P) is correct, you should next see the Admin Control Panel (Figure 5-2).

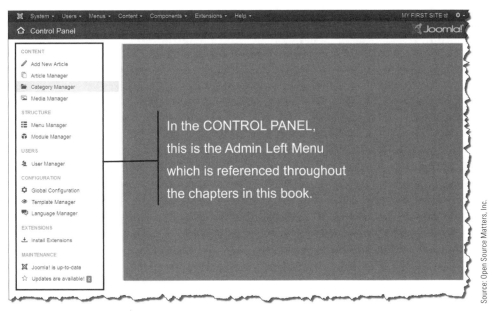

Figure 5-2 *This is the central location for administration of the website via Joomla! 3 back-end. The most frequently used managers are accessible via the Admin Left Menu. All other managers are accessible via the Admin Top Menu.*

Every time you log in, the page shown in Figure 5-2 will open as the starting point to perform backend tasks. Some features in the backend must be accessed in a different way; they are discussed as they come up in this book. Now then, before you have an "OMG" moment when looking at the backend for the first time, here's what you'll when you log in as the super user:

◆ The Control Panel is the starting point for all Joomla! 3 backend tasks.

◆ The display in the center of the screen is mostly information about content.

◆ The menu along the top of the screen (in the dark blue bar) will take you to every manager location in the backend, along with its sub-functions.

◆ The Admin Left Menu contains convenient links to the most frequently used managers in the backend. You will use these links constantly when managing the website and content.

◆ You can access all of the managers either via the top menu or using the Admin Left Menu. They both go to the same backend areas, although the top menu has more links to more management task areas.

◆ The super user can edit her profile information by accessing the super user at the top-right of the screen. There is also a Log Out button to exit the backend.

◆ Information about site access and another Log Out button appear at the bottom left of the screen. You can use either one to exit the backend.

Before proceeding, let's take a look at the Admin Left Menu. Their primary functions are pretty obvious so I won't waste time explaining them in depth at this point. Each will be explained in greater detail later in other chapters. You are on a "fast track" here, so let's not dwell on them individually for now. They will be thoroughly covered in the respective topical chapter later.

The objective of this chapter is to get you into the backend, overcome your "OMG" reaction, and learn, through the following exercises, how to do the basic tasks in the backend. You'll learn how to create a category, an article, and a menu link item to display the article on the website's front-end.

Understanding the Joomla! 3 Content Structure

The majority of the content on a Joomla! 3 website consists of articles. *Articles* are assigned to *categories*. Other content comes from components, modules, and plug-ins, and each has a chapter dedicated to its use.

At this point categories, articles, and menu link items are created on a "fast track" to help you understand their relationship and how easy it is to create viewable content. In fact, you can complete the exercises in this chapter in less than 30 minutes. Do the exercises, step-by-step. When you're done, you'll probably say, "Heck, that was easy. How do I do more stuff?"

General Rules Relating to Categories, Articles, and Menu Link Items

Joomla! 3 has many fixed configuration rules that govern and manage how content is created and displayed. Here are some general rules pertaining to those items:

◆ Categories are the "top level" of content management for articles.

◆ Categories can have articles assigned to them, but only articles.

◆ Articles must be assigned to a category, regardless of its hierarchy or level.

◆ Sub-categories (child categories) can be created and associated with any Category above (a parent category).

◆ Articles can be assigned to sub-categories.

◆ There is no limit to the number of categories that can be created.

◆ There is no limit to the number of sub-categories, or sub-sub-categories, that can be created.

- There is no limit to the number of child levels that can be created within a parent category.
- There is no limit to the number of articles that can be assigned to any level of category.
- Articles can be assigned to only one category, although extensions can be added, and they allow a single article to be assigned to multiple categories.
- Articles cannot be assigned to articles, but they can be associated by reference to each other by creating an automatic link to the associated article.
- There is no limit to the number of menus that can be created.
- There is no limit to the number of menu link items a menu can contain.
- Articles are opened by menu link items.
- Menu link items can be associated with only one article at a time, although there are other actions that can be associated with menu link items.

As explained, Joomla! 3 structures content primarily into articles, which are assigned to categories. Categories may have sub-categories, and sub-categories may have sub-sub-categories built into the structure (Figure 5-3).

Figure 5-3 *Categories contain the articles. The "parent" category can have any number of "child" categories (called sub-categories or sub-sub-categories). Although there is no limit to the number of child categories, too many can complicate the organization of the content.*

Once a category structure is created, articles can be assigned to it. This process of structuring content is similar to a file cabinet. Within the drawers of the file cabinet, there are hanging folders (the categories), and within those folders are file folders (sub-categories and sub-sub-categories), and within the folders there are documents (articles) (Figure 5-4).

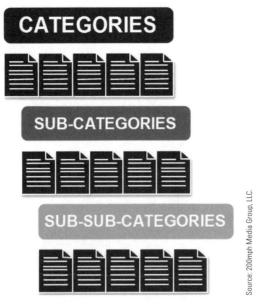

Source: 200mph Media Group, LLC.

Figure 5-4 *Articles must be assigned to categories, which can be parent or child categories at any level. There is no limit to the number of articles that can be assigned to a category.*

How the Content Structure Is Created

This section helps you get started by executing the actions necessary to create content:

Action 1. Create a category using the Category Manager.

Action 2. Create an article and assign it to the category in the Article Manager.

Action 3. Create a menu link item to the article in an existing menu.

While you're performing the steps involved, you'll see that the explanations cover only what's needed to complete the tasks. On the admin pages, you will see many other things such as controls, options, buttons, fill-in boxes, and other parameters. For these "fast track" exercises, you can ignore most of what you see there and focus on the basics. Later in the book, you will find out more about the skipped items. You will also learn how to add more content elements and how to administer all aspects of the website.

For the most part, articles are the mainstay of Joomla! 3 websites. Almost all content that is accessible via menu link items are articles, or the content links to another type of layout that leads to categorized articles. You will learn all about the different display formats in Chapter 6, "Front Page Content and Layout."

As you are completing the exercises, go through the steps as outlined and perform only those tasks. The idea here is to guide you through the most frequently used tasks on a Joomla! 3 website.

Also, content built in earlier chapters of this book is used in exercises in later chapters, so make sure you complete the tasks as you go along. Therefore, any references to previous exercises will have meaning. It is important that you complete the tasks so you can build future content on top.

Ready? Let's do it.

EXERCISE 5-2: CREATING A CATEGORY

Objective: This exercise creates a category into which articles will be assigned. Categories are similar to file folders in a file cabinet. You may have as many of them as you want and may add sub-categories as needed to catalog your information (articles) that comprises the content of the website.

Let's create a category now:

Step 1. In the Admin Control Panel, open the Category Manager from the Admin Left Menu to the right. Spend a couple of minutes looking around the screen in Figure 5-5 to gain familiarity with locations of the controls. There is no link to the Featured Articles Manager in the Admin Left Menu.

Figure 5-5 *The* **[A]** *Category Manager displays all the categories and sub-categories automatically created when Joomla! 3 was installed.*

The control buttons for the Category Manager appearing in the upper menu (Figure 5-6) are discussed in detail and used in exercises in Chapter 17, "Categories." For the purposes of the "fast track" exercises, only those needed to create a single category are discussed.

Figure 5-6 *This* **[B]** *menu appears only when the Category Manager opens. Note that directly under New, there is a menu that has links to articles and featured articles. The featured articles (articles specifically designated to appear on the front page of the website) may be accessed here or via the Content Menu drop-down.*

Step 2. Click the green New button **[C]** at the top left (Figure 5-7). This opens the manager to create a single category.

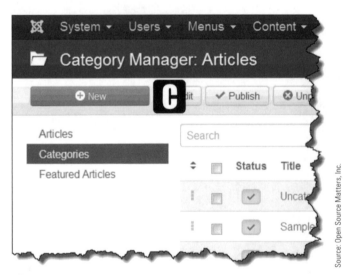

Figure 5-7 *The* **[C]** *New button, which you'll see throughout Joomla! 3, creates a new item in whichever manager is open at the time.*

Step 3. Note the new tab bar that opens along with a change in the third menu row, which now applies only to the particular category being created (Figure 5-8).

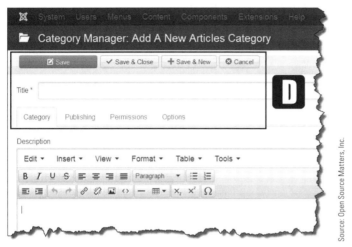

Figure 5-8 *When an individual category manager is open, two new* **[D]** *button rows display. They offer more opportunities to administer different aspects of the category.*

REPEATING DESCRIPTIONS AND EXPLANATIONS

Throughout Joomla! 3, the menu buttons typically function in the same manner, but contextually within the Administrative Manager areas in which you are working. When future menus or manager areas are explained, only new buttons are defined and described. This will save you time so you aren't re-reading the same information over and over again. The information will be repeated from previous instruction only when it's unique or special in its use and there is a compelling need to define it further.

Step 4. In the Title text box, enter **[E] My First Category** (Figure 5-9).

Step 5. In the Description text area, enter **[F] This is my first Joomla! 3 Category.**

Step 6. Click on the **[G]** green Save button at the top left, which results in the screen displaying the success message (Figure 5-10).

Source: Open Source Matters, Inc.

Figure 5-9 *To create a category, only a* **[E]** *title is required. The* **[F]** *description need not contain any content. However, in larger, complex Joomla! 3 websites that display categories in certain formats, the description will be helpful to site visitors to locate content. It will also be helpful for other administrators who may have access to the backend.*

Source: Open Source Matters, Inc.

Figure 5-10 *When the category has been created and* **[G]** *saved, a message will appear, in a* **[H]** *green shaded area, indicating that the action was successful. This happens in other managers in the backend, each time to let you know that the item has been created.*

Step 7. Click the Save & Close button at the top to exit this category and return to the Category Manager screen.

Step 8. Expand the number of items displayed, by clicking the **[I]** drop-down box to the top right and changing the value 20 to All, which expands the list and will display "My First Category" at the bottom after scrolling down (Figure 5-11).

Source: Open Source Matters, Inc.

Figure 5-11 *All lists in Joomla! 3 can be displayed by changing the value to All in the* **[I]** *drop-down box to the upper right of the screen. When new items are added, they are generally* **[J]** *listed in the order in which created, so new items are generally at the bottom of the list. Regardless of type, each item in Joomla! 3 is also assigned a unique ID number. You can use filtering to display selected lists; it's addressed in another chapter.*

Step 9. Click on the Joomla! logo in the top left portion of the screen, which will take you back to the Control Panel, which displays immediately after logging in (Figure 5-2). This is a fast way to get back to "home base" when working within content managers.

When a list view is displayed, another set of buttons appear at the top that allows management of the content at the higher level of display (Figure 5-11). The other managers in the backend have similar buttons with similar functions, although there may be instances where those are different, which is dictated by which manager is being viewed. As you move forward in learning Joomla! 3, these differences will be more obvious.

In exercises later in the book, when there are buttons that apply only to specific managers, they are identified and explained as needed.

When you're done with this exercise, there will be a category (that you created), into which you can assign an article for classification purposes.

ABOUT THE SAVE BUTTONS

Joomla! 3 has a number of similar administrative features and functions in the backend that relate to buttons or tabs within the different content managers. Here are a few things to remember, which are consistent throughout the backend:

- ◆ **The Save button**—Saves the current screen content and the screen remains open for further editing.
- ◆ **The Save & Close button**—Saves the current screen content and returns to the list view of the respective manager.
- ◆ **The Save & New button**—Saves the current screen content and opens a new or blank manager screen to create another similar type of content.
- ◆ **The Save & Copy button**—Saves the screen content and copies the current item to the list view; it's identified as "item name (#)" for indexing purposes. The copy then automatically remains open for any changes to be applied, such as a title change, and so on. Using the copy function saves repetitive work; you should immediately rename the new version to remove the "copy" name status.
- ◆ **The Close button**—Closes the item and typically returns to the list view.

If changes have been made to the content, but have *not* been saved, those changes will be lost when the Close function is executed. Be aware of this danger when managing content, regardless of which manager you're in. Always perform some sort of "saving" action before closing a manager, if you want to keep the changes. If there is no need to save, simply close the manager; this will revert the content back to the previously saved version.

EXERCISE 5-3: CREATING AN ARTICLE AND ASSIGNING IT TO A CATEGORY

Objective: This exercise creates an article that will be assigned to the "My First Category" you created. This function is probably the one that is used the most when administering a Joomla! 3 website, because the general content is in the form of articles, and they need to be assigned to a category.

UNDERSTANDING THE UNCATEGORISED CATEGORY

This might sound confusing, but it is a rational function. By default, Joomla! 3 creates a place for articles to be assigned that isn't a category in the traditional sense. This location is called "Uncategorised." Okay, so there is a category into which articles can be assigned—it's called Uncategorised—but it really isn't a category *per se*. It's a category alright, but it really isn't, and you will still find it on the Category List Manager. It's just the name that creates confusion.

The Uncategorised category should be used as a "parking place" to put articles if there is no named category. Or, on smaller websites, all articles can be assigned into that category and remain there. An article can always be created and placed into the Uncategorised, and then a category can be created at any time and the article re-assigned (moved) into it, removing it from the Uncategorised category.

The term "Unassigned" might be a better name for it, but you can live with "Uncategorised" because you now understand it. *Right*?

As you use Joomla! 3 more and more, you'll notice this use of British English in many places, such as with "uncategorised." You'll see other uses of British English spelling, such as with colour.

Let's create an article and assign it to a category now:

Step 1. Go back to the Admin Control Panel and select Add New Article using the topmost link in the Admin Left Menu (Figure 5-12).

Source: Open Source Matters, Inc.

Figure 5-12 *The* **[K]** *Add New Article link is in the Admin Left Menu because it is one of the most frequently used actions on a Joomla! 3 website. Immediately upon logging into the backend, clicking this link opens the New Article Manager.*

Before going to Step 2, take a quick look the **[L]** control buttons for the Add New Article Manager creation area that appear in the upper-left area of the screen **[M]**. Notice that these are not much different than the category control buttons and function in a similar manner, but they apply only to the creation of a new article (Figure 5-13). This menu array appears only when you're in the New Articles view or admin mode for existing articles.

Source: Open Source Matters, Inc.

Figure 5-13 *Most managers in the backend have somewhat similar but different functioning menus when opened. The* **[L]** *top menu generally deals with "saving" actions, while the* **[M]** *lower tabbed menu deals with the actual content item's optional parameters and settings.*

At this point, the actual article creation process can begin. The Add New Article Manager is now open and information can be added that is part of the article.

Step 2. In the Title box, enter **My First Article**. This field is required when creating an article (Figure 5-14).

Source: Open Source Matters, Inc.

Figure 5-14 *Every article in the creation process must have a* **[N]** *title and be assigned to a* **[O]** *category. Both items are required before you can enter and save the article content.*

Step 3. Open the Category drop-down and scroll to the bottom of the list. Select My First Category, which is the category you created in Exercise 5-2.

Step 4. At this point, save the article by clicking the **[P]** green Save button at the top left. The green "Article Successfully Saved" message should appear. The action saves the article with a title and a category assignment, and the screen remains open for further editing (Figure 5-15).

Figure 5-15 *The **[P]** Save button, in all managers, simply saves the current screen, which will remain open for further editing and/or changes in the parameters of the item.*

Note the two other buttons shown in Figure 5-15. Save & Close will close the current window and revert back to the list view, while Save & New will close the current article and open a new blank article screen. After saving, a Save as Copy button will appear (not shown).

CREATING ARTICLES AND MANAGING LIST LENGTH

Notice that only two items were needed to create an article and that no content, or other information, was needed to add the article to the article list, which can be viewed by clicking on Save & Close. You can extend the number of articles displayed by changing the 20 value in the top right drop-down to All. The article will appear in alphabetical order and display the article title and the assigned category (Figure 5-16).

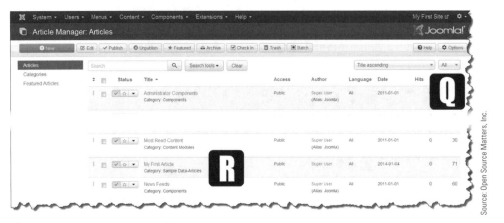

Figure 5-16 *You can set the* **[Q]** *number of items to view all items in the list view. Articles on the list show the* **[R]** *assigned category, as well as information about who and when it was created. The list can also be filtered to pare down the number of articles displayed.*

Step 5. Click on the article title in **[R]** the Article List to open it. The screen opens to the Article Content tab (Figure 5-17). This is a good time to look around the manager at the different administration sections in the top tabs, the drop-downs on the right, under the content window and the input areas below it.

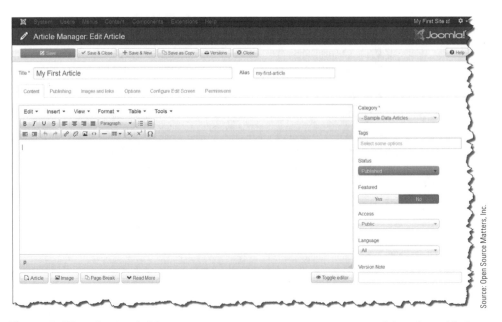

Figure 5-17 *In the Article Manager view, you can open or activate some of the tabs and link buttons and view the contents.*

Chapter 18, "Articles," covers all of these sections in detail. All these parameters are discussed in their respective chapters.

The next step is to add some text to the article. Normally, actual content would be added at this point, but you'll add some "lorem ipsum" text, which is simply dummy Latin text. The dummy text can be generated online, then you can use Copy & Paste to capture the text. Go to:

http://generator.lorem-ipsum.info/

which is a good online resource to obtain or create the dummy text.

Step 6. Select a paragraph or two of "lorem ipsum" text from the text area. Note that you can create many different types of dummy text to use in place of real text when designing articles. Copy the text and paste it into the Article Editor box. Ignore the "spelling error" highlights when you're using dummy text (Figure 5-18).

Figure 5-18 *The default* **[S]** *text editor in Joomla! 3 is a minimal version with only basic word processing features.*

Step 7. Click the Save & Close button at the top to complete this task and exit the Article Manager area.

If the default Joomla! text editor can't give you what you need, there are several other text editors with more features and functions that you can install as extensions. They are covered in Chapter 7, "Adding and Managing Extensions."

So far, you've created a category and assigned an article to it. The next step is to create a menu link item that opens the article when you click on an item in a menu. In this case, it will be the top menu, which is located between the website name and the sample image on the front-end.

EXERCISE 5-4: CREATING A MENU LINK ITEM TO AN ARTICLE

Objective: This exercise connects the article you created in Exercise 5-3 to a menu link item, located in the top menu. The link will open the article and display it in the front page content area of the website.

MENU LINK ITEMS

Joomla! 3 has many different menu link item types that can be created, which allows the display of many different content types on a website. In this exercise, the menu link item type is a single article, which is one of several article-associated link types that can be created.

How to create the menu link item:

Step 1. Open the **[T]** Menu Manager in the Admin Left Menu section of the backend Control Panel (Figure 5-19).

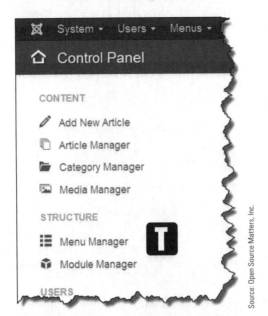

Figure 5-19 *The Admin Left Menu on the Control Panel can be used to access nearly all of the managers used to administer content. The **[T]** Menu Manager is the starting point for all menu-related actions.*

Step 2. Click on the menu named **[U]** Top to open it (Figure 5-20). You should see a list of three menu link items that comprise the links available in that menu as part of the default installation (Figure 5-21).

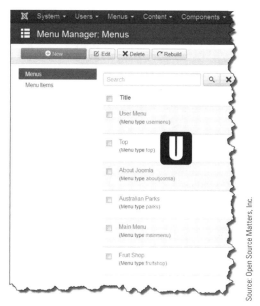

Figure 5-20 *In the Menu Manager, all menus are listed, indicating the type of menu and other information. Each* **[U]** *menu opens to display the menu link items for each.*

Figure 5-21 *The default installation top menu has* **[V]** *three link items. Note the different types and the Status indicator. If it's checked, the menu link item is active and visible within the menu. The* **[W]** *New button opens a new menu link item in the respective open menu.*

SOME MANAGERS SHOW DIFFERENT LINKS

Notice that Add New Menu Item was not available in the Admin Left Menu, as for Add New Article. It is available, however, in the top menu bar (menus). For this exercise, the New method is being used so you can learn how items are created via that method. Keep in mind that the Add New fly-out menus can always be opened via the top (black bar) menu. As you learn how to get around the Joomla! 3 backend, you will likely use the quicker methods of creating content.

Step 3. The New Menu Item Manager opens (Figure 5-22) when the New button is clicked. To create a menu link item, only three actions need to be performed:

Action 1. Select the menu item type to be used.

Action 2. Select the article to which the item will connect.

Action 3. Name the menu link item.

Step 4. Enter **[X] My Menu Item** for the title (Figure 5-22).

Figure 5-22 *The New Menu Item Manager has progressive actions that involve the link name, the type, and the article to be connected to the link.*

Step 5. Click the blue **[Y]** Select button to select the type of menu link item to create (Figure 5-22). This opens the menu type pop-up screen.

Step 6. Select **[Z]** Articles on this screen (Figure 5-23).

Figure 5-23 *This pop-up window also shows other "types" that you can create, in addition to articles.*

Step 7. Click on the **[AA]** Single Article type, which will open a drop-down list (Figure 5-24).

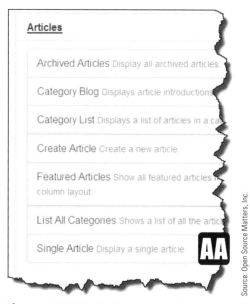

Figure 5-24 *The drill-down into the Articles option displays seven additional content options that can be created. In this instance, pick* **[AA]** *Single Article.*

Step 8. When you click on the Single Article link, the screen changes back to the New Menu Item Manager and displays a new section called Select Article (Figure 5-25).

Figure 5-25 [CC] *Select Article is one of the progressive options that appears based on the previous action of selecting the menu item type, as an* **[BB]** *Article > Single Article.*

When the **[CC]** Select button is executed, a new window opens with a list of all articles that have been created on the website, from which you can choose an article (Figure 5-26).

Step 9. Filter the list by selecting **[DD]** My First Category in the Category drop-down. The list should display only one article entitled **[EE]** "My First Article." Select the article by clicking on the name. This action reopens the New Menu Item Manager with the article name displayed in the Select Article text area.

Figure 5-26 *Before filtering, the other articles listed were added during installation of Joomla! 3.* **[EE]** *My First Article was created in a previous exercise.*

Note that future exercises will refer back to content you create now, which is why it is important that all of the exercises be completed in order.

Step 10. At this point, execute the Save & Close action. The Save & Close action takes you back to the list of menu items in the current menu (top). Save & New saves the menu link item, and opens a new, blank screen. This allows several menu link items to be created in the respective menu during only one series of administrative tasks.

The **[FF]** Success screen that displays is the updated menu item list for the top menu, and should display the **[GG]** My Menu Item as the last item (Figure 5-27). If there are any issues, a different message will appear indicating the problem with the action.

Figure 5-27 *When creation actions are executed, the* **[FF]** *green success message will appear when the task is completed, and the* **[GG]** *menu link item will appear on the list.*

At this point, return to the front-end of the website and refresh the monitor screen. The new menu link item (called My Menu Item) should display in the top menu bar (Figure 5-28). Note that the top menu is a horizontal layout. Any additional menu link items added to that menu will be added to the bottom.

Source: Open Source Matters, Inc.

Figure 5-28 *The new* **[HH]** *menu link item is now available in the menu.*

Step 11. On the front-end, click **[HH]** My Menu Item in the top menu. This will open and display **[II]** My First Article (Figure 5-29). By default, all articles include details. You can modify or remove these details, on a global default basis or on an article-by-article basis. See the online supplement at joomla3bootcamp.com.

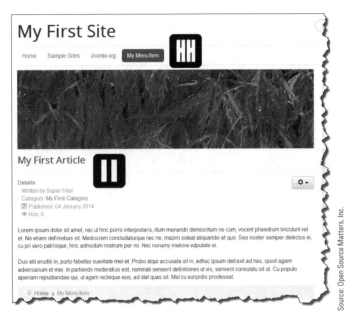

Source: Open Source Matters, Inc.

Figure 5-29 *As shown, the* **[HH]** *menu link item opened the* **[II]** *article.*

Summary

In this chapter, you learned:

◆ How to access the Administrator backend.

◆ How to create and save a content category.

◆ How to create and save an article.

◆ How to assign an article to a content category.

◆ How to access an existing menu.

◆ How to link a menu link item to an article.

◆ How to display an article on the website front-end.

Source: Open Source Matters, Inc./200mph Media Group, LLC.

Chapter 6

Front Page Content and Layout

Learning Objectives

What's included in this chapter:

- Information about the website's front page.
- Information about the front page layout.
- Information about the Protostar template layout.
- Identification of different parts of the template.
- Identifying the Home Page menu link item.
- Understanding the types of page layouts for content.
- Designating articles in categories as featured.
- How to change the order of articles in the Featured Articles category.
- How to rearrange the layout of the featured articles on the front page.
- Identifying template frameworks.
- Using responsive templates and mobile devices.
- Using Google Fonts.

First Impressions Count

The opening page of a website sets the stage for visitor interest. If the visitor does not like what they immediately see, they will not click any links to go deeper into the website's content. If you can't get visitors to browse around your site, or look for specific content, you might as well just shut the website down. It's not serving any useful purpose if the visitors look and then leave in a hurry.

On the other hand, if they like what they see, they will likely spend time prowling around website content and visiting the interior pages. Therefore, the Front Page and layout are very important factors that make websites popular or just so much Internet fodder. Joomla! 3 has the internal horsepower to build a stunning and magnetic front page. It also has the ability to make every web page for every menu link item completely different. These are times when the page layout of interior pages of a website can, and often should, be different from the opening front page. This can be accomplished in Joomla! 3.

Front Page Anatomy

Before considering the content of a front page, which can be fully controlled by the super user with many different types of layout configurations, let's take a look at the anatomy of the front page.

> **JOOMLA! TERMINOLOGY**
>
> Within this chapter and for the remainder of the book, many terms will be used or introduced. Some terms apply globally across the Internet. Others apply only to Joomla! The terms are defined and explained as needed.

Understanding the Protostar Template Layout

If you recall from previous chapters, templates are the Joomla! 3 extensions that determine the layout, look, and physical characteristics of the website. The template architecture, or anatomy, is made up of a number of building blocks, all controlled by the main page coding and the Cascading Style Sheet (CSS) associated with it.

If you think of templates as "structures," understanding their layout and how to manage or manipulate them will be easy. The layout can be changed and adjusted using built-in controls within the different content managers for components, modules, and other content-generating features. The most important of these layout options are controlled via the Type menu link item.

Understanding templates and the Joomla! 3 content-generating functions can make management of a website's visual layout easier. The structure of a typical, fully-coded, Joomla! 3 template, built upon a configurable "framework," is illustrated in Figure 6-1. The default

Joomla! 3 Protostar template is based on Twitter's bootstrap and the new Joomla User Interface (JUI) Library.

The template's colors, font selections, and layout can be selected within the template's Options area, if the template is set up to allow those changes.

The new Joomla! 3 "core" and "framework" also allows for other templates to be assigned to different menus and different menu link items. This gives the super user the option of using different templates for different layouts within the same website. This topic is thoroughly covered in Chapter 21, "Templates."

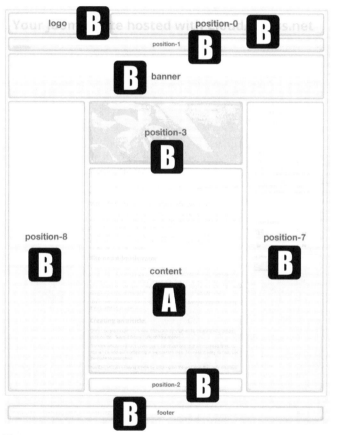

Source: Open Source Matters, Inc.

Figure 6-1 *The Joomla! 3 Protostar template module positions. This type of guide is also called a "module map." The Protostar template has, by default, a simple three-column layout, but can be used to create a variety of content layouts.*

Figure 6-1 shows the layout of the Protostar template. There are two essential parts: the **[A]** main content area, and **[B]** many modules in various positions. This layout is a good example of an uncomplicated three-column layout, wherein modules displaying different types of content can be located in different positions on the page, with the main content in the middle.

If there are no modules actually assigned to position-8, the content area appears shifted to the left of the page. Likewise with position-7, which displays modules on the right side. So, when the module positions are adjacent one another, and one does not have any modules assigned, the other positions with modules assigned expand to fill up the allotted space. There's more on this topic in Chapter 19, "Modules."

ABUNDANCE OF TEMPLATES AVAILABLE

Joomla! 3 websites are not limited to the use of the default templates. There are hundreds, if not thousands, of templates available. Additionally, there are several programs that allow the site managers to create their own templates from scratch.

When looking for templates for a Joomla! 3 website, it's a good idea to always look closely at the template demo provided by the developers, and to review the available module positions. Most all quality template demos include the module map, usually called "module positions" in one of the menus of the template demo page.

Always spend time looking at template demo pages when considering any template for inclusion into your website. This is especially important when the templates are not free. Take a test-drive of the template before putting your money on the table to make sure it is the right one for your site.

Types of Page Layouts

Every website has a Home location, which is the opening page. In Joomla! 3, the layout and content of the opening page is determined by what type of menu link item is in control by being designated as the default menu link item, which can be any one of a number of content display formats.

Joomla! 3 has many built-in features that control the layout of pages, or better stated, they allow content to be displayed in many ways. In fact, if an extension is installed that generates a certain type of content or layout, it can be designated as the Home page layout. Such would be the case of a shopping cart extension, and the open website page would feature certain products. The certain products screen is designated as the default and shows the desired content.

In short, any kind or type of content, whether from the default Joomla! 3 installation or from installed extensions, can be designated as the opening Home page of the website.

HOME CAN BE ANYTHING

The opening page of a website does not need to be called Home. The menu link item that controls the Main Page layout can be named anything, and can be any kind of content layout format. The controlling factor is which menu link item type is designated as the default for the opening page, or opening screen of the website.

By setting the menu link item as the default for the opening page, whatever content layout is assigned to it displays when the website is opened. Joomla! 3 allows any number of Home page layouts by selection and then setting some additional parameters.

What Kind of Layouts?

The layout of the "My First Site" opening page has a top menu, into which the "My Menu Item" was added in the "Fast Track Start" exercises in Chapter 5. This menu is located between the site banner and the content area. However, on this template, the actual main menu is located on the right side of the page, and the format-controlling Home button is in that menu.

Let's clarify that some more. The website's main menu is on the right, located in the This Site menu module, and actually controls the format of the opening page.

The Home menu link item in the top menu does nothing more than mimic the Home menu link item in the main menu, and it does so as an *alias*. This functionality is covered in Chapter 24, "Using the Menu System."

Which brings up another point. The main menu with the Home menu link item does not need to appear in any standard location, such as at the top, below the site banner, with the Home button on the left. The main menu can be anywhere on the screen where there is a module position to hold it, and the Home menu link item can be called any name.

How and why certain menus are used and their locations isn't really important right now. Chapters 8 through 22 cover many topics that include components, categories, articles, modules, plug-ins, templates, menus, and more. So for the time being, be assured that these topics will be covered in depth later.

LOOK FOR ICONS, STARS, AND CHECKMARKS

The menu that contains the default or home item is found by looking in the Menus drop-down in the backend. Open any menu via the Menus button in the top menu and look at the list in the drop-down section. The menu that has an image of a house next to it contains the default menu link item and controls the front page content display.

When that menu is open, one menu link item in the list of menu link items in that menu has a "gold star" in the Home column. This star indicates the menu link item that controls the format of the front page. Any menu link item on the list can be designated as Home, which would change the front page layout accordingly.

Types of Front Page Content and Layouts

When a menu link item is created in any menu, the first action is to select a menu item type in the manager for an existing menu. Every website must have at least one menu. Joomla! 3 websites can have many menus, and these can be set to display or not, given the settings in other menu link items. This can get very interesting for creating website pages, and is discussed in greater detail in Chapter 24.

Here are the default menu item types and variations that can be created within the standard Joomla! 3 default installation:

Contacts—Allows the creation of different types of contact lists that can be used to communicate with the individuals added to the Contacts component.

> Featured Contacts
>
> List All Contact Categories
>
> List Contacts in a Category
>
> Single Contact

Articles—Manages all types of content relative to categories and articles.

> Archived Articles
>
> Category Blog
>
> Category List
>
> Create Article
>
> Featured Articles
>
> List All Categories
>
> Single Article

Smart Search—Creates a feature to search the website for specific content.

> Search

Newsfeeds—RSS feeds from other websites can be displayed in different combinations or as a single feed.

> List All News Feed Categories
>
> List News Feeds in a Category
>
> Single News Feed

Search—Offers the option of creating a more advanced method of searching the website.

> Search Form or Search Results

Tags—Allows adding tags to articles and other content, which is simply a label attached to a content item. Content tagging is covered in Chapter 15, "Components: Tags."

Compact List of Tagged Items

List of All Tags

Tagged Items

Users Manager—Organizes users and allows the use of the Joomla! 3 Access Control Manager (ACL) to manage user permissions relative to website content.

Edit User Profile

Login Form

Password Reset

Registration Form

User Profile

Username Reminder Request

Weblinks—Similar to the Contacts component except this deals with links to other websites.

List All Web Link Categories

List Web Links in a Category

Submit a Web Link

Wrapper—Allows external URLs to be displayed within the content area of the website.

iFrame Wrapper

System Links—These functions can create link items that have specialized uses within the Joomla! 3 menu structures.

External URL

Menu Heading

Menu Item Alias

Text Separator

These menu link item types are representative of the default installation. When additional extensions, such as components, modules, and plug-ins, are added to a website, more menu link type choices are automatically added, depending upon the nature of the extension. After an extension that generates content to be displayed on the website has been added, a new menu link type is added to the Type list, specific to the extension.

Another interesting thing about module extensions is that they can be associated with a menu link item. As an example, if the menu link item type is for a single article, when the item is clicked in a menu, the article opens, and then, one more thing happens. The associated module will appear in the assigned module position. When another menu link item is clicked, the module does not appear if it has not been assigned to that link item.

Content or Main Body Area, Which Is It?

By default in Joomla! 3, the content or main body area is where articles, categories, and certain menu link item types are automatically displayed. If a menu link item is connected to an article, the article will appear in the physical area on the template (called content or sometimes called main body) when it's clicked. The terms may be used interchangeably.

This default placement is important for other content also. For example, when you're viewing the My First Site front page, and you click the Example Pages link in the This Site Menu Module, the result will display in the Content area, leaving all modules intact in their assigned positions.

Note that the About Joomla! module now expands to include more menu link items within the list. This is an excellent example of how one action in one menu can affect the page layout, the space used and arrangement of modules, and the actual display of module content. In the case of About Joomla!, it's a Menu Module.

This change of the menu display was accomplished using the Module Assignment for this Menu Item option, which is found as a tabbed parameter area on each menu link item that is created, and offers many different options for displaying information. Chapter 19, "Modules," covers the dynamics of hiding or showing modules in association with menu link items.

Creating Featured Articles

Articles are assigned to categories, and menu link items are used to open the article, which displays in the content area of the website. Most websites have specific articles to be displayed on the front page, and these articles may be assigned to one, or many, different categories. This does not mean articles can be assigned to multiple categories at the same time, but that several articles in different categories can be displayed.

Displaying articles from multiple categories on the front page is a daunting task. It would be, that is, if it were not for the Featured Articles option within the individual Article Manager. This configuration is the only instance where a single article can be assigned to two categories at the same time. For content-display purposes, featured articles are treated as a category.

Let's look at how this is accomplished.

On the front page, there is a leading article called Joomla! Here are some facts about that article:

◆ The category assignment for the article is **Category = Joomla!** and it's found in the Category list.

◆ The article is also designated as a featured article, which automatically makes it visible on the front page **[C]** (Figure 6-2).

◆ The Featured Article designation is set in the Article Manager for the individual article **[F]** (Figure 6-3).

◆ The visual layout of the article on the front page is dictated by the Layout parameters of the Featured Articles menu item type in the main menu (Figure 6-4).

Source: Open Source Matters, Inc.

Figure 6-2 *The* **[C]** *full-width article, in the Layout setting, is called the # Leading Articles and can have any number, with each article displayed in a one-column layout. In this case, the "# of…" is set to one article.*

Source: Open Source Matters, Inc.

Figure 6-3 *Any individual* **[D]** *article in any* **[E]** *category can be designated to appear on the front page as a featured article by selecting Yes in the* **[F]** *Featured parameter.*

Figure 6-4 *Within the menu link item's* **[G]** *Layout tab, you can set the layout for the display of the featured articles content, which is a Category Blog layout. The settings shown here generate the layout seen in Figure 6-2.*

The settings for the Category Blog layout parameters are:

[H] Select which categories the featured articles will come from. This can be one, several, or all categories, and offers a wide range of options for sourcing articles for the front page. If you choose several, click on the current category, and a drop-down will show all the categories. Select another and repeat the procedure until you've selected all the desired categories.

[I] Leading articles appear at the top of the content area as the full width of the column. If the value is 0, all of the articles will appear as defined in the # Columns value. The # Columns can be 1, 2, 3, or any value that is practical for a good visual display.

[J] This parameter sets the value of the # Intro Articles, which are articles displayed after the leading articles. In the default installation, these are the three articles underneath the Joomla! leading article. If you need more, the number can simply be increased.

[K] Allows the entire display of articles, or just the # Intro Articles, to display in one or several columns. If the # Leading Articles is set to 0, the entire display will be based on the value in the # Columns parameter, which should be a practical number given the width of the content area and article column width.

[L] After the leading and intro articles, there can be text links to additional articles within the scope of the categories to be displayed. This is just a list of the articles as links to open them. This feature is discussed again in several following chapters.

[M] The way articles are presented is set by the Multi Column Order parameter, either down or across. This is a helpful parameter setting if the articles are all of the Leading type with none designated as the Intro type.

[N] If several categories are used to source the articles, they can be displayed in a specific way with this parameter.

[O] The order of article display is set with this parameter, which has many different options.

The other parameters that may be applied are covered in Chapter 24, where each menu item type is discussed with examples and exercises.

To better understand how the Category Blog layouts can be changed and the presentation of articles can be altered, complete the following exercises.

EXERCISE 6-1: DESIGNATING MY FIRST ARTICLE AS A FEATURED ARTICLE

Objective: This exercise will make the previously created article (My First Article) a featured article, which means it will appear on the front page, in addition to its classification in My First Category.

Step 1. Log in to the Administrator backend as the super user.

Step 2. In a New Browser tab, display the My First Site front-end for your domain.

Step 3. In the backend, open the Article Manager via the Admin Left Menu.

Step 4. Scroll down the list of articles and find My First Article.

Step 5. Next to the green checkmark, click on the star icon. The result should be as shown in Figure 6-5.

Figure 6-5 *On article lists, if the* **[P]** *star next to the checkbox is gold, the article has been assigned, not only to its respective category, but also to the Featured Articles category.*

EXERCISE 6-2: CHANGING THE ORDER OF MY FIRST ARTICLE IN THE FEATURED ARTICLE LIST

Objective: This exercise will move My First Article to the top of the article ordering list.

Step 1. Scroll to the top of the Article Manager list page.

Step 2. Click the Featured Articles link at the top left (Figure 6-6).

> The resulting screen from Step 2 is a list of the articles that have been designated as featured, which should include My First Article on the list.

Figure 6-6 *When in the Article Manager, the links to the top left provide fast access to the categories and to the* **[Q]** *Featured Articles Managers.*

Step 3. On the results screen, click on the column heading called **[S]** Ordering (Figure 6-7).

> The resulting screen will display the featured articles and their numerical order. The order may not be the same on your website. As long as there are five articles, all is well.

Figure 6-7 *When **[R]** the Featured Articles column heading **[S]** called Ordering is clicked, the column becomes a control with parameter settings to move articles up or down, or assign them numerical orders.*

To change the actual ordering of the items, you can use two methods. First, the Up/Down arrows in the Ordering column can be used to move the articles on the list. This can be a bit cumbersome if the article is at the bottom of the list and the list is long. Second, the numeric values in the boxes can be changed to reflect the order, which is what you'll do in the next step.

Step 4. Set the My First Article order to 1, meaning you want it to be first.

Step 5. Set the Joomla! article order to 5, which will place it as the last article.

Step 6. Click the **[T]** small box at the head of the Ordering column to change and save the new order of the articles (Figure 6-8). *This is important! Don't forget to do it.*

Figure 6-8 *Once the desired ordering has been set, click the **[T]** icon shown to save the resulting order. There is no Save button to do this; this icon saves the new order.*

EXERCISE 6-3: SETTING THE LAYOUT OF THE ARTICLES

Objective: This exercise demonstrates how to alter the actual layout of the front page, which is a Featured Articles Category Blog layout for the sample data that was installed.

Step 1. Click the Menus link at the top of the screen in the dark blue bar. Then, open the main menu with the house icon.

Step 2. Click on the Home menu link item, then open the Layout tab.

Step 3. Set the Category Order (about half way down the screen), to No Order in the respective drop-down. This removes any effect the article categories may have on the order.

Step 4. In the Article Order drop-down, select the Featured Articles Order option, which will arrange the articles as set in Exercise 6-2, Steps 4 and 5.

Step 5. Execute the Save action. This will save the changes and keep you on the same screen.

Step 6. Go to the front-end and confirm that My First Article is being displayed as the only leading article on the page display. If it is not, go through Exercise 6-2 again, and then check the items in Exercise 6-3 to make sure the settings are the same.

In the next exercise, you'll learn how to alter the visual arrangement of the page.

EXERCISE 6-4: CREATING FULL-COLUMN WIDTH LAYOUT FOR ALL FEATURED ARTICLES

Objective: The goal of this exercise is to demonstrate how to make all of the featured articles appear column-wide. At present there is one article column-wide, and four articles displayed in a two-column format, using two rows. This exercise will change the layout to five full column-width articles (Figure 6-9).

Step 1. In the Menu Manager of the main menu, and with the Home menu link item, open the Layout tab.

Step 2. Change the settings of the items as indicated here:

Leading Articles = 5

Intro Articles = 0

Columns = 0 or 1 (technically, there cannot be 0 columns)

Step 3. Execute the Save action, to save the changes and remain on the same screen. The result should be all five articles displayed the full width of the content area (Figure 6-9).

Source: Open Source Matters, Inc.

Figure 6-9 *Based on individual article content, the depth of the articles may vary, which can result in undesired whitespace, as seen in the Upgraders/Professionals article presentation. Upgrades does not have a "read more" insert, thus the disparity in vertical space between the articles.*

EXERCISE 6-5: CREATING A THREE-COLUMN WIDTH LAYOUT FOR THREE FEATURED ARTICLES

Objective: The goal of this exercise is to demonstrate how to make only three of the featured articles appear in three-columns. At present, the layout is one column-wide, and there are five articles displayed. This exercise will change the layout to three columns using three articles.

Step 1. In the Menu Manager for the main menu, and with the Home menu link item, open the Layout tab.

Step 2. Change the settings of the items as indicated here:

Leading Articles = 0

Intro Articles = 3

Columns = 3

Step 3. Execute the Save action, to save the changes and remain on the same screen. The result should be three articles displayed in three columns within the content area (Figure 6-10). Note that because only three of the five featured articles are designated to display, the system automatically creates a **[U]** paginated location for the articles not displayed in the main content area on the main page.

Source: Open Source Matters, Inc.

Figure 6-10 *Column depth is dependent upon actual article content, which can be adjusted to be of equal lengths. If the number of articles exceeds the layout parameters, the* **[U]** *page navigation is automatically generated to allow access to those articles.*

EXERCISE 6-6: CREATING TWO-COLUMN WIDTH LAYOUT FOR FOUR FEATURED ARTICLES

Objective: The goal of this exercise is to demonstrate how to make four of the featured articles appear in two-columns. At present there are three columns using three articles, with additional articles accessed via the pagination links below.

Step 1. In the Menu Manager for the main menu, and with the Home menu link item, open the Layout tab.

Step 2. Change the settings of the items as indicated here:

Leading Articles = 0

Intro Articles = 4

Columns = 2

Step 3. Execute the Save action, to save the changes and remain on the same screen.

On the website front-end, the result should be four articles in two-columns in the content area (Figure 6-11). The fifth article is accessible by using the pagination links.

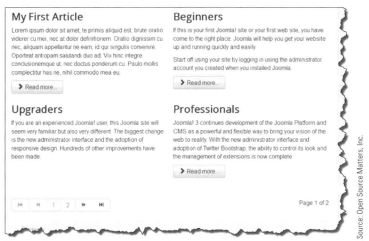

Source: Open Source Matters, Inc.

Figure 6-11 *This layout suffers from content-depth issues because the articles were not created with opening text, which would help balance the page.*

To set up a layout of the featured articles, for future exercises, complete this step:

Step 4. Change the featured articles parameters to these values:

> # Leading Articles = 1
>
> # Intro Articles = 4
>
> # Columns = 2

Step 5. Execute the Save action, to save the changes and remain on the same screen. The result should display My First Article one-column wide, and the four other articles in two columns below it. Keep this order and layout; do not change it. The layout will be used in future exercises.

CONTENT DISPLAY OPTIONS

A good point to keep in mind, when considering layouts, is that many different combinations can be used to display content. The Featured Articles function is only one of the many ways content can be displayed. Exercises in other chapters cover the different methods with working examples.

You can also install and use extensions, which allow content to be displayed by different assigned parameters to categories and articles, based on the display options desired for the website. These are also discussed with examples or exercises.

Templates Built Upon Frameworks

The default Joomla! 3 templates are built upon the core framework of the program. This provides basic template configurations as a core feature and allows novice Joomla! 3 users to get a website up and running immediately upon completing the installation process. But, after that, the templates fall a tad short of further enhancements. Templates are covered in Chapter 21.

Developers and Frameworks

Most of the upper tier Joomla! 3 templates are built upon a framework. The developers have created unique frameworks specific to their template designs and this adds an abundance of features and functionality, along with layout and configuration options.

Generally, in previous Joomla! versions, modifying a template required an advanced knowledge of PHP, CSS, along with several other codes to make the front-end display visually appealing. As Joomla! evolved past version 1.5, developers began to construct frameworks upon which their advanced templates could be programmed. This is a good thing.

Very much like building a house, it is built upon a foundation (Joomla! 3 core), and the walls are added (template frameworks), which give the house a nice, appealing look.

Consider Template Frameworks

Here are some template frameworks to look at and research, which will help you understand how they work with Joomla! 3. Some of these are free and some are commercial, which means you need to pay for them.

When you acquire a template from the developers, the framework is usually built into it. This way, the framework does not need to be installed separately from the template.

Most of these frameworks can be downloaded so you can build your own custom templates, but this isn't a good idea unless you are proficient with programming, HTML, and CSS. Some frameworks are free; others require either a direct purchase or a subscription to access extensions. Table 6-1 shows a list of template frameworks you might consider.

Apologies to any framework developers whose package is not listed. The best plan of action is to visit joomla3bootcamp.com to review additional information about frameworks.

TABLE 6-1 Joomla! 3 Template Frameworks

Template Framework	Template Developers
Bootstruct	JoomlaEngineering
Expose	Themexpert
Gantry	RocketTheme
Gavern	Gavick
HD	Hyde-Design
Helix	JoomShaper
JV	JVFramework
T3	JoomlaArt
Vertex	Shape 5
Warp	YooTheme
Wright	JoomlaShack
XTC	Joomla XTC
YJ Simple Grid	YouJoomla
Zen Grid 2	JoomlaBamboo

Source: 200mph Media Group, LLC.

Templates Compatible with Mobile Devices

This chapter would not be complete without mentioning the adaptability of Joomla! 3 templates to display websites on mobile devices—including laptops, pad devices, and phone devices—regardless of manufacturer or operating system.

Generally, most of the high-quality Joomla! 3 templates have what is known as *responsive design*. This means the template fits the criteria of compatibility identified in the previous paragraph. In fact, if a website does not have the ability to display properly on mobile devices, it is considered inferior.

Good websites can either have a separate mobile device page layout, or a responsive design. The separate page layout means more work in creating the website, which leads to more work if changes are made to the content and so on. Therefore, a website template with a responsive design is the best way to make a Joomla! 3 website visible on desktop browsers, tablets/laptops, pads, and mobile phones.

Mobile devices have different screen resolutions, different screen widths and heights, in addition to portrait and landscape (rotated) views. This, in itself, is a challenge to overcome on any website. But, thanks to fluid template widths and responsive design, one template can meet the display requirements of desktop, laptop, and mobile devices at the same time.

When considering a template for any Joomla! 3 website, make sure it can generate fluid layouts and tackles responsive design. Modern day websites should always offer proper content display on any device capable of accessing the website.

Fonts on Joomla! 3 Websites

Showing different and unique fonts on a website, at least in the past, was a problem because websites could only display fonts that were resident on the client-side computer. Fancy or decorative headline fonts generally could not be used.

A lot of font solutions have been offered, but one of the biggest problems was that specialized fonts needed to be downloaded with the website files. In the case of purchased and licensed fonts, this was not permitted because the fonts were licensed to be used on only one (the buyer's) computer. There were so many complications involved with embedded and downloadable fonts that a universal solution was desperately needed.

Along Came Google Fonts

Google created a free font library and any website can access the library and use their fonts on a website. This solved the problem to the extent that as long as they provide the service, the fonts can be used.

Most all modern-era (Joomla! 1.5, 1.6, 1.7, 2.5, and 3.1.x) templates have a built-in feature that allows you to use fonts from that library, and interact with the parameters of the template. If the template does not specifically have the ability to incorporate Google Fonts, there are a number of extensions that you can use to take advantage of using the non-resident Google Fonts on a Joomla! 3 website. More information about using Google Fonts can be found in Chapter 27, "Using Fonts with Joomla! 3," and at joomla3bootcamp.com.

Summary

In this chapter, you learned:

◆ About the website's front page.

◆ About the front page layout.

◆ About the Protostar template layout.

◆ How to identify different parts of the template.

◆ How to identify the Home Page menu link item.

◆ The types of page layouts for content.

◆ How to designate articles as featured.

◆ How to change the order of articles in the Featured Articles category.

◆ How to rearrange the layout of the featured articles on the front page.

◆ Template frameworks are often used to manage template features.

◆ Responsive templates can be used with mobile devices.

◆ Google Fonts can be used with templates.

Chapter 7

Adding and Managing Extensions

Learning Objectives

What's included in this chapter:

◆ The functions of extensions.

◆ What versions of extensions to use.

◆ What are the different types of extensions.

◆ How to obtain and download extensions.

◆ How to install extensions using each method.

◆ How to change the website's default editor.

◆ How to change an individual user's editor.

◆ Extending the duration of the user's session.

◆ Disabling an extension.

◆ Uninstalling an extension.

Extensions Amp Up the Power of Joomla! 3

Extensions add more horsepower and features to Joomla! 3. Essentially, extensions change Joomla!'s six-cylinder engine to eight cylinders and crank up the ability to create virtually any type of website. Extensions can change the entire makeup of a website by presenting more content and displaying it in many different ways, all on top of the basic features of Joomla! 3.

Chapters 3, "Joomla! 3 Default Installation," and 4, "How Joomla! 3 Works," outlined the Joomla! 3 core installation. The default installation is more than sufficient to create and deploy many varieties of general-content websites. Many different displays of content can be created, but there is a point at which the default installation runs out of options to the point where more features are needed.

That's where extensions come into play. Using extensions allows website managers to add features, functions, content displays, and a whole range of related parts. The list is almost unending, with many types of extensions across a wide spectrum of formats and content creation ability.

In this chapter, extensions are discussed in-depth. Exercises will guide you through the relatively simple process of adding extensions to the website and also demonstrate how the super user configures them via the Administrator backend.

Where Extensions Come From

Extensions are created by independent, third-party developers. The Joomla! 3 developer team does not develop extensions, beyond those included in the default installation of the software on the website. Mostly, independent developers create extensions for their own use, then share them with the Joomla! community via the Joomla! Extensions Directory (JED). The JED lists thousands of extensions that you can add to earlier and current versions of Joomla! These extensions are used on hundreds of thousands of websites across the world.

Some developers create extensions because they want to, and contribute them to the world community. They do this because developing extensions to perform certain functions, or to display certain types of content, is good coding practice.

Other developers have made a business out of extensions and provide either specialized ones, or a range of extension products that work alone or in unison. It is safe to assume that if you want an extension to do something specific, it is available somewhere in the JED. The JED classifies extensions by category, and simple searching will narrow them down so you can select the appropriate one to fill your website's needs.

EXTENSIONS FOR JOOMLA! VERSIONS

This is important! Extensions are version-specific. What this means is that extensions created for Version 1.5 will not work with Version 3.x. For this reason, the JED has icons for each Joomla! version. When you're searching for extensions to use, always make sure the extension is compatible with the version of Joomla! you are using. In this case, Joomla! Version 3.x.x. Use the Advanced Search feature of the JED to find extensions by Joomla! version.

The joomla.org JED

The joomla.org website has an entire section devoted to extensions. This library of extensions is categorized by use category and is located on the website. You choose the Extend link in the dark blue top menu bar, and then the Extension Directory link (Figure 7-1).

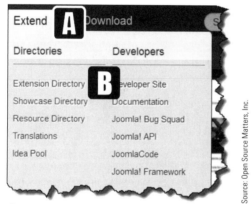

Figure 7-1 *The* **[A]** *Extend tab opens the links to the* **[B]** *Extension Directory link to the JED.*

Commercial versus Non-Commercial Extensions

To pay or not to pay for extensions, that is the question. There are many, many extensions that are absolutely free to use, donated to the Open Source community *gratis* by developers. Other extensions require a flat fee payment or a paid membership to the developer's website. The JED shows extensions by the broad classifications of non-commercial and commercial. This is where things start to get fuzzy.

When you're searching for an extension, you might run upon one that fits the function just the way you want it, and it's listed as non-commercial. So you follow the JED links to the location to download the extension, and you run into one of these four situations:

Situation 1. All is well. The extension is free and can be immediately downloaded from the developer's website.

Situation 2. The extension is free, but you must register as a user on the site, which will often require an email confirmation. When you click on the link in the email that was sent to you, you gain access to the site. You may then log in and download the extension.

Situation 3. The extension, which was listed as a non-commercial, is free, but you must pay for a membership to access the download area on the developer's website. Technically, the extension is free, but the rub is that you must pay for a subscription to the website to download any free extensions. This combination comes in many different forms, so be aware that payment may be required, maybe not for the extension itself, but to access the download area on the developer's website.

Situation 4. The extension is free, but there are missing parts needed to make it fully functional. These add-ons must be purchased. There are many extensions that fall into this scenario—the basic functions are available at no cost, but to add the meat and potatoes to them, some payment is required. Templates often are of this type—part of it free, and the full-featured version needs a payment.

There are some other scenarios for downloading and using extensions, whether they are commercial or non-commercial. These situations deal with using the website itself. Here are those situations:

Situation 1. The extension can be used on an unlimited number of websites.

Situation 2. The extension can be used only on a specified website, which means that the use, which is likely the case with commercial or paid extensions, is strictly limited only to the website that is specified at the time of acquiring the extension. After downloading, there is usually some sort of registration required wherein the use-domain is specified, and a license code is issued, which is entered in the Extensions plug-in via the Admin backend. In this case, if you want to use the extension on another site, you have to purchase a new use license for that domain.

Situation 3. The extension is limited to use on three or more websites, and you must get a serial number for each installation. This is easy enough to do in most cases. You log in to the site, enter the domains for the use of the extension, and get a license key. You enter this key in the Extensions Manager after installing it on the website. Multiple-website-use extensions are available, but not that common, unless the developer is trying to gain a market edge on another, similar extension.

Situation 4. There are other limitations, such as a limit to the number of times the extension can be downloaded; the subscriptions are in tiers whereby the updates are allowed for a given period of time based on the level of subscription purchased; no updates or upgrades are offered after the initial download; or downloading of upgrades or updates are limited to specific lengths of time based on the payment level of the subscription.

Is the Extension Supported?

The whole point of this discussion was to clarify the various methods by which extensions can be acquired and the circumstances that may arise when doing so. Another point to consider about extensions is the level of support. Usually, free extensions have little or no support from the developers. In some instances this can be good or bad. For simple extensions, support probably isn't needed. However, for more complex extensions, support is almost essential, and without it, you can run into trouble getting the extension to work properly, especially if you are not a code-savvy person.

When you're purchasing an extension or a subscription to the website, you should expect a certain level of support included in your purchase. In some cases, the support is excellent with proper responses within a reasonable time limit. In other cases, requests for support issues never receive responses.

If a developer's website has support that includes a ticketing system, chances are that their responsiveness to support questions or assistance requests is good.

Be Aware of Monetary Units When Purchasing

One other item to consider when purchasing extensions or subscriptions is the monetary value. Be aware that many times the price of the extension/subscription is listed in Euros (€) and not U.S. dollars ($). You might need to do a quick conversion to get the actual dollar amount you are paying. Chances are you will be buying extensions that use the Euro monetary unit because the developers are in a Euro Zone country. As a general rule, a Euro is 130% the value of a U.S. dollar, where €10 Euros is equal to $13 U.S. dollars, thereabouts. If you are offering services to clients, make sure you don't short-change yourself by using the wrong monetary value when quoting extension costs.

Types of Extensions: A Quick Review

In Chapter 4, extensions were defined as add-ons that expand the function of Joomla! 3 in the areas of content and operation. Extensions can be readily installed by the super user to display website content.

Joomla! 3 consists of six types of extensions (Figure 7-2), and each extension has unique characteristics regarding how the content is displayed or accessed by website visitors.

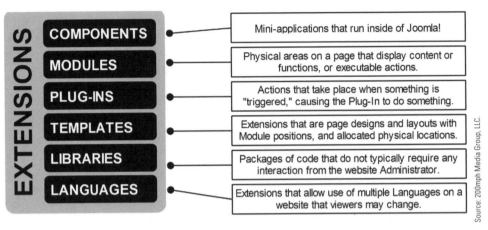

Figure 7-2 *With the exception of libraries and languages, website content is controlled by the super user and based on the respective parameters of each extension. This allows a wide and varied range of content to be displayed on a Joomla! 3 website.*

What's the Purpose of Extensions?

At the risk of stating the obvious, Extensions extend Joomla! 3's functions and content management/display capabilities. They work on the building-block principle, where the core installation sets the foundation, and then extensions are added to extend that foundation. The number of extensions you decide to add can be few or many.

There are six types of extensions of Joomla! 3. Each extension type installs the same way via the Admin backend by the super user. Based on the type of extension, they need to either be configured to manage their content display, or simply enabled.

Some extensions actually install several other parts. For example, a component may also install a module and a plug-in at the same time, with each being used to display the content. Of course, you should always check the individual parts of an extension to make sure they are enabled for use. You would be surprised by how many times administrators miss that simple step.

In general order of most used, components top the list, with modules and plug-ins a close second. It's likely that no more than two templates are actually used on a typical Joomla! 3 website. There are, however, websites that might use a different template for each page, as distinguished from simply altering the layout with the Module Hide/Show features. Chapter 21, "Templates," covers how to implement and use multiple templates and different styles to display content in different ways.

Extensions were discussed and defined in Chapter 4, so let's get into how extensions are installed in the Admin backend.

Method for Installing Extensions

Every extension is installed the same way, following a process that goes like this:

Step 1. The extension is located/selected in the Joomla! JED, or

Step 2. The extension is sourced and downloaded from a developer's website.

Step 3. The extension ZIP file is typically downloaded to the super user's computer.

Step 4. The Extension Manager in the backend is used to select and install the extension by one of three built-in alternative methods.

Step 5. The extension is then enabled or configured as needed to produce the desired result.

There are three ways to connect to an extension in the Extension Manager when installing it:

Method A. Download the extension package file to the super user's computer. This is the conventional way of installing extensions. Exercise 7-2 will install an extension via this conventional method.

Method B. Install the extension from a directory on the website server. This is an alternative method for installing an extension if Method A does not work for one reason or another. The file is downloaded in Method A, and then moved to the webserver via FTP. Exercise 7-3 will guide you through an example of this method.

Method C. Install the extension from a URL location. There are not a whole lot of extensions that are set up to download from their hosting location on the developer's webserver. This may be a prelude of an extension center on the JED, which might function the way that mobile apps are downloaded to mobile devices.

Method D. In addition to Method C, an option to Install from Web has been added in Joomla! Version 3.2. When this tab is added in the Extension Manager, Install area, it automatically connects to a web location that has extensions listed that may be installed directly. This is a very new and innovative way to install extensions. Read more about this new method at joomla3bootcamp.com.

It's best to use Method A to install your extensions, because it gives your anti-virus software a chance to take a look at the file that is being downloaded, in order to make sure it is safe and does not contain any malicious code.

If the extension is a commercial version, by all means, secure a downloaded copy of the extension to store on your computer. Whether it's a direct purchase or a subscription purchase, ensure your ability to reinstall any extension that you paid for by having a hard copy of the file in your Joomla! 3 resource library on your computer.

FILE TYPES FOR TYPICAL EXTENSIONS

Extensions that you are likely to download include components, modules, plug-ins, and templates. They are often identified by their prefixes, such as:

pkg—Typically a package file for a component.

mod—Indicates that the extension is a module.

plg—Indicates the extension is a plug-in.

This is not a steadfast rule, however. An extension may just be a ZIP file with a name; it makes no matter what it's called. They all install the same way, regardless of their name or type.

Obtaining an Extension to Install

The obvious first step before installing an extension is to download one from the JED. As your administrator skills increase, obtaining extensions will be an easy and familiar task. But for now, this section guides you through the process.

Adding a Content Editor

Joomla!'s default content editor is a minimalist tool, as you saw when you created the categories, articles, and modules in previous exercises. Let's replace the default editor with something that has a bit more functionality and more features.

First, it is necessary to obtain and install the new editor from the JED, which will then replace the default editor (but not remove it). You'll need to download and install the extensions, and then change the website's configuration settings.

EXERCISE 7-1: OBTAINING AN EXTENSION FROM THE JED

Objective: This exercise walks you through the acquisition of an extension from the joomla.org JED. This extension will add an additional, selectable, editor to the website as the default editor, which will appear whenever a text area is available for entering content or information. The new editor (called JCK Editor) will replace the default (TinyMCE).

Step 1. Go to joomla.org and click on the Extend link in the top menu; then open the Extension Directory link.

Step 2. In the leftmost menu, which is the Categories list of extensions that are grouped by their use, and click on the "Editing" link.

Step 3. If the JCK Editor icon is displayed in the Popular section of the page, click on it. If it is not displayed, click on the Editors link in the Editing section. Scroll down the page and click on the **[C]** JCK Editor name, or on the **[D]** JCK Editor icon (Figure 7-3).

Figure 7-3 *The first screen of an extension in the JED gener-ally provides a brief explanation of the extension, including the Joomla! versions with which it may be used, along with dates and other relevant information.*

DOWNLOAD THE CORRECT EXTENSION VERSION

Note the **[E]** Joomla 3.x image for this extension (Figure 7-3). The gold colored icon will be displayed for every extension in the JED that is compatible with Joomla! 3. There are different colors for each version of Joomla!, and the gold Joomla 3.x icon means the extension works only for this specific version. Be sure to download the proper one; others will not install correctly.

Step 4. Notice in Figure 7-4 the **[F]** Non-Commercial License indicator. Click on the **[G]** Download button to display information about the extension. This link goes to the joomlackeditor.com website (Figure 7-5).

Figure 7-4 *On the extension details page in the JED, additional information is displayed. You can usually demo the extension on the developer's website and access the documentation, if any, as well as ask pre-sale support questions about commercial extensions.*

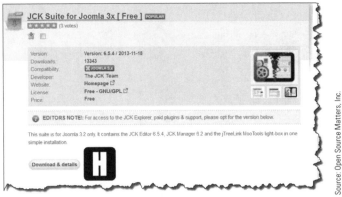

Source: Open Source Matters, Inc.

Figure 7-5 *Sometimes, the download link opens another screen with the actual download button, as is the case with this extension. Others use a file manager extension that is a bit clumsy with one or two screens to get through before the actual download link is accessible.*

Step 5. Click on the **[H]** Download & Details button (Figure 7-5). This will open the Download Details page for the JCK Suite (Figure 7-6).

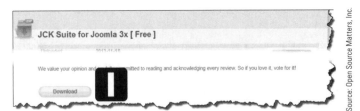

Source: Open Source Matters, Inc.

Figure 7-6 *When downloading extensions, double-check to make sure the extension is for a native Joomla! 3.x website. This screen will have a compatibility line indicating the version.*

Step 6. Click on the **[I]** Download button, which should open a pop-up window on your browser.

Step 7. Make a note of the name of the **[J]** extension file, and then choose **[K]** Save File to save it to the downloads folder on your computer (Figure 7-7). Notice that this is a PKG file, meaning it probably also contains a component, module, or plug-in.

YOUR BROWSER MAY BE DIFFERENT

It is possible, depending on which browser you are using and which type of computer you have, that some of the pop-up boxes or utility screens might not appear the same as the ones shown in the screenshots in this book. Also, some of the buttons have different names for functions that do the same thing.

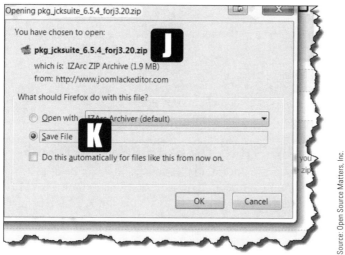

Figure 7-7 *Save your downloaded files to the local computer. Before you execute the Save File action, make a note of the filename and the location where it is being saved on your computer.*

At this point, a copy of the extension file should reside on your computer. Take a couple of minutes to find exactly where it is located—which folder it's in. Make a note of the location so you can quickly access it during the installation process in Exercise 7-2.

Installing an Extension

In Exercise 7-2, the JCK Editor Suite extension will be installed. This process will install a component and a plug-in or two at the same time. The procedure in Exercise 7-2 is the same procedure used to install any other extension from the JED, or from private developers, into Joomla! 3. Once you have gone through your first extension installation, you will have pretty much mastered the technique. All extensions install via the Extension Manager/Install function, as explained.

Although there may be several ways that extensions can be installed, the most common method is the download/install directly type. You can also install from a directory, and install from a URL.

Installing from a directory is typically used only when the normal method fails. Exercise 7-3 will take you step-by-step through this alternate extension install method. This method also involves downloading the files to your local computer, similar to the process described in Exercise 7-1.

Installing from a URL is not used much by website managers when adding extensions. This is probably because that method has not been explained to website managers like it should be to gain greater acceptance. Exercise 7-4 covers the steps needed to install an extension from a developer's website. Some developers have their extension downloads set up on their sites to allow URL downloading/installation. Most, unfortunately, do not and require the multistep processes to acquire the extension.

REINSTALLING EXTENSIONS

What about reinstalls? Although installing from a URL is fine, what happens when you need to reinstall an extension, and the URL isn't available any longer? That situation makes a strong case for actually downloading an extension, which puts the files in your possession, and then you can reinstall it any time later on if needed. Just keep that in mind. Sure, install via URL, but download an actual file copy anyway.

EXERCISE 7-2: INSTALLING AN EXTENSION BY NORMAL METHODS

Objective: This exercise installs the JCK Editor onto the website so it can be used as the default editor, or the editor of choice by content administrators. The default TinyMCE Editor will not be removed or uninstalled and will still be available for content managers who may elect to use it under their preferences for the level of administration.

Step 1. Open the **[L]** Extensions > Extension Manager either via the top Extensions Menu or in the Admin Left Menu on the backend following a proper login (Figure 7-8). The screen will open to Extension Manager: Install.

Figure 7-8 *The starting point for adding extensions to a website is always via the Extension Manager, which can be accessed via the Admin Left Menu or via the Extensions drop-down in the upper Menu: Extensions > Extension Manager.*

Step 2. Click the **[M]** Browse button to locate the package file that needs to be installed (Figure 7-9). Then, locate the file on your computer and click on the filename (pkg_jcksuite_6.5.4_forj3.20.zip). The name of the file might be slightly different depending upon when you downloaded it and whether it has been updated or given a new name by the developers.

BUTTON NAMES, DIFFERENT BROWSERS

In most browsers, the button used to open the folders on your computer is called Browse. But in the Chrome browser, for example, it is called Choose File. Let logical choices prevail if you encounter these differences.

Step 3.   With the file selected, click the Open button.

Step 4.   The screen should now display the **[N]** filename next to the **[M]** Browse button (Figure 7-9). Execute the **[O]** Upload & Install action by clicking the blue button.

Figure 7-9 *The file selected via Browse should be the same file as was downloaded from the JED or the developer's website. Be sure that the correct extension is selected. There may be a slight delay before the filename appears after selecting it.*

The actual process of installing the extension can be fast, or possibly take a minute or so to complete. Sometimes, when the extension files are large, a progress indicator may display on the screen while it is downloading.

In the case of the JCK Editor, this opens a Setup Wizard for the extension after the download is completed (Figure 7-10). Most extensions do not have this, but this one does.

Source: Open Source Matters, Inc.

Figure 7-10 *This particular extension requires a few additional steps after the installation is completed. Some extensions have these additional configuration actions, but most do not.*

Step 5.   Click the **[P]** Next >>> button to continue configuring the extension. This will start a series of actions taken by the extension to ensure it is operating in the proper webserver environment. Continue to click the Next >>> button to progress through the steps. Simply accept the defaults on the various screens. There is no need to change the settings. Be sure to read the screens so you can understand the many configuration options for this particular extension. The last button displays Finish >>, so click on it. When it's complete, the Success message will display in a green area near the top of the screen (as is the case with all extensions).

Step 6.   At this point, under the Components tab in the top menu, the JCK Manager should be listed.

   The installation process is not yet complete. The next series of steps in this exercise designates the JCK Editor as the default editor in all managers that have text areas.

Step 7.   Click on the Joomla! logo at the top left of the screen to return to the backend Control Panel.

Step 8.   In the Admin Left Menu of the backend screen, click on the Global Configuration link.

Step 9.   Under the Site tab, about half way down the page, open the Default Editor drop-down and select "Editor – JoomlaCK" from the list. Note the other editors are still on the list and have not been removed.

Step 10.   With Editor – JoomlaCK showing as the default editor, click the green Save button at the top left of the screen.

Step 11.   Under the Content menu at the top of the screen, click on the link and when the drop-down opens, mouse over the Article Manager, which will display a fly-out entitled Add New Article. Click on that link to open a blank article screen.

Step 12.   A screen entitled Article Manager: Add New Article should open with the JCK Editor having replaced the default Editor (TinyMCE), as seen in previous exercises. Many of the controls for this editor are similar to word processors on your computer. Many of the functions are explained in exercises in other chapters of the book.

Step 13.   Close the Article Manager: Add New Article window.

The JCK Editor is now the primary editor for all content that has a Content area for entering descriptions or actual information.

Installing Plug-Ins

The previous example installed a component as well as its accompanying plug-ins. While the JCK Editor component was being installed, several global plug-ins were also automatically included. There are no settings that require attention or parameter changes in the plug-ins for this extension.

Additionally, several core plug-ins for the Editor were installed. You can view them by opening the Components > JCK Manager > Control Panel > Plugin Manager. These particular plug-ins interact and function only with the editor. They are not used anywhere else, as are traditional Joomla! 3 plug-ins. What makes this so good is that you can activate or deactivate the plug-ins, and you can also acquire more, based on your content-editing needs.

Degree of Difficulty

If this were an Olympic event, the degree of difficulty for installing an extension would be a 2, because it's really easy to do so.

Other than the additional steps needed to customize the extension, the installation was rather straightforward and not particularly difficult. Most extensions just cruise right along and install in a jiffy, without undue drama or difficulty.

However, there are times when, for complex technical reasons, an extension cannot or does not install using the preferred conventional method. Joomla! 3 recognizes this and has provided another method for installing extensions.

EXERCISE 7-3: INSTALLING AN EXTENSION FROM A DIRECTORY

Objective: This exercise demonstrates how to install an extension from a directory location. This directory location is on the webserver where Joomla! 3 is installed. During installation, Joomla! 3 creates several directories, one of which is one named /tmp/. Files are moved into this /tmp/ directory via FTP or the Control Panel, and then installed from that location rather than directly from your local computer. The extension still needs to be downloaded to your computer, then uploaded to the /tmp/ directory on the webserver. Once there, the file needs to be unzipped, which then shows the extension as a regular folder, versus a ZIP file.

The Install from Directory function is used when the webserver does not have the unzip function activated. This is a webserver-level control that you cannot access or change. You can upload the ZIP file into the /tmp/ directory, then unzip it as a folder that contains the extension files. This process allows files to be uploaded into directories and unzipped or extracted without doing it on the local computer, then uploading via FTP.

The extension being installed is called "Modules Anywhere." It allows modules to be inserted into any type of content on the website and it's discussed more in Chapter 19, "Modules," so make sure that you install it exactly as outlined in the following steps.

UPLOAD FILES TWO WAYS

To upload files to the webserver location of a website, you can use an FTP program, which connects to the webserver. If FTP is not available, log in to the control panel for the website and open the target directory/folder location (/**tmp**). Then, use the upload feature of the control panel folder management area to add the file to the target location. Once the zipped file is located in the /**tmp**/ folder, go through the exact procedure so that the Extensions folder is also displayed there.

Step 1. Go to the JED and use the Advanced Search feature to find an extension named "Modules Anywhere." Just type the name into the Extension Name box. Then, select the Joomla! 3.x version compatibility by checking the box next to the icon. Execute the Search action.

Step 2. The search results should display one or more extensions that match the search criteria. Select the extension created by the NoNumber developer, as shown by the website URL, by clicking on the Modules Anywhere title.

Step 3. On the next screen, click the Download button.

Step 4. When the NoNumber web page opens, select the free version of the extension and click the Download button in the green column (top or bottom button is OK). The extension file will be saved to your computer in the same manner as experienced in Exercise 7-1.

Step 5. Navigate to the folder into which the extension was downloaded, and then right-click on the filename and execute the unzip function. This will create a folder with the same name as the extension file.

UNZIPPING FILES USING WINDOWS

If you are using Windows and do not have a specific unzipping utility, right-click on the file and select Extract All from the context menu. Browse to the destination directory where the file should be extracted and click Extract. A progress bar will display and disappear once the extraction is complete.

Step 6. By your method of choice, upload the extension's unzipped folder to this location on the webserver for the website: /location name/myfirstsite/tmp/ directory, where /location name/ is the path name for the webserver files. Use either an FTP program or the website's control panel, File Upload, feature. Move the contents of the entire folder. The ZIP file, as used in the previous exercise, *does not* get uploaded via this method, unless you are using the alternative method of unzipped via the control panel described earlier.

THE LOCATION NAME ON WEBSERVERS

Depending upon which webserver control panel is being used, the location name can be **public_html**, or **httpdocs**, or sometimes **htpdocs** or a variation thereof. The **/myfirstsite/** should appear under the root folder. The **/tmp/** directory is located within that folder where Joomla! 3 is installed.

Step 7. Go to the Admin backend (click the Joomla! logo at the top left). Then, in the Admin Left Menu, open the Extension Manager: Install page (Figure 7-11), and select the **[Q]** Install from Directory option. Notice that when the tab is opened, the path to the **[R]** Install Directory /tmp/ is automatically displayed, and it ends in /tmp.

Step 8. In the Install Directory box, add the complete filename of the extension's folder that was copied into the **[S]** /tmp/ folder path location on the webserver (Figure 7-12). Note the (1) in the folder name in the example. If you download extensions with the same filename as one already on your system, the download will be numbered incrementally. In this case (1) means it is the second download of the file with the same name on your computer. Make sure a / follows /tmp before adding the folder name.

Figure 7-11 *When installing from a directory, this is a location on the website that is accessed by either FTP or via the file manager in the website control panel. In the root file structure for the website, the location is the* /tmp/ *directory or folder.*

Figure 7-12 *The extension filename is shown after selection of the location. This path must exactly match the path to the file uploaded via ftp. If the path is not correct, the install attempt will fail.*

Step 9. Execute the action by clicking the **[T]** Install button (Figure 7-12).

Step 10. When the installation is complete, the Success message should appear near the top of the page in a light green background. The installation of the "Modules Anywhere" extension via the directory method is complete.

Difference Between Installation Methods

The package file method downloads the extension installer ZIP file to your computer, and to install it, that file is accessed by the built-in installer. This is the easiest method to use when installing extensions.

The directory method also downloads the extension ZIP file to your computer. Then you must unzip it and copy the unzipped folder to the **/tmp/** folder on the webserver website location. The folder name must then be entered into the Install Directory path after the **path/myfirstsite/tmp/** folder location. Remember, you can FTP the unzipped folder to the **/tmp/** directory, or upload the zipped file via the control panel uploads and unzip it there.

The exact path may vary among the different types of webservers. The website location and the temporary directory should be indicated automatically. The name of the extracted folder that was uploaded should be added at the very end. Be cognizant of - and _ in the filenames, along with the use of capitalization. The name of the folder being entered must be exactly the same as the uploaded folder name.

EXERCISE 7-4: INSTALLING AN EXTENSION FROM A URL

Objective: This exercise installs an extension that is located on a developer's website and identified by a URL, which is copied and pasted into a location identifier, and the install action initiated. If the developer's extension files are set up for download only, this method will not work. There must be a complete URL for the package file that contains the extension. The package filenames always end in .ZIP or .zip.

Step 1. Go to the JED and use the Advanced Search feature to find an extension named "Custom CSS." Just type the name into the Extension Name box. Then, select the Joomla! 3.x version below by checking the box next to the 3.x icon (gold color). Execute the Search action. There might be a slight delay before the search results are displayed.

Step 2. The search results should display one or more extensions that match the search criteria. Select the extension created by Hyde-Design by clicking on the Custom CSS title.

Step 3. On the next JED screen, click the Download button.

Step 4. When the download page opens, mouse over the "Download for Joomla 2.5 & 3" link to the right of the screen under the Hyde-Design logo. When the mouse is over the link, an underline will appear. *Do not click the link*, which would initiate a normal download action.

Step 5. With the mouse over the link, right-click your mouse, and in the pop-up dialog box, select Copy Link Location. This copies the URL address to your computer's copy/paste utility. The Chrome browser calls this action Copy Link Address, so do that if you are using Chrome.

Step 6. Go to the Admin backend (click the Joomla! logo at the top left), and open the **[U]** Extension Manager: Install page (Figure 7-13), which is the start page for uploading any type of extension.

Step 7. On the tab row next to the left Menu Install, click on **[V]** Install from URL.

Step 8. In the **[W]** Install URL box, right-click your mouse and paste the link into the Install URL box (Figure 7-13). When installing from a URL, the complete URL must be defined, with the name of the extension file at the ending of the string. By default, the **http://** appears in the text input box. When pasting the URL, make sure the default text is removed first, otherwise the link will fail.

Step 9. Click the **[X]** Install button to initiate the action.

Figure 7-13 *Paste the link into the* **[W]** *Install URL box.*

Step 10. When the installation is complete, the Success message should appear near the top of the page in a light green background.

That completes the exercise for installing an extension from a URL location. You can use this method only when the extension file location on the developer's website is a URL. The path to the extension may also be typed in manually, but the URL needs to actually exist to do the URL installation.

The new "Install from Web" method can also be used if the extension is within the web location that is set up for that kind of download/install method.

Designating the JCK Editor as the Default

When an editor is designated as the default, it becomes so for all areas where text is added, such as category or module descriptions, articles, and the like. This designation makes the JCK Editor the default throughout the entire website for all users with editing privileges.

Some editors might not want all the bells and whistles of the JCK Editor, so there is an option in each editor's personal profile to select which of the installed editors they want to use other than the default. Exercise 7-7 explains how to make this selection.

Housekeeping on the Session Settings

Before proceeding, this is a good time to do some housekeeping on the website's Admin configuration. These kinds of activities will be part of future exercises and will involve altering some configuration or system settings, such as:

◆ Session Time Out settings
◆ Default List Limit settings
◆ Permission settings
◆ Text-Filtering settings
◆ List Filtering settings

Rather than just include a bunch of exercises dealing with all these items at once, these configuration settings will be covered as the chapters dictate.

Many of the settings apply to such areas as components, articles, modules, menus, and others, and are conveniently altered in the Global Configuration area. As these setting changes are needed, they will be explained with appropriate exercises.

Let's take care of one right now that you may have already encountered.

Did You Need to Log In Again?

At some point during the previous exercises, you may have been required to log in again as the super user, even though you thought you were already logged in. This happens when a certain amount of idle time passes. There is no reason displayed as to why you had to log in again. Before changing the default editor on the website, let's fix this time out-log in issue.

EXERCISE 7-5: SETTING THE USER SESSION DURATION

Objective: The purpose of this exercise is to change the Session Lifetime setting in the System configuration. This is called the Session Settings, which is the amount of time the system can remain idle, with no actions executed (keystrokes or mouse clicks), before requiring the user to log in again. The default time is 15 minutes. If you are working on a website, and get interrupted with a phone call or something else, then return to the task after 15 minutes, you will be required to log in again. This exercise shows you how to extend that time to 90 minutes.

Perform the following steps to change the Session Settings time value:

Step 1. If you're not already there, log in to the Admin backend of the website.

Step 2. Access the Global Configuration link in the Admin Left Menu.

Step 3. Open the System tab at the top, which opens the System Settings.

Step 4. At the bottom of the right column, there is an area for **[Y]** Session Settings (Figure 7-14).

SESSION LIFETIME VALUES

In the Session Lifetime box, the default value of 15 is displayed, and the Session Handler is set to Database. The 15 value indicates the number of minutes during which a user may be logged into the system without executing an action of some sort. After the set value has expired, and no action has been executed, the user will have to log in again.

Step 5. In the Session Lifetime box, enter the number of minutes you want before time-out. A value of 60 will limit the time to one hour, 120 two hours, and so on. Because you will be reading and performing tasks in the exercises, set the value to 90 **[Z]**.

Step 6. Execute the Save action.

Source: Open Source Matters, Inc.

Figure 7-14 *The Session Lifetime determines the length of time before the system will log the current user out, requiring the user to log in to the backend again. This setting applies to all users who have login privileges, if they're allowed to access and edit content.*

Step 7. After the Save action is completed, open the System tab and check the value in the Session Lifetime to confirm the setting is set to 90 minutes.

Now that the Session Lifetime has been increased, let's continue with the task of setting the JCK Editor as the default for the website.

EXERCISE 7-6: SETTING THE DEFAULT EDITOR

Objective: The goal of this exercise is to learn how to set the default editor, which will apply throughout the website's Admin backend. It will also be the editor used if content is accessed via the front-end following a user login. The objective is to set the same editor to be used across the website wherever content can be edited using the text editor.

This exercise assumes that the default installation editor is designated, but that you want to designate a different editor as the default. Recall that you installed the new editor in Exercise 7-2.

Step 1. Remain in the Global Configuration area with the **[AA]** Site tab open (Figure 7-15), and find the parameter setting for **[BB]** default editor, about half-way down the column. The selected editor at this point should be Editor – TinyMCE, which Joomla! 3 added during the installation process.

Figure 7-15 *The default editor is displayed on this screen; right now, it's the editor that was added during the installation process.*

Step 2. Change the **[CC]** value of the parameter to Editor – JoomlaCK (Figure 7-16).

Figure 7-16 *All editors installed on the website will display in the Default Editor drop-down list. Select any one of them to designate it as the default for all Content Managers that have text editing areas.*

Step 3. With the Editor – JoomlaCK visible in the drop-down, execute a Save & Close action.

Step 4. A Success message will display when the configuration has been changed to the new editor. The JCK Editor is now designated as the default editor for the website.

Allowing Editor Selection by Other Administrators

Recall in Exercise 7-6 that the default editor was changed for every editing screen where content can be added. However, if your site has many editors or publishers of different content, who administer it themselves, there may be a case where one of those individuals may want a less complicated editor, along the lines of the TinyMCE Editor that was installed as part of the Joomla! 3 core files.

Joomla! 3 has a pretty neat feature to accommodate this scenario. Even when the super user has set a specific editor as the default, administrators can use another editor as a personal preference, provided it is installed. This is done in the individual's profile.

There are several high-quality editors available for Joomla! 3, and more than one can be installed at the same time, but only one can be designated as the global default editor. In Exercise 7-2, the JCK Editor was installed. The JCE Editor is another many-featured editor, and administrators might elect to use one over the other. When JCK is the default editor, JCE can be selected as a personal preference, or the other way around.

Why Would You Do This?

The JCK and JCE Editors are full-featured editors with many functions, along the lines of a typical word processor. For someone who is just adding and editing simple content, these two editors may be somewhat complicated to use.

As an alternative, administrators may elect to use a less complicated, easier to use editor, by selecting TinyMCE as the default. By doing so, they can edit content in a less-complicated text management extension in the backend. The process of making an alternative editor your default is straightforward. You do so within your personal profile, which is accessible after you log in. A logged in administrator, with the correct privileges assigned, can set preferences via parameters in their My Profile area, as explained in Exercise 7-7.

EXERCISE 7-7: EDITOR SELECTION BY INDIVIDUAL ADMINISTRATORS

Objective: This exercise demonstrates the way that administrators can select a different editor as the default when managing content.

Step 1. Log in to the Admin backend of the website.

Step 2. Click on the User Name at the top-right corner of the screen.

Step 3. Click on the Edit Account link in the user's drop-down menu.

Step 4. Open the Basic Settings tab in the My Profile area.

Stop! At this point, *do not change your super user personal settings*. The action in Step 5 would do that, so stop at this point, and exit with the knowledge that you can make this change for individual users.

Step 5. Select any alternative editor in the Editor selection drop-down.

The alternative editor is the one the individual user would see when accessing any content under their responsibility, had the change been Saved.

Before executing Save & Close, and while you're in the My Profile area, review the other personal choices available for administrators for the following:

My Profile Details:

Name: The user's name can be changed by users.

Login Name: Cannot be changed here, but the super user can change the Login Name of any user via the User Manager: Edit Profile. Only the super user can make this change.

Password: The login password can be changed by the user in the My Profile section.

Email: The user's email address can also be changed by the user without the involvement of the super user.

My Profile Basic Settings:

Backend Template Style: Any backend template that's been installed by default or as an extension can be selected on a per-user basis, similar to the editor selections. This will be discussed in Chapter 21.

Backend Language: On multi-language websites, the backend language can be set by the user, if it's different than the default language. Instructions on adding/changing languages is available at joomla3bootcamp.com.

Frontend Language: The front-end language can also be set as desired.

Editor: Here is where the backend editor can be selected, as described previously.

Help Site: This sets the location of any Help Site that has been made available. This setting is in the Global Configuration of the website.

Time Zone: It is possible that content administrators may be located in different parts of the world, so the users might want to set this to their own local times.

These parameters, when altered, only affect the individual user's preferences. Changes in an individual's profile do not alter the global or default settings for any parameter applied on a global basis.

Step 6. Execute the Save & Close action, which takes you back to the Admin Control Panel.

Uninstalling Extensions

It stands to reason that if extensions can be installed, they should also be able to be uninstalled. You might uninstall them if you no longer need them or they no longer meet your website content needs. Joomla! 3 has a utility function that will render extensions inactive or remove them from the website.

Why Would You Want to Uninstall an Extension?

Immediately after you install a new extension to the website, you notice that problems arise. When that happens, the new extension and one that is already installed are acting like two bobcats in a burlap bag, and not playing nice with each other. To quickly check the issue, you should disable the new extension. If that doesn't solve the problem, you should uninstall it.

Two Ways to Uninstall an Extension

There are two ways to make extensions—which includes components, modules, plug-ins, templates, languages, and libraries—inoperative.

Disable the extension—The extension can simply be disabled, and then re-enabled later if you need it (Exercise 7-8). The extension remains part of the website installation.

Uninstall the extension—This action actually removes the extension from the website (Exercise 7-9). It cannot be reactivated without reinstalling it; it's as if it were never installed to begin with.

EXERCISE 7-8: TEMPORARILY DISABLING AN EXTENSION

Objective: This exercise guides you through the process of temporarily disabling an extension by making it inactive, but still keeping it installed as part of the website. At the end of this exercise, you will reactivate the extension.

Step 1. Log in to the Administrator backend as the super user.

Step 2. In the Admin Left Menu, click on the Install Extensions link.

Step 3. In the left menu, click the Manage link. This opens the unfiltered list of extensions that are installed in both the Site and the Administrator areas.

Step 4. Extensions can be visually identified as to their current operating state in the **[DD]** Status column (Figure 7-17).

EXTENSION STATES

Extensions that are installed on a Joomla! 3 website have three possible status states regarding their operation:

◆ **Green Checkmark:** The extension is active or enabled for use.
◆ **Red X Circle:** The extension is inactive or disabled.
◆ **Lock Symbol:** The extension is critical to the website operation and cannot be removed or uninstalled. The extension is in a protected state.

Source: Open Source Matters, Inc.

Figure 7-17 *The status of every installed extension can be determined at a glance in the list view, along with where it is used—Site or Administrator—and its type.*

Filtering Lists

On the left side of the screen, there are filters that can be applied to the list of extensions, which comes in handy when you're looking for a specific extension, or for a type of extension. Most all the managers in the Admin backend have the same or similar filtering capabilities, making it convenient to find an extension, especially when there are many of them installed.

The list of extensions can be filtered in several ways, or in any combination of filtering options that can be invoked. These particular filters apply only to the Extension Manager: Manage list view. Other managers in the backend may have more, or fewer, of the same or different filters that can be applied to the list display.

From top to bottom, here are the filters in the Extension Manager (they are not named or titled in Joomla!):

Filter 1:   Used to select the extensions that are installed for the site or administrator; basically filters for the front-end and the backend.

Filter 2:   Selects the status of the extension as Disabled, Enabled, or Protected.

Filter 3:   Allows the type to be filtered, to narrow the list somewhat. This lists the extensions by their common-use type category.

Filter 4:   Allows filtering by folder, which is actually filtering by groups that have a common installation location.

In the following steps, you will filter the list for ease-of-use in selecting extensions:

Step 5. Filter the list using these settings:

Filter 1: Select Site in this filter.

Filter 2: Select the Status as Enabled.

Filter 3: For Type, select Module.

Filter 4: Do not select any folder for this option.

> The result of this filtering should show only a list of the modules that are installed.

Step 6. In the top-right corner of the screen, change the list display from 20 to All.

Step 7. In the **[EE]** Status column, scroll down to the Wrapper module, which might be located on page two of the list, and click on the green checkmark (read the mouse over message), to change the status of the extension (Figure 7-18).

Source: Open Source Matters, Inc.

Figure 7-18 *The list view of extensions displays information about the use and the type of extension, along with the version, the date it was created (not installed), and the ID number. Notice that the Wrapper as a component is locked, but the module is not and can be changed.*

> The extension has now been disabled, which means it cannot be used without changing its status. Because it is a module, when a new module creation action is initiated, the wrapper will not appear on the list of choices for types of modules to create.

Step 8. To view and enable a disabled extension, you must filter the list by Disabled. It's always a good idea to return filters to a default or not-used state so you are not befuddled trying to find something that might be in another state. This happens frequently, so reset any filters to their defaults before leaving the manager section.

> At this point, the extension should be enabled to make it accessible for use. This action is just the opposite of disabling the extension. The action is a typical ON/OFF function. This function applies to every item displayed on list views in all of the managers.

Step 9. Click on the red circle X and change the Status back to Enabled. The green checkmark should display when this action is completed. When changing the status, you don't have to save the new configuration. The Status item saves itself to the selected state automatically as a toggled selection.

MORE THAN ONE PART

It was previously mentioned that extensions sometimes install several other extensions upon which they rely.

The "Modules Anywhere" extension falls in that group. When the main extension was installed, it also installed these additional plug-ins:

◆ **System:** NoNumber Framework
◆ **Button:** NoNumber Modules Anywhere

The framework is necessary for the plug-in to operate. The Button adds a button to the bottom of all of the installed and active editors to easily perform the module insertion into content.

Removing or Uninstalling Extensions

After a time, you may have installed a good number of extensions, especially when you're testing to determine which will work the best in any given situation. Extensions that are not being used and are disabled for an extended period of time should be uninstalled. Therefore, if you install an extension, test it, and then decide not to use it, you need to get rid of it using the Remove/Uninstall feature of the Extensions Manager.

TAKE CARE WHEN UNINSTALLING EXTENSIONS

Are you sure you want to uninstall the extension? Some extensions, such as components and modules, have content that is generated by the extension, or control the display of the content on the front-end. If the extension is uninstalled, the generated or displayed content goes away. That content usually cannot be recovered by reinstalling the extension.

When you're uninstalling extensions, there is no confirmation message that asks if you are sure you want to remove the extension. Be absolutely certain that the extension you're removing does not cause content generation and/or display issues when it's no longer part of the website. Always double-check your intended actions when uninstalling extensions.

Removing an extension is a relatively easy task, as outlined in Exercise 7-9.

EXERCISE 7-9: REMOVING/UNINSTALLING AN EXTENSION

Objective: The exercise demonstrates how extensions are removed from the website. The Extension Manager has a built-in feature to accomplish it. Take care when you're removing or uninstalling extensions and be sure the correct extension is being removed. Double-check yourself when removing any extension—remember, you don't get a confirmation message!

You can uninstall the Extension Random Image extension by following these steps. (This extension module isn't used often and there are better extensions available in the JED that do the same, with more display parameter options.)

Step 1. Log in to the Administrator backend as the super user.

Step 2. In the Admin Left Menu, click on the Install Extensions link.

Step 3. In the left menu, click the Manage link. This opens the unfiltered list of extensions that are installed for both the Site and the Administrator areas.

Step 4. Filter the list of installed extensions using the -Select Location- drop-down in the Filter: Area to the left. Select Site as the extension types to view.

Step 5. Filter the list using the Select Type drop-down filter, by selecting Module.

Step 6. Change the number of items to display on the list from 20 to All using the utility in the upper-right corner of the screen.

Step 7. On the list, scroll down and check the **[FF]** box next to the Most Read Content extension (Figure 7-19).

Figure 7-19 *For this exercise, the Most Read Content extension is uninstalled.*

When you're scrolling long lists within the various managers, note that the action buttons for the manager stay in position and the list scrolls under the button bar. When lists are long, this feature comes in handy for administering the files on the list.

Step 8. In the button bar for this manager, near the top of the screen, select **[GG]** X Uninstall to execute this action. The action will begin immediately. There is no confirmation message or Proceed button. When you click the button, that's it; the extension is uninstalled permanently. More than one extension can be selected at a time, so make sure the correct ones are selected before clicking the button. Also make sure you have not accidentally checked more than the extension to be removed.

Step 9.   The "Uninstalling Module Was Successful" message will display in a green panel when the process is completed.

Step 10.   View the list again to verify that the Most Read Content extension has been removed.

SOMETIMES...

Occasionally you might uninstall an extension and then decide to reinstall it, but when you try, you get an error message along the lines of "Already exists," or "Cannot install because it is still present on the website," or something along those lines.

In this case, you might need to physically delete the extension files from the website. This can be a daunting action if you are not code-savvy or do not want to dig into the files on the server. These files cannot be accessed via the backend of the website. They must be accessed via FTP or via the website's control panel.

If you are not confident about performing this task, seek assistance in removing the files so that you can reinstall the extension.

Summary

In this chapter, you learned:

◆ About the functions of extensions.

◆ Which versions of extensions to use.

◆ Where to obtain and download extensions.

◆ About the different types of extensions.

◆ How to install extensions by using the methods available.

◆ How to change the default editor globally.

◆ How to change the default text editor for an individual user only.

◆ How to extend the user's session duration.

◆ How to disable an extension.

◆ How to remove an extension from the website.

forum.joomla3bootcamp.com

Network with other Joomla! 3 Administrators
in the United States and Worldwide.

JOIN THE JOOMLA! 3 BOOT CAMP

**Sign up and participate in the
Joomla! 3 Boot Camp FORUM,
a place where you can ask questions
about administration of a Joomla! 3
website and share information with
other users in the United States
and in the worldwide user community.**

 **ASK JOOMLA! 3 QUESTIONS**    **NETWORK WORLDWIDE**

 **CONTRIBUTE WITH ANSWERS**    **HELP IDENTIFY RESOURCES**

USE THE JOOMLA! 3 BOOT CAMP
HELP DESK! FOR PERSONAL ASSISTANCE

Joomla! 3 Boot Camp FORUM is powered by

Website: www.kunena.org

Chapter 8

Components: Banners

Learning Objectives

What's included in this chapter:

- ◆ Understanding components.
- ◆ The 10 components of Joomla!
- ◆ The Banner component.
- ◆ How banners are organized.
- ◆ Details of banners and their management.
- ◆ How to create and display a banner.

Understanding Components

The best way to describe components in Joomla! 3 is that they are "mini-programs" that run on the Joomla! core platform. Each default installation component is a small application that performs certain functions and helps generate and manage content.

Additionally, more components can be installed as extensions and there are hundreds upon hundreds of them available in the JED. Just figure out what you want to do, find the component extension to do the job, download it, and perform an install. Installations are usually uncomplicated.

There are ten components in the default installation. Each performs different functions and offers different types of content and management, such as:

◆ Banners
◆ Contacts
◆ Joomla! Update
◆ Messaging
◆ Newsfeeds
◆ Redirect
◆ Search
◆ Smart Search
◆ Tags
◆ Weblinks

This chapter covers the Banner component. The remaining components are covered in depth in following chapters. This will make it more convenient for you to study each component and to perform the exercises, guiding you through the "how-to" aspects of each.

The Joomla! Update component is not covered in this chapter. Information about that component is available at joomla3bootcamp.com.

Understanding the Banner Component

Joomla! 3 provides a banner-management mechanism. These are not "site" banners, but rather advertising banners, whereby clients advertise on your site by displaying promotional banners.

Quite honestly, this Banner component isn't used all that much, but when it is used, it can be an effective way of putting ad panels on your website. If you don't need external advertising banners, you can also use the Banner Manager to generate banners to promote or showcase some of the items on your site.

The same banner displays can be accomplished with modules, which are covered in Chapter 19, "Modules," with information and exercises. The difference between using the Banner Manager and using regular content modules is the ability to track information about click-throughs when someone clicks one of the banners. The normal Joomla! 3

modules do not have that ability. However, the modules created and associated with the Banner Manager do have that tracking ability.

At the end of this chapter, Exercise 8-1 will guide you through the creation of a Banner module that will appear on the front page when a menu link item is clicked.

How Banners Are Organized

As you will find throughout Joomla! 3, most all content is generally organized in categories. This means that each content area has its own set of categories by which you can organize the information. As you have already learned, articles have categories. These are not the same as the categories for banners. Keep content area categories separated mentally when working within different content areas in the Admin backend.

Using the Banner Manager

The Banner Manager is accessed in the same way as all other components, via the Components link in the top menu (Figure 8-1). When accessing components via that menu, most have fly-outs that allow you fast access to the different management areas of the component.

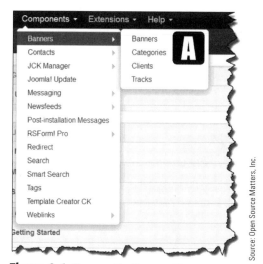

Figure 8-1 *To open the Banner Manager, go to the* **[A]** *Components > Banners > Banners fly-out, which will open to the screen that lists all banners, whether their status is Published or Unpublished.*

Three banners were added to the website during the installation process. These banners are used on different pages of the sample data that was installed (Figure 8-2).

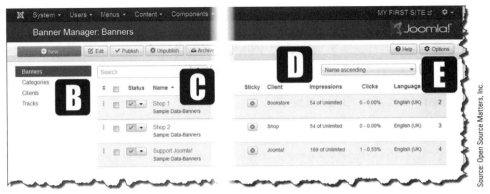

Figure 8-2 *The list of* **[B]** *banners is displayed* **[C]** *along with* **[D]** *columns that indicate information about each. In the top menu of the Banners Manager, there is an* **[E]** *Options button, which opens a sub-manager for some of the attributes of banner management.*

ALWAYS CREATE CATEGORIES

Note that categories must be created first. Throughout Joomla! 3, a content item, such as an article, banner, contact, and so on, cannot be created unless there's a category to contain it. Most content areas have an "uncategorized" category, which can be used to temporarily assign content. However, a named category should be created to help keep content orderly and easier to manage. So, for banners, a category must exist before a banner can be created. Keep this rule in mind throughout the administration of Joomla! 3 content. See Figure 8-3.

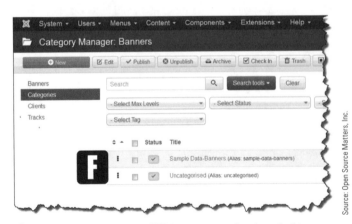

Figure 8-3 *As mentioned,* **[F]** *banners can be classified into categories. This screen enables you to add a new category or manage the existing ones.*

Banners have one category that other components do not include, the Clients category (Figure 8-4). The Banner component is intended to allow "outsiders" to post advertising panels on the website, and the Clients category allows those banners to be assigned, not only to content categories, but to individual advertisers as well.

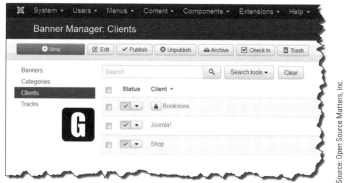

Figure 8-4 *Another method of classification of banners is called "By Clients." The* **[G]** *Clients tab opens the Clients Manager, where you can add a new client or manage existing client accounts.*

Advertisers always want information about the ad panels they display. The Banner component allows you to track the visitor's viewing activity (Figure 8-5).

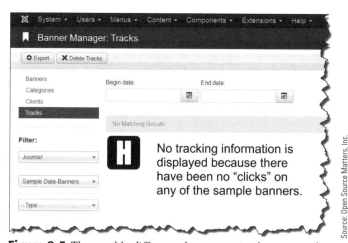

Figure 8-5 *The notable difference between using banners and using modules to contain banners is the ability to track information about user click-throughs and when, by date. The* **[H]** *Tracks tab opens the Tracks Manager screen. Note at the top, there is a button to export the information. None of the banners on "My First Site" have yet to be clicked, so there is no information display.*

Banner Manager Options

One way Joomla! 3 gives the website administrator the ability to manage the many parts is via options within the content managers. The Banner Manager is no exception. The options for the Banner Manager are accessed at the top-right of the screen. When you open it, you'll see three tabs: Client Options, History Options, and Permissions (Figure 8-6).

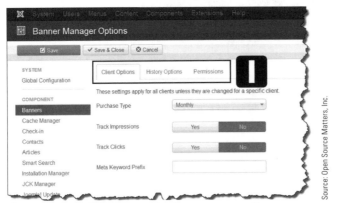

Figure 8-6 *The* **[I]** *Options tab allows you to configure parameters relative to client options and banner history options. The permissions relate to access control.*

One of the most powerful features of Joomla! 3 is access control lists, which are covered in depth in Chapter 23, "Access Control List and Permissions." There aren't many parts of a Joomla! 3 website that do not have such permissions. The Banner Manager has permissions under the Permissions tab (Figure 8-7).

Figure 8-7 *The* **[J]** *Permissions tab is connected to the Joomla! 3 Access Control (ACL). The main ACL settings control which permission can be configured in the Permissions tab for the Banner Manager, and this setting applies to each banner globally. It cannot be overridden at the individual banner level.*

Individual Banner Parameters

Each banner has its own group of parameters that can be set, which affects how the banner is displayed on the website. There are three parameter tabs. The parameter settings for banners are not too complicated, and include the following.

Details—Selects the image from a banner category and sets the size and toggles the Published setting (Figure 8-8).

Banner Details—Configures the client and type of banner tracking, counting impressions (number of times displayed) and clicks (actual user mouse clicks on the banner) with their associated settings (Figure 8-9).

Publishing—Controls the start/finish date for the banner and provides the ability to add metadata for search engine optimization settings (Figure 8-10).

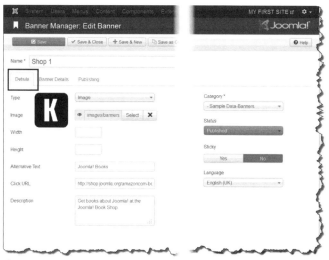

Figure 8-8 *In this screen view, the individual banner* **[K]** *details are shown for Banner Shop 1. There are many setting or parameters that can be set per banner, the main two being Name and Category, which are required parameter settings. The source of the image banner is selected in the Image Select box, which connects to the images/banners in the Media Manager.*

Figure 8-9 *Under the* **[L]** *Banner Details tab, there is information about the statistics of the banner. This tab contains the tracking information.*

CONTROLLING THE DURATION OF THE DISPLAY

Almost every content manager in Joomla! 3 has a parameter setting that allows the administrator to set the Start Publishing and Finish Publishing settings for the content. This means that content can be created in advance, and set to begin to display based on the Start Publishing setting. It also allows content to stop being displayed by setting the Finish Publishing date.

Source: Open Source Matters, Inc.

Figure 8-10 *The **[M]** Publishing tab allows you to control the dates the banner is published and add metadata for search engines.*

COMPLETE THE EXERCISES

Because the exercises in upcoming chapters rely on the content of your practice website, it is important that you do each exercise in each chapter. Quite often, there will be references to previous exercises, so make sure you do each one in each chapter.

Banner Placements

Banners must initially be set up in the Banner Manager by creating a category, adding a banner to it, and completing other information. This establishes the existence of a banner, but it does not place it anywhere on the website.

The use of banners requires two actions by the administrator:

Action 1.   Create the banner in the Banner Manager.

Action 2.   Create the module that will display the banner on selected web pages.

In the default installation with sample data, Action 1 was completed automatically. Exercise 8-1 outlines the steps you need to execute in order to complete Action 2.

EXERCISE 8-1: DISPLAYING A BANNER ON THE FRONT PAGE

Objective: This exercise guides you through the process of creating a Banner module and displaying it on the front page. The banner, called "My First Banner" will be created on the front page of the website, in the left column, and will display only when a certain menu link item is clicked. This effort takes place in the Module Manager, where a module for a specific banner is created and placed into a module position on the front page and assigned to a menu link item.

Step 1. Log in to the Administrator backend as the super user.

Step 2. Open the Module Manager via the Admin Left Menu.

Step 3. Click the green New button in the top menu. This will open the screen so you can select a module type from those available (Figure 8-11).

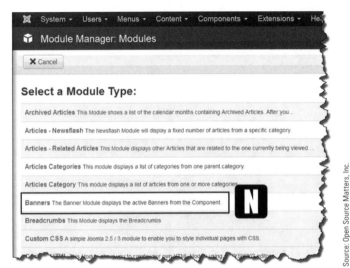

Figure 8-11 *You must select a module type when you're creating a new module content item. The* **[N]** *Banners option creates the module that will host an existing banner created in the Banner Manager.*

Step 4. In the **[O]** Title box, enter **My First Banner** (Figure 8-12).

Step 5. Execute a Save action. This saves the module immediately.

Step 6. Open the **[P]** Position drop-down and select Left [position-8] within the Protostar template option group. *Do not* select the Banner position under the Protostar template. Make sure to select the Left [position-8] module position.

Step 7. Immediately below the position selector, set the **[Q]** Status drop-down to Published.

Step 8. Execute a Save action.

Step 9. In the left column, set the **[R]** Count value to 1 so that only one banner from the client or category will display.

Step 10. For **[S]** Client, select Bookstore. Because All Categories is the default for the Category selector, you don't need to change this setting.

Step 11. Execute a Save action.

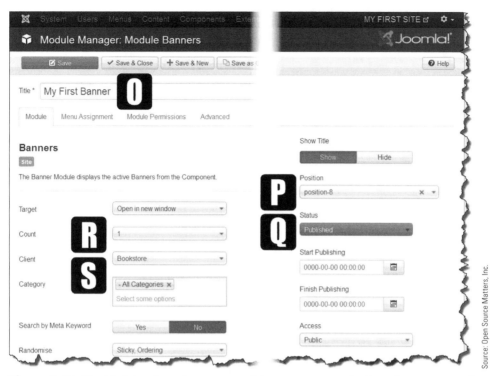

Figure 8-12 *The Module tab configures most of the parameters to display a banner in a module position and other key settings.*

Step 12. Open the Menu Assignment tab.

Step 13. In the drop-down, select **[T]** Only On The Pages Selected, which will open a list of all of the menu link items for each page on the website (Figure 8-13).

Step 14. At the top, select **[U]** None as the selector option, which will unselect each item.

Step 15. Scroll down near the bottom of the list and select **[V]** My Menu Item. The objective of this task is to show the banner *only* when that menu link item is selected.

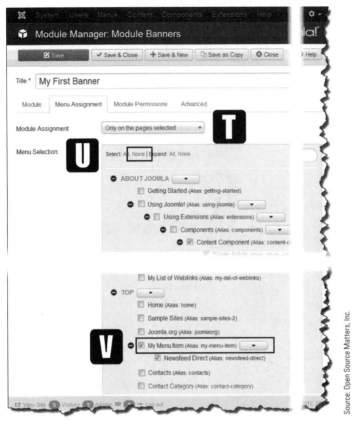

Figure 8-13 *This screen, throughout the admin areas and content managers, allows you to select specific pages on which a module will display when the item is clicked.*

Step 16. Execute a Save action.

Step 17. Go to the website front-end and refresh the screen.

Step 18. Click on the My Menu Item link in the top menu. The result should show the page associated with that item, with the **[W]** banner module in the left column (Figure 8-14).

Figure 8-14 *Clicking any other menu link item in the top menu will not display the Banner module. Only the My Menu Item link will display the Banner module. The banner will not display for any other menu link item because of the Menu Assignment setting.*

Banners Summary

Banners can be an asset to your website, particularly if you have a large following of users. The Banner component can be used to display important content, be it text or graphics, or combinations of the two. It's a good, but underutilized, component, mostly because website administrators simply do not understand how to use it.

If you are managing your own personal website, it isn't likely that you'll use the Banner Manager. But, if you are selling banners on your site, it's quite possible you may want to. However, the Banner Manager is a tad clumsy in some regards, especially in generally managing banners.

A better choice is to find and install an extension from the JED. There are several very good ones. Most of these extensions, however, are commercial and not free. But if you will make money selling banners on your website, investing a few dollars might be necessary.

Summary

In this chapter, you learned:

◆ Which components are part of the default installation.

◆ What the Banner component is and what it does.

◆ How banners are organized and managed.

◆ About the details of banners and how to manage them.

◆ How to create a banner.

◆ How a banner can be displayed on a screen.

◆ That banners can be associated with menu link items.

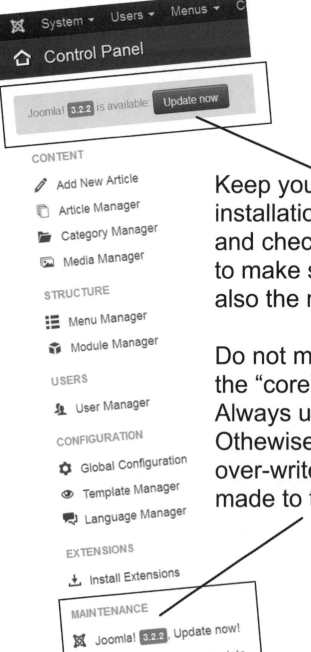

Keep your Joomla! 3 installation up-to-date and check extensions to make sure they are also the most current.

Do not modify any of the "core" files directly. Always use overrides. Othewise, updates will over-write the changes made to the files.

Chapter 9

Components: Contacts

Learning Objectives

What's included in this chapter:

◆ Use of the Contacts component.

◆ Organizing contacts and Contact categories.

◆ Accessing the Contact Manager.

◆ Creating a Contact category.

◆ Creating an individual contact.

◆ Displaying the individual contact via a menu link item.

◆ Displaying a Contact category via another menu link item.

◆ Creating a list of categories to display.

◆ Paginating large lists of categories or contacts.

Understanding the Contacts Component

It is possible you might be the administrator of a company website that may have a number of people whom users may need to contact. To help with that, Joomla! 3 has a Contact Manager.

The Contacts component operates in such a way that categories of contacts are created and then individual contact information is added and categorized for display. The Contact Manager is dramatically much easier to use than the Banner Manager. However, there are many more options that may be invoked within the Contact Manager.

This chapter covers the Contact Manager so that, when called upon, you can create a list of contacts for your website, or for the website of a company. It's a powerful component and can be used in different ways.

How Contacts Are Organized

Contacts are organized in categories. No surprise there, as almost every type of content has some type of Category Manager to help organize the individual pieces of content. For the Contact Manager the categories are key, especially if you have a large number of contacts to list and display.

If you are only going to list yourself as a "contact" on the site, you can do that easily enough. If you are going to list many, many contacts, the task is a bit more complicated, but doable if you follow the instructions in this chapter and use a little "organizational imagination" to create the structure for the contacts and categories (Figure 9-1).

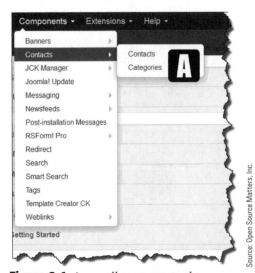

Source: Open Source Matters, Inc.

Figure 9-1 *As are all components, the Contact Manager can be accessed via the* **[A]** *Components drop-down. There is no Contact Manager link in the Admin Left Menu of the Control Panel, so you must access this component as shown.*

146

Accessing the Contact Manager

Let's start learning about the Contact Manager by accessing it in the Components menu (choose Components > Contacts). This opens the Contacts list, which shows the contacts that Joomla! 3 installer added.

If you switch to the Categories tab on the left, the list displays the categories that were also installed as part of the default configuration.

To help you master the use of the Contact Manager, there are three important parts you need to familiarize yourself with:

Create Categories: All contacts must be assigned to a Category, and if there is not a suitable one already created, you must create one.

Create Contacts: A contact must be created for display, and this contact must be assigned to a category.

Manage the Appearance: The "look" of the contact and the contact lists can be controlled using options, which allow you to control the actual information displayed for each contact.

Let's begin by creating a Contact category.

EXERCISE 9-1: CREATING A CONTACT CATEGORY

Objective: The objective of this exercise is to demonstrate how to create a category into which you can assign contacts.

Step 1.   If you're not already there, log in to the Administrator backend of the website.

Step 2.   Open the Contact Manager: Contacts via the Components tab in the top menu.

Step 3.   Click on the **[B]** Categories link in the left column, which opens the Contact Category Manager (Figure 9-2).

Figure 9-2 *When the Categories area is open, clicking the New button will open the individual Category Manager.*

Step 4.   Click the green **[C]** New button at the top left of the screen.

Step 5.   Enter **Contact Category A** in the Title field.

Step 6.   Click the Save & Close button to save the information and close the screen.

At this point, when returning to the Categories tab view, you should check to ensure the Contact category was created.

Step 7. In the Contact Categories screen view (the Categories link on the left is high-lighted blue), click on the column head Title, which will sort the list alphabetically. The Contact category should be the fourth item down, in alphabetical order following the C category. The status should show a green checkmark to the left of the name, which means it's active.

It's now an active Contact category into which a contact can be assigned.

EXERCISE 9-2: CREATING A CONTACT

Objective: In this exercise, you learn to create a contact.

Step 1. Make sure the **[D]** Contacts tab is active in the left column. It should be high-lighted blue.

Step 2. Click the green **[E]** New button at the top left of the screen (Figure 9-3).

Figure 9-3 *The New button opens a Contact Manager when in the Contacts section of the Contacts Component Manager.*

Step 2 should have opened the Contact Manager for creating a new contact, which is indicated by the **[F]** New Contact tab at the upper-left part of the screen (Figure 9-4).

Step 3. Enter **[G] Contact A** in the Name field.

Step 4. In the **[H]** Category drop-down, select Contact Category A, which is likely at the very bottom of the list. You may need to scroll down to select it.

Step 5. Click the green Save button to save the information and remain on the screen.

No other information is needed in this section of the contact information. Note the Linked User drop-down field. If you have registered users on the website, you can select from among those users to populate this information. We are not doing this at this time, but note that you may do this if desired.

Step 6. Switch to the **[J]** Publishing screen. Review the information and note the ability to control the Start and Finish Publishing dates. Normally, these fields are left blank.

Step 7.   Switch to the **[F]** New Contact screen. This is where the detailed information about Contact A is entered. Go ahead and enter some information in all of the fields except the Sort field at the bottom. Any information will do, but make sure you fill in all the fields.

Step 8.   Click the green Save button to save the information and remain on the screen.

Step 9.   Switch to the **[K]** Display screen. This screen is abundant with setting options and the ability to add customized information. At this time, *do not change* any of the settings. Look through the list and relate the selections to the items in the New Contact screen, entered in Step 7.

Step 10. Switch to the **[L]** Form screen. The settings on this screen control some aspects of contact form management, including the ability to ban email addresses, subject matter, and text from being sent to the recipient. By default, the contact form is set to show when the contact menu link item on the front-end is clicked.

Step 11. Switch to the Metadata Options screen which, like all other metadata screens, allows you to enter information that Internet search engines can read and list as search results, based on specific queries that contain those words.

Figure 9-4 *Most of the settings for an individual contact can be set in the Contact Manager by opening the different sections of the manager.*

The contact has been created and is assigned to a category, which was also created. Note that the Contact Status is automatically set to Published, so if you don't want it to be available immediately, make sure to change it to Unpublished.

Contact Manager Options

As is the case with many other managers in the Admin backend, the Contact Manager has options that you can set, which control how information is generated or displayed on the front-end. The options are accessible via the Options tab in the top menu, when the Contact Manager is open to either the contacts or the categories sections.

The parameter settings, which affect both the backend management and the front-end display on a global basis, consist of these areas:

Contact: Determines exactly what is displayed globally for all contacts. This control can be overridden for each contact under the Display Options tab when the individual Contact Manager is open.

Icons: Several of the information fields for contacts can display an icon image next to the data display field. These are global settings. This cannot be overridden for an individual contact. It's all or none.

Category: Deals with how a Contact category is displayed on the front-end. Review the options available. Menu link item types have some settings that may override the default settings.

Categories: Offers options as to how the categories are displayed with respect to sub-categories and empty categories, as well as other settings.

List Layouts: When there are many contacts on a list of contacts, the list can be very wide. These controls allow you to hide or show list columns. Simply toggle the item's settings.

Form: If a contact form is to be used, you can show it as such, along with setting other parameters, which can also be set at the individual contact level.

Integration: Some extensions integrate with the Contact Manager, such as extensions that deal with social media. This allows integration with those extensions.

Permissions: Allows management of the Access Control List (ACL) aspects of Joomla! 3 to be invoked for the Contact Manager. This is a global setting.

Displaying Contacts on the Front-End

Now that you've created a Contact category and assigned a contact to it, the next challenge is to display this information on the front-end.

The same procedure used to display other content, such as articles, is used to display a contact or Contact category list that is accessible via a menu link item in a menu. In previous exercises in earlier chapters, this process was used to display "My First Article" by clicking the My Menu Item in the top menu.

Displaying a Single Contact

Complete the following exercise to display the Contact A information on the front-end, using a menu link item called "My Contacts."

EXERCISE 9-3: DISPLAYING A SINGLE CONTACT ON THE FRONT-END

Objective: This exercise takes you through the process of creating a menu link item that will connect to a single contact in the Contacts directory.

Step 1.   If you're not already there, log in to the Administrator backend of the website.

Step 2.   From the Admin Left Menu, click on the Menu Manager link.

Step 3.   When the Menu Manager opens, click on the top menu.

Step 4.   Click the green New button at the top left of the screen. This will open the Menu Manager: New Menu Item screen (Figure 9-5).

Step 5.   For the Menu Item Type, click the blue **[M]** Select button to open the list of types that can be created from the ones installed.

Step 6.   Select Contacts in the pop-up window, then choose Single Contact from the accordion list that drops down.

Step 7.   In the Select Contact field, use the grey **[N]** Select button to open the list of Contacts and select Contact A, which was previously created, from among the list.

Step 8.   The **[O]** Menu Title is required, so enter **Contact Us**.

Step 9.   Click the Save & Close button to save the information and close the screen.

Figure 9-5 *Two items are required to create a menu link item— the **[M]** menu item type and the **[N]** select contact choice. There must be a **[O]** menu title. By default, the menu link item should be in the **[P]** Published status, but it should be checked when executing a Save action.*

Step 10.   Go to the website front-end, refresh the screen, and make sure the Contact Us menu link item appears on the right end of the top menu.

Step 11.   Click the Contacts link. The Contact A page should appear with the contact information displayed. Notice the icons next to the information items.

Step 12. Click the Contact Form below the Contact area, which will open the actual contact form for this contact.

Step 13. Go back into Contact Manager > Contacts > Contact A, and go into the Display Options tab. Hide the fax number using the drop-down setting.

Step 14. Click the Save & Close button to save the information and close the screen.

Go back to the front-end and refresh the screen. The fax number field should no longer appear. Most all data fields for contact information can be toggled on/off to alter the display.

Showing a Category of Contacts

Complete the following exercise to display a contact list from a Contact category.

EXERCISE 9-4: DISPLAYING A CONTACT CATEGORY LIST ON THE FRONT-END

Objective: As an alternative to showing a single contact, this exercise shows you how to display a list view of the contacts in a category.

Step 1. If you're not already there, log in to the Administrator backend of the website.

Step 2. From the Admin Left Menu, click on the Menu Manager link.

Step 3. When the Menu Manager opens, click on the top menu.

Step 4. Click the green New button at the top left of the screen. This will open the Menu Manager: New Menu Item screen (Figure 9-6).

Step 5. For the Menu Item Type, click the blue **[Q]** Select button to open the list of types that can be created from those installed.

Step 6. Select List Contacts in a Category in the pop-up window. You will be returned to the previous screen for the Details page for the Menu Link Item.

Step 7. In the Select a Category field, open the drop down and select **[R]** Contact Category A, which is at the bottom of the list.

Step 8. The **[S]** Menu Title is required, so enter **Contact Category**.

Step 9. Click the Save & Close button to save the information and close the screen.

Step 10. Go to the website front-end, refresh the screen, and check to see if the Contact Category menu link item appears on the right end of the top menu.

Step 11. Click the Contact Category link. The Contact Category A page should appear with the Contact A information displayed.

Step 12. Click the Contact A name link, which will open the individual's contact information. In this instance, notice that the link is opening the Contact screen for a single contact, as per Exercise 9-3. The contact form is identical to the one created previously, with the same parameter settings.

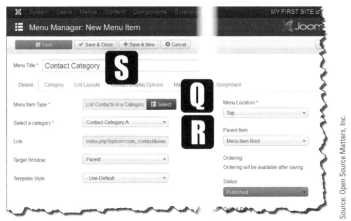

Figure 9-6 *The* **[Q]** *menu item type and* **[R]** *category that will be displayed. In this case, it is a list of contacts in a category and the category is Contact Category A.*

If there were 10 or 15 individual contacts assigned to that Contact category, the list would display them all, if the parameters were set that way.

Step 13. Go back into the Menu Manager: New Menu Item and open the Advanced Options tab.

Step 14. Open the List Layouts section and hide the phone number.

Step 15. Click the Save & Close button to save the information and close the screen.

Step 16. Go to the website front-end, refresh the screen, and check the Contact Category list view. Verify that the phone number that appeared on the right no longer appears. However, the phone number still remains on the individual contact listing. In this way, lists can be modified to show limited information without affecting the appearance of the individual contact display.

Other Contact List Displays

In the previous exercises, a Contact category was created, along with a single contact. Then, the contact, by itself was set up as a menu link item. Next, the Contact category was displayed with another menu link item. These are not the only types of displays available in the Contact Manager. There are more, such as:

List All Contact Categories: If there are many Contact categories, this can list all of the categories on one screen. They can then be opened individually, essentially displaying a list of contacts in a category. If there are many categories, the list is easier to view and more convenient to access using this layout type option.

List Contacts in a Category: When all contacts are in one Contact category, they can be displayed as a group in a list-type view. Parameters can be set for the category and the contact. Almost any combination of category and contact settings can be employed in generating this view.

Single Contact: This is a display of an individual contact with no frills. Just a listing for one individual with the various parameter settings adjusted as desired. This works well with a simple Contact Us link on the website.

Featured Contacts: This is how, from among a list of contacts, some contacts can be listed as "featured." This option generates a contact list of all the contacts, in any/all categories, that have one of their parameters set to Featured. The contacts do not need to be in any specific Contact category; they just need to be designated as Featured, in addition to their regular category assignments. For example, if you have five categories of employees and one of them in each list is a manager, the managers can be set to Featured and displayed together on one screen, even though they are each in separate categories.

Paginating Large Contact Lists

One of the problems that comes up in large corporate websites that list employees by their departments or job areas, is that the lists can be incredibly unwieldy and make the screen displays complicated and hard to read.

The solution to this problem is to paginate the display, which is typically done by limiting the display to a given number of Contact categories, or by a given number of individual contacts.

The pagination setting takes place within the Contact Manager options, in the List Layouts section. Keep in mind that the settings in the Category section can also affect the layout.

Summary

In this chapter, you learned:

◆ How to use the Contacts component.

◆ How contacts and Contact categories are organized.

◆ How to access the Contact Manager.

◆ How to create a Contact category.

◆ How to create an individual contact.

◆ How a menu link item is used to display a single contact.

◆ How a menu link item is used to display a Contact category.

◆ Lists of categories can be displayed if needed.

◆ About the different types of display options for contacts/categories.

◆ Pagination can be used to break large lists into multiple pages.

Chapter 10

Components: Joomla! Update

Learning Objectives

What's included in this chapter:

◆ How to update the Joomla! 3 installation.

◆ Joomla! 3 structure is defined.

◆ How to tell if updates are available.

◆ How to update Joomla! 3.

◆ How to tell if extension updates are available.

◆ How to update the extensions, if updates are available.

Updating the Joomla! 3 Install

One of the many great things about the Joomla! 3 platform is the ability to update any installation. As is the case with most software, there are updates to make the program operate better, add new features, and insert security patches.

In the past, Joomla! provided "patches," which were created to upgrade from one version to another, and was somewhat confusing for administrators who were not technically savvy. The update process was easy enough, but still had that degree of confusion for administrators.

So, to solve all that, the Joomla! developers included a way to automatically update any Joomla! 3 installation.

How Joomla! 3 Is Structured

The way Joomla! 3 is structured was briefly discussed in previous chapters. There are three layers involved in the Joomla! 3 platform:

Core Platform—This is the invisible part of Joomla! 3 that you don't see. It is the underlying code that connects to the database and contains the program files and the interfaces.

CMS—The CMS is where the administrators work, and displays the content on the frontend of the website. Administrators manage the content through articles, modules, and components as part of the CMS.

Extensions—These are added, through the core to the CMS, to enlarge and enhance the ability to display more types of content than what is provided in the default CMS part.

What Gets Updated?

When Joomla! 3 is updated, only the core platform is affected. The new files are added as needed at that level of structure. The CMS part usually isn't affected, unless there is something small in nature that needs to be changed. If that happens, the operation of the backend doesn't change.

If extensions are updated, the changes are at the Administrator level, which means that the extension itself can change. After an extension is updated, you should open it to check to see what has changed, if the change is in the "manager" part of the extension.

It is safe to say that Jooma! 3 updates do not generally affect the CMS or the extensions, unless some security issue needs fixing.

Don't "Hack" the Core!

If you are an advanced user and you want to change something on your website, don't ever—it's forbidden!—change any of the core platform files.

Why? You don't want to change the core platform files because when an update is performed, there is a good chance the files will be overwritten, and there go your changes. If you have made those changes via an "override," the update *will not* alter those changes.

If you need to make any changes, consult the **joomla3bootcamp.com** website for guidance about the Update feature.

What Happens After Login

When the super user logs in to the Admin backend, the Control Panel opens. Immediately after that, the internal functions of Joomla! 3 start to check the installation and extensions to compare the installed version with the latest available version.

If no updates are available, Joomla! 3 does nothing and awaits any actions by the administrator to manage the website content. If updates are available, a notice is displayed at the bottom of the Admin Left Menu under the Maintenance heading. Both the Joomla! core and the installed extensions will be flagged if there are any updates.

The "check for updates" process is best explained this way:

1. Joomla! 3.2.4, as an example, is the current installed version on a website.
2. The development team has made some improvements and the new version is Joomla! 3.2.5.
3. When accessing the Admin Control Panel, Joomla! 3 automatically does two things:

   A. Checks for Joomla! 3 updates.

   B. Checks for updates to extensions.
4. Alerts display when any updates are available, and identify which ones.
5. The option to automatically install the updates is presented.
6. An Update action is executed.
7. The website is now operating as Joomla! 3.2.5.

The figures of the Joomla! 3 updating process in this chapter briefly describe what happens as part of the process, and what action is needed by the administrator to make the update happen. There isn't much involved in doing it, other than clicking a few links and letting the system do it's job.

At the bottom of the Admin Left Menu, there are two entries that indicate the system is checking for updates (Figure 10-1). This check is performed automatically immediately after the administrator login is completed.

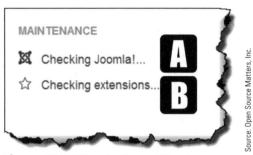

Source: Open Source Matters, Inc.

Figure 10-1 *When the Control Panel opens, at the bottom of the Admin Left Menu, the program checks the* **[A]** *Joomla! installation and the installed* **[B]** *extensions to determine if there are any updates.*

When the update check is complete (the program checks a fixed URL location), the message changes to notify the administrator whether updates are available (Figure 10-2). Joomla! splits this checking process so that administrators can install the updates individually.

Source: Open Source Matters, Inc.

Figure 10-2 *If updates are available, the display indicates which version for* **[C]** *Joomla! 3 or the* **[D]** *extensions. The text also turns into a link that opens the updater. At the time of this screenshot, Joomla! 3.2 was being updated to version 3.2.1.*

The update check can also be initiated at any time in the Admin backend by clicking the Joomla! Update component, which is accessed in the top menu (Figure 10-3).

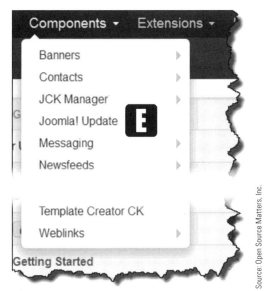

Figure 10-3 *The update features are also accessible via the* **[E]** *Components menu, which opens the same update as before.*

When the Joomla! Update link is clicked, the information screen displays all of the information relative to the update (Figure 10-4). The administrator can start the update by clicking the **[K]** Install the Update button.

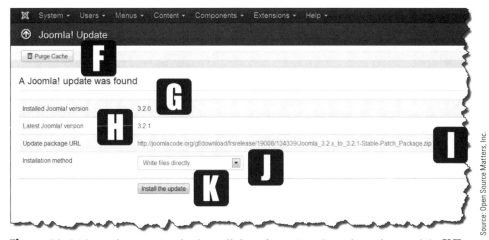

Figure 10-4 *The updater screen displays all the information about the update, and the* **[K]** *Install the Update button executes the action. The* **[F]** *notice tells you that an update was found. The* **[G]** *installed version is identified. The* **[H]** *Joomla! updates are also identified The* **[I]** *URL from which the update is taken is also listed. The* **[J]** *installation method is shown, which is typically to write the files directly into the installation or to use FTP.*

If something looks familiar about the updating process, it's because it is akin to something else you've already read about. In Chapter 7, "Adding and Managing Extensions," there was an installation process called "Install from URL." Well, that is exactly how the Joomla! 3 platform is updated. It grabs the file from a URL and installs it—but it does so automatically.

Sometimes, when programs are being updated, the activity takes place in the background. You might sit there wondering if anything is actually happening. Fortunately, the Joomla! developers thought to provide a screen that lets you know what is happening, as it happens (Figure 10-5). As you can see, there are a lot of files involved in the updating process, but it doesn't take too long on cable-provided Internet access. If you're updating via a slower Internet connection, well—it might take a while.

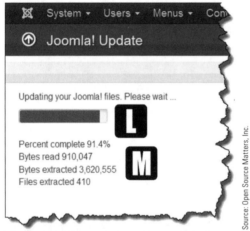

Figure 10-5 *During the update, you'll see an* **[L]** *progress bar, along with a* **[M]** *written display.*

When the update is completed, the system lets you know. If there is an issue, the issue will be identified and you can take action as needed. If there is no issue and the update is completed, the success message (Figure 10-6) will display, indicating which version was installed.

You typically won't need to change the updating options (Figure 10-7). The default location is fixed in the core platform files, and works just fine in most cases. The policy of "if it works, don't fix it," might be a good one to follow for the updating options.

Source: Open Source Matters, Inc.

Figure 10-6 *When the update is complete, a* **[N]** *status display indicates whether the update was successful. If it was successful, you'll see the* **[O]** *current operating version listed.*

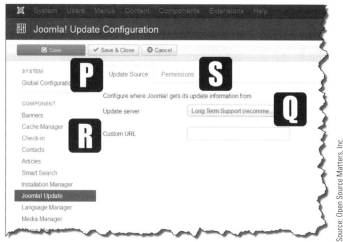

Source: Open Source Matters, Inc.

Figure 10-7 *The Options button on the update screen opens the* **[P]** *Update Source tab. The* **[Q]** *Update Server can be changed from here (the default is Long Term Support). A* **[R]** *Custom URL can be entered if it's from another source. The* **[S]** *Permissions tab also links to the ACL to allow or deny certain administrator levels to perform the updates.*

Always Do It!

As you can see, updating Joomla! 3 isn't a very traumatic process. It's easy to do, requires almost no intervention by the administrator, and takes only a minute or two to complete.

If platform updates are available after the Control Panel opens, go ahead and perform the update immediately. This is especially important if it's a security update, which will patch some sort of issue with hackers or others who may try to disable your website.

Updating Extensions

If there is a message in the Admin Left Menu area indicating that extension updates are available, the display will tell you how many (Figure 10-8), but not which extensions have updates. There are a few more steps involved in updating extensions than when updating the core platform, but the basic process is the same.

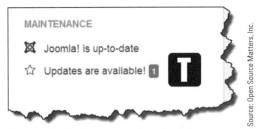

Figure 10-8 *The system also checks extensions for updates, and in this case,* **[T]** *one update was found.*

When you open the Extension Manager: Update screen, all of the extensions that have updates are shown (Figure 10-9). The idea behind this is to allow the administrator to select which extensions to update by checking the selection, then executing the update action.

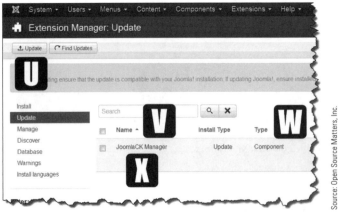

Figure 10-9 *After viewing the* **[V]** *Name and* **[W]** *Type lists, select the* **[X]** *Joomla CK Manager. Click the* **[U]** *Update button at the top to start the update.*

It's a good idea to update only one extension at a time. The list of remaining extensions to be updated isn't going to disappear. You can update them one at a time if you like—which is the best way to do it, especially if your Internet connection is on the slow side.

Again, when the administrator initiates the update action, the process begins and usually requires no intervention. When it's complete, a success message will display (Figure 10-10). That's it. No complications, no issues. Just a nice clean extension update.

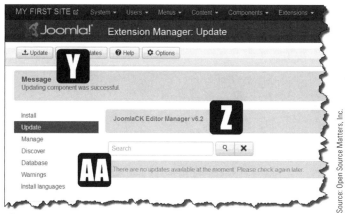

Figure 10-10 *As in all add-in actions, a* **[Y]** *success message is displayed. The* **[Z]** *updated extension is identified and a* **[AA]** *No More Updates message is displayed.*

For the most part, Joomla! 3 updates and extension updates are seamlessly performed by the system, and the administrator only needs to execute the action, or pick which extension updates to perform.

Summary

In this chapter, you learned:

◆ How to update the Joomla! 3 installation.

◆ About the Joomla! 3 structure.

◆ How updates are identified on the Control Panel.

◆ The process by which Joomla! 3 is updated.

◆ The way extension update notifications are displayed.

◆ How to update the extensions.

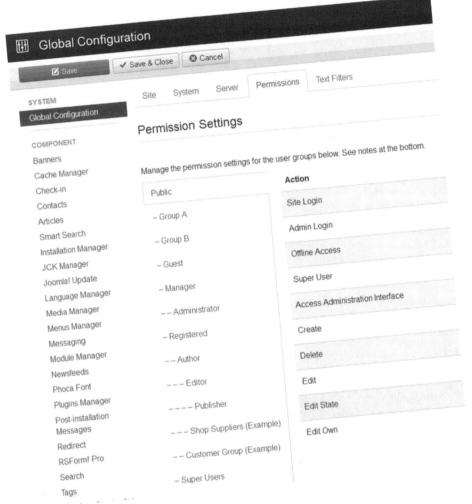

If you are the Administrator of a large, corporate website, you should master the use of the Joomla! 3 "Permissions" system's viewing and actions for Users in User Groups.

Chapter 11

Components: Messaging

Learning Objectives

What's included in this chapter:

- ◆ Why the Messaging component is available.
- ◆ How the component is used.
- ◆ Sending messages.
- ◆ Receiving messages.
- ◆ Responding to messages.
- ◆ Managing the component's settings.
- ◆ Managing messages.

Understanding the Messaging Component

Joomla! 3 has a simple messaging system that the administrator can use to send messages to users of the website, designated as administrators and super users. Think of the messaging feature along the lines of a system administrator sending messages to individuals, or to everyone on the network. That's the sum and substance of the Joomla! 3 Messaging component.

For sites that only have a super user, there is no one to message to. But, for sites that have a number of administrators, you might need to message any one of them, or all of them, more often than one might think.

For example, let's say the administrator needs to take the site offline for some reason. It would be good to send all site administrators a notification to that effect. In this case, the Messaging component would come in very handy.

Skip This Chapter if ...

The Messaging component is designed to be used so that super users and administrators can send messages to each other. If you are the only super user and the sole administrator of your website, you won't have a need to use this component.

Therefore, you can skip this chapter and read it later if you want to learn about the Messaging component at a later time.

However, if you have many administrators, by all means, continue reading.

How the Messaging Component Works

This is another one of those components that is not accessible via the Admin Left Menu in the Control Panel. It must be accessed via the top Components menu (Figure 11-1).

When the Messaging component opens, it automatically puts the Messages view on the screen. This is where messages are displayed (Figure 11-2).

166

Figure 11-1 *You open the Messaging component from the* **[A]** *Components > Messaging
menu.*

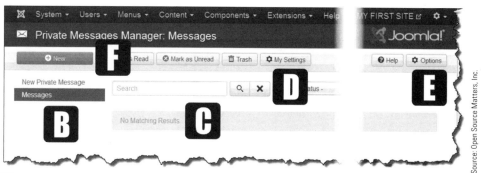

Figure 11-2 *The main screen of the* **[B]** *Messages view lists any received* **[C]** *messages and
includes the* **[D]** *My Settings and* **[E]** *Options buttons. The green* **[F]** *New button and the
New Private Message link open the same message screen.*

Messages Menu Items

The **[D]** My Settings button takes you to the parameters that you can set. As the super
user, you can lock the inbox or receive emails when a new message arrives. These settings
can be disabled (Figure 11-3). Whenever the super user logs into the system, there is an
indicator in the bottom left corner of the Admin backend that will display a notification
that new messages are in the inbox.

The **[E]** Options button in the Messaging menu (Figure 11-2) is simply a connection to
the permissions for this component. It can be used to limit access to administrators who
are in certain permission groups.

Entering Settings

The My Settings parameters allow a super user or an administrator to **[G]** lock the inbox, to stop receiving messages. The **[H]** Email New Messages controls whether an email notification will be sent to you when a message has been received. The **[I]** Save & Close button puts the settings into effect.

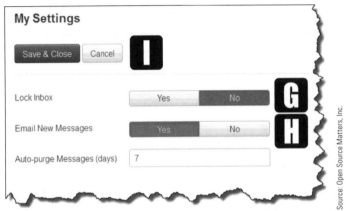

Figure 11-3 *Both the* **[G]** *Super Users inbox and the* **[H]** *Email Notifications can be enabled or disabled in the My Settings parameters.*

Sending a Message

A message can be sent to other super users and administrators. When the green New button or the New Private Message link is clicked, it opens the Message Editor (Figure 11-4).

When you click the **[J]** icon next to the Recipient field, it opens the list of possible recipients, controlled by the **[N]** User Group selector (Figure 11-5). Then, simply clicking on the **[O]** name of the individual will enter them into the Recipient box.

You can then add a subject to the message and compose the message using the text area of the JCK Editor.

After you click the Send button, the message is sent and the success message appears.

Figure 11-4 *Clicking on the* **[J]** *recipient icon opens the list of super users and administrators. Choose one* **[M]** *recipient to receive the subject message* **[K]**. *The content editor* **[L]** *works the same as a standard email program, requiring a subject and text.*

Figure 11-5 *When the recipient icon is clicked, a list of users appears and can be filtered* **[N]**. *The* **[O]** *recipient can be selected by clicking on the name.*

Reading and Responding to Messages

Reading and responding to actions applies to all users. When the recipient logs in to the Admin backend, there is an indicator and an envelope icon display in the lower-left corner of the screen. When it's clicked, the message list will open (Figure 11-6). You can open the individual messages by clicking the **[P]** subject's name.

After a message is opened, there is a Reply button to initiate a response to the sender.

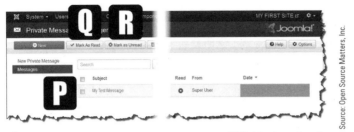

Figure 11-6 *You can designate messages as* **[Q]** *Mark as Read or* **[R]** *Mark as Unread, by checking the box next to the message's subject and then clicking the appropriate button. Open the* **[P]** *message by clicking on the subject.*

Removing Messages

Messages can easily accumulate to the point where the lists get long. If it is not necessary to keep the messages, it's good practice to delete them. In the Messaging Manager, items can be placed into Trash, from which there is no return.

Once you select a message and click the Trash button, that's it. The message is gone (Figure 11-7). There is no recovery from this action.

Figure 11-7 *You* **[S]** *check a message and click the* **[T]** *Trash button to permanently remove the message. There is no warning; the message is simply deleted.*

Is This a Functional Component?

The answer to this question depends on the nature of the website you administer. If the website is small, with only one or two super users or administrators, this component probably isn't going to be used much. This might explain why the Messaging component isn't listed in the Control Panel's Admin Left Menu, where the "frequently used" admin areas are accessible via links.

The bottom line on this component is that it's useful on larger websites, where the super users and administrators have a need to communicate quickly and efficiently with each other to exchange information or instructions.

Summary

In this chapter, you learned:

◆ The use of the messaging component.

◆ How to send messages.

◆ How messages are received.

◆ How to respond to messages.

◆ Which parameters can be set.

◆ How to manage messages in the inbox.

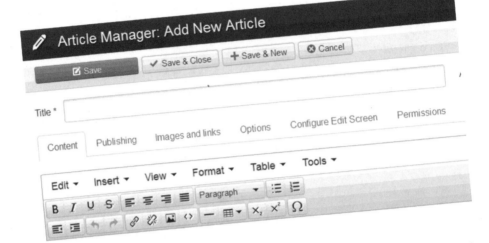

Joomla! 3 has a new "editor" that is easier to use to format text in both Articles and Custom HTML Modules.

The < > in the bottom row allows you to view and edit the HTML code for the content.

If you know HTML, you can modify individual content layouts.

Chapter 12

Components: Newsfeeds

Learning Objectives

What's included in this chapter:

◆ Newsfeeds can provide website content.

◆ Newsfeeds and RSS are the same thing.

◆ How to use newsfeeds.

◆ How to obtain a newsfeed link.

◆ How to add newsfeeds using a link item.

◆ How to add newsfeeds using a module.

◆ What content on your website can be a newsfeed.

◆ How to create a newsfeed from your content.

◆ How to find and use newsfeed extensions.

Understanding the Newsfeeds Component

Newsfeeds work in a very simple way, which is actually the basis for their real name, which is RSS (Really Simple Syndication). This chapter discusses newsfeeds and provides exercises that you can use to implement feeds on your website.

Syndication, in Joomla!-speak, means taking content from another website and displaying it on your website. There are thousands of websites that generate content for syndication, or for RSS, and are more than happy to share their information.

THE SAME MEANING

The terms *newsfeeds* and *RSS* are used interchangeably in this chapter, because they mean the same thing. When pulling feeds from other websites, you may see both terms, or even a term particular to an individual website, as many have their own terminology.

Using Newsfeeds

Way back when, newsfeeds were all the rage because they allowed sites with very little original content to display a lot of information for free. Almost every website had a newsfeed of one sort or another. This helped websites devoted to single subjects, such as fighting hunger, to pull in articles on the same subject from other websites. Actually, some websites consist exclusively of newsfeeds culled from a wide spectrum of websites.

In this chapter, you will be pulling newsfeeds from the "RSS Feeds" section of the joomla .org website.

Types of Newsfeed Generators and Readers

Here is where using newsfeeds gets complicated. There are an abundance of newsfeed generators, which are utilities that make content on a website available to other websites. There are an equally large number of readers (over 2,000), which allow website visitors to see the RSS feeds available on a website. In short, there are many options for both generating and reading newsfeeds. It can get confusing.

Problems Solved and Confusion Gone

Joomla! 3 has solved at least one of these problems. The Newsfeeds component allows the website administrator to import newsfeeds that display website content from other websites. It does so in the traditional Joomla! 3 manner—you create a category, create a newsfeed, assign it to a category, and then link to it from a menu link item.

This has been stated before, a couple of times, but it needs to be said again. Joomla! 3 has content that is based on displaying individual items that are "classified" into categories.

The Newsfeeds component is no different. Let's start learning about the component by creating a category.

EXERCISE 12-1: CREATING NEWSFEED CATEGORIES

Objective: The purpose of this exercise is to demonstrate how newsfeed categories are created using the Newsfeeds section within the Categories Manager.

Step 1.   If you're not already there, log in to the Administrator backend of the website.

Step 2.   Open the **[A]** Newsfeeds Manager via the Extensions tab in the top menu (Figure 12-1). This is another component, used less frequently than some others, that's not listed in the Admin Left Menu of the Control Panel. The manager opens to Categories Manager: Newsfeeds by default.

Source: Open Source Matters, Inc.

Figure 12-1 *As are all components,* **[A]** *newsfeeds are accessed in the top menu. There is no Newsfeeds link in the Admin Left Menu.*

Step 3.   Change the manager to Categories using the link to the left of the screen.

Step 4.   Click the green New button at the top left portion of the screen.

Step 5.   Enter **My Newsfeeds Category** into the Title box. Content can be entered into the Description area, but it is not required.

The other tabs in the manager have minor settings that do not need to be changed to create a Newsfeeds category.

Step 6.   Click the Save & Close button to save the information and close the screen. The green success message will display near the top of the screen.

The new category should appear on the list screen that opens after executing the action. If you want to put many newsfeeds on your website, and classify them into some sort of order, simply repeat the steps in Exercise 12-1 as many times needed.

Now that you've created a category, the next thing to do is create an actual newsfeed item. This requires you to obtain a link from the website that is generating the RSS feed.

The Joomla! website uses FeedBurner as the utility to generate the RSS feeds. So, go to http://www.joomla.org/rss.html to grab a newsfeed.

EXERCISE 12-2: GETTING A NEWSFEED URL

Objective: Before you can display an actual newsfeed item on your website, you need to grab the URL from the Joomla! website. For the next two exercises, the Joomla! Announcements newsfeeds will be used.

Step 1. Go to http://www.joomla.org/rss.html. At the top of the screen there are an abundance of links to social media and other destinations. This is the way Joomla! helps syndicate the newsfeeds across the Internet.

Step 2. Click on the URL for the "Joomla! Announcements," which will open to the FeedBurner generated page. The main topics listed on that page will be the items that will display using this newsfeed link.

Step 3. Copy the URL in the browser location bar. It should be http://feeds.joomla.org/JoomlaAnnouncements. This feed will be used in the next exercise.

NEWSFEEDS WILL CHANGE

This chapter was written in January 2014, and so it shows the Joomla! Announcements newsfeeds during this time period. When you create yours, the newsfeeds will be different, depending on what the Joomla! team has designated for the feed topics.

Now that you've created a category and selected a newsfeed category from the Joomla! website, the next step is to create a newsfeed item to display.

EXERCISE 12-3: CREATING A NEWSFEED ITEM

Objective: The objective of this exercise is to show you the steps used to create a newsfeed item.

Step 1. Change to the News Feed Manager: News view.

Step 2. Click the green New button at the top-left portion of the screen.

Step 3. Enter **My Newsfeeds One** in the Title box (Figure 12-2).

Step 4. Enter **http://feeds.joomla.org/JoomlaAnnouncements** in the Link box.

Step 5. Select My Newsfeeds Category from the Category drop-down.

Figure 12-2 *The* **[B]** *Title,* **[C]** *Link, and* **[D]** *Category options must be entered on this screen to create a newsfeed item.*

Step 6.   Click the Save & Close button to save the information and close the screen. The green success message will display near the top of the screen.

Step 7.   Review the list of newsfeeds and verify that "My Newsfeeds One" is on the list.

Displaying the Newsfeed

For the most part, newsfeeds can be displayed in one of two ways, depending on how you want the display to work with the menus on your website. They are:

Displayed by a Menu Link Item: By creating a single menu link item that is of the Newsfeeds type, the feeds can be displayed in the main content area, the same way an article is displayed. The actual newsfeed display is about the same as what is on the Joomla! website feeds page. The newsfeed displays internally to your website in the main content area and does not link out to the actual website page on the Joomla! website.

Displayed by a Module: Displaying a newsfeed as a module allows the information to be displayed anywhere on the page where there is a module position. This differs from the direct method in that the module needs to be associated with an existing menu link item, and does not require a new menu link item to be created. The display is also different in that it displays only the main topic names on the newsfeed. When one of those is clicked, a new browser window opens to the page on the Joomla! website. It does not display the newsfeed on your website, as with the Displayed by a Menu Link Item method.

Let's create a newsfeed using both methods.

EXERCISE 12-4: CREATING A MENU LINK ITEM FOR A NEWSFEED

Objective: The objective of this exercise is to guide you through the steps needed to display a newsfeed that displays as the result of clicking a menu link item.

Step 1. Under the Menus tab at the top of the screen, mouse over the top menu and click on the Add New Menu Item fly-out. This opens the Menu Manager: New Menu Item screen.

Step 2. For the menu item type, click the blue Select button and the Newsfeeds link, which then opens the list of choices available.

Step 3. Select Single Newsfeed as the choice.

Step 4. Click the grey Select button for the feed.

Step 5. Click My Newsfeeds One, which you created previously.

Step 6. Enter the Menu Title as **Newsfeed Direct**.

At this point, you will add this menu link item under an existing one, by selecting a parent item for it.

Step 7. Open the Parent Item drop-down and select My Menu Item.

Step 8. Click the Save & Close button to save the information and close the screen. The green success message will display near the top of the screen.

In order to show sub-menu items under an existing link, the Show Sub-menu Items option must be activated in Module Manager: Module Menu.

Step 9. Go to the Extensions link in the top menu, and click on the Module Manager.

Step 10. In the Filter area on the left, open the Select Type drop-down.

Step 11. Select Menu and click on it. The result is a list displaying all of the menus on the website. This is verified in the Type column, where all should be Menu.

Step 12. Click on the top menu name, or click the drop-down next to the name and select Edit.

Step 13. Click on the Modules tab for the menu.

Step 14. Change the Show Sub-Menu Items from red No to green Yes.

Step 15. Click the Save & Close button to save the information and close the screen. The green success message will display near the top of the screen.

Step 16. Go to the website front-end and refresh the screen.

Step 17. Mouse over the My Menu Item and the Newsfeed Direct link should appear. Click it.

The result of this action should display the newsfeeds in the main content area. Note that the banner panel does not show. Why? Because that Banner module isn't associated with this new menu link item. Keep that in mind should you run across the same situation in the future and you want the association to continue with new items. Change the settings in the module for the particular display item.

Step 18. Click on Home to go back to the front-page display without the newsfeed.

EXERCISE 12-5: CREATING A MODULE TO DISPLAY A NEWSFEED

Objective: This exercise demonstrates an alternate way to display newsfeeds.

Step 1.   Open the Module Manager from either the Admin Left Menu, or via the Extensions Menu Module Manager link.

Step 2.   Click the green New button at the top left of the screen.

Step 3.   Select Feed Display from the list of module types that appears.

Step 4.   Name the module **Newsfeed Module**.

For the module position, you want the display in the main content area, above any content, such as articles. If you use the ?tp=1 code at the end of the URL in the browser location bar, on the front-end, you will find that position-3 is a module position directly above the content area.

Step 5.   Under the Protostar Template positions, select Top Center [position-3].

Step 6.   Click the Save button to save the information and remain on the screen.

Step 7.   Open the Module tab.

Step 8.   Insert the **http://feeds.joomla.org/JoomlaAnnouncements** URL in the Feed URL box.

Step 9.   Change the Feed Items value from 3 to 1. This number determines the number of newsfeeds that will be displayed.

Step 10. Click the Save button to save the information and remain on the screen.

Step 11. Open the Menu Assignment tab for this module.

Step 12. Select Only on the Pages Selected for the Module Assignment.

Step 13. In the list area, clear the selection list by clicking None for the Select options. This clears all of the checkboxes.

Step 14. Scroll down the list near the bottom and check My Menu Item. Below it should be the sub-item Newsfeed Direct, created previously.

Step 15. Click the Save & Close button to save the information and close the screen. The green success message will display near the top of the screen.

Step 16. Go to the website front-end and refresh the screen.

Step 17. Click the My Menu Item, which will display the red graphic, the newsfeed's module content, and the article assigned to that menu link item. My First Banner should also appear in the left column.

As you can see in the previous exercises, you can add newsfeeds in several ways. There are many, many variable ways to display newsfeeds. They can be sourced from many sources, can be assigned to categories, and then the list of categories can be displayed, which is another way to show newsfeeds.

Use Them, Please!

If you are low on content and need to add some that is relevant to the topics on your website, by all means, use the RSS features. Remember, you can have many categories of newsfeeds, add many different feed topics, and then associate them with menu link items on your site. The possible combinations allow you to do almost anything using the Newsfeeds extension.

Creating Your Own Newsfeeds

Let's flip the newsfeeds coin over. What if you wanted the content on your website to be available for display on other websites? Joomla! 3 has a feature called Module Syndication Feed, which is a way of creating outbound newsfeeds.

NOT ALL CONTENT CAN BE SYNDICATED

Within the Joomla! 3 Syndication structure, not all the content items can generate a newsfeed. When you're setting up a syndication feed, only those content areas that consist of more than one item can generate the Syndication Feed Module.

Those that can be syndicated are (menu link item types):

◆ Category Blog
◆ Category List
◆ Featured Articles

Those that cannot be syndicated are:

◆ Single Articles (see the sidebar near end of chapter)
◆ Contacts of any type
◆ Weblinks

To create a syndication feed for the category blog content, you must create a module of the proper type, place it into a module position, and associate it with a menu link item—the one for the category blog display.

EXERCISE 12-6: CREATING A SYNDICATION FEED

Objective: This exercise shows you how to create a syndication feed.

Step 1. If you're not already there, log in to the Administrator backend of the website.

Step 2. From the Admin Left Menu, open the Module Manager.

Step 3. Click the green New button at the top left of the screen.

Step 4. Scroll to the bottom and select Syndication Feeds, which will open the Module Manager: Module Syndication Feeds screen (Figure 12-3).

Step 5. Enter **[E]** Newsfeed A in the Title box.

Step 6. For the position, select **[F]** Right [position-7] from the Protostar template. This will place the syndication feed at the top of the right column.

Figure 12-3 *An outbound Newsfeed module needs a* **[E]** *title, and must be assigned to a* **[F]** *module position.*

Step 7.   Click the Save button to save the information and remain on the screen.

Step 8.   Open the **[G]** Menu Assignment tab for the module (Figure 12-3).

Step 9.   Set the module assignment to **[H]** Only on the Pages Selected (Figure 12-4).

Step 10.   Clear the selection list by clicking **[I]** None.

Step 11.   In the About Joomla! menu, select the **[J]** Article Category Blog menu link item by checking the checkbox. This is the only item that should be checked on this list.

Figure 12-4 *The default installation created content of different types. The* **[J]** *Article Category Blog will be used for this syndication newsfeed.*

Step 12. Click the Save & Close button to save the information and close the screen. The green success message will display near the top of the screen.

Step 13. Go to the front-end of the website and refresh/reload the browser window.

Step 14. Drill down in the About Joomla! menu, on the right, as follows:

Click > Using Joomla! (second link item)

Click > Using Extensions

Click > Components

Click > Content Component

Click > Article Category Blog

At this point, the First Blog Post article should appear in the Main Content area and the Newsfeed A module should appear at the top of the right column.

Step 15. Click on the Feed Entries link in the Newsfeed A module. The screen should open to the article category blog syndicated feed with two articles. The syndication feed is now live for this content.

If the browser you are using does not have an RSS reader installed, you may not see a nicely formatted web page, but rather, a page that shows markup code. If that happens, add an RSS reader to your browser.

What was shown here is that the content items, which consist of something more than a single item, can be syndicated from your website. The Syndication module will display only on the content item via a menu link item because it must be associated with one.

The Syndication module will appear on the screen only if the content item qualifies for an outbound feed, as defined earlier.

A SYNDICATION NEWSFEED FOR A SINGLE ARTICLE: LET'S CHEAT THE SYSTEM!

The rule is that a syndication newsfeed cannot be created for a single article. But it can!

You must create a separate category and assign the article to it. Then, you can create a Category Blog menu link item, which connects to the category. Next, you create the Syndication Feed module and assign it to that menu link item.

Because the menu link item is a category blog and not a single article, it will display all of the articles within that category. But there's only one article! Yes, that's the point. A syndication feed has been created for a single article in a roundabout manner. You can trick the system into displaying a single article as a newsfeed.

Considering a Syndication or RSS Extension

The default syndication feed that comes with Joomla! 3 is adequate for smaller websites. However, if you have a lot of content that you want to feed to other websites, consider using an extension from the JED.

Go to the JED and search for "syndication" or "rss." Use the Demo feature for extensions in which you have an interest. The extensions generally provide more control and parameter settings to make your feed better and easier for other websites to grab.

Summary

In this chapter, you learned:

◆ Content can be provided by newsfeeds.

◆ Newsfeeds and RSS are the same.

◆ How to use newsfeeds.

◆ Where to obtain a newsfeed link.

◆ Newsfeeds can be added using a link item.

◆ Newsfeeds can be added/displayed using a module.

◆ Website content can be a newsfeed.

◆ How to create a newsfeed of your content.

◆ How to create single article syndication feeds.

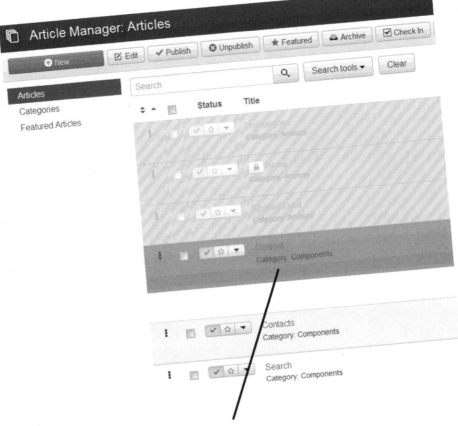

After enabling the content ordering feature, selecting a content item turns the selection green, which then may be moved up and down to "re-order" the item within the Category.

Chapter 13

Components: Redirects

Learning Objectives

What's included in this chapter:

- ◆ How redirects are used on websites.
- ◆ How to enable the Redirect plug-in.
- ◆ Configuring site parameter settings to use a redirect.
- ◆ How to simulate a failed bookmark to an article.
- ◆ Unpublishing an article and redirecting from it.
- ◆ Creating a redirect and testing it.

Understanding the Redirects Component

A *redirect* does exactly what the name implies. It sends a URL that previously existed but is no longer available to a content item that has replaced the previous content, but has a different name.

Joomla! 3 recognizes the possibility of such occurrences by providing the Redirect component. This component allows the super user or administrator (with the proper permissions, of course) to create and manage the change of URL locations/names of content.

According to Joomla!, a redirect's main function is "…to provide a mechanism to give an administrator the ability to redirect the URL of a web page that no longer exists to a working web page."

They go on to say, "This component is primarily used for redirecting URLs for web pages that no longer exist on your website to web pages that are working."

Okay, so what does that mean, and can it apply to your website?

Let's say users have bookmarked a page of content from your website. Then, for some reason or other, a new page of content with a different name replaces that page. When the users try to use their bookmark links, it will take them to the dreaded "page not found" message screen. This is not good.

As the website administrator, you have either unpublished that content or placed it into the archive. In either case, the exact bookmark link no longer goes to the destination on your website—it does not find the page and displays an error to the users.

The solution is to create a redirect from the web page that's no longer available to the new web page that's in the published state.

EXERCISE 13-1: ENABLING THE REDIRECT PLUG-IN

Objective: By default, the Redirect plug-in is disabled, which means that the extension is installed in the system, but it is not available. It needs to be enabled before you can use it. This exercise shows you how to make the Redirect plug-in available for use.

MANY EXTENSIONS ARE DISABLED OR INSTALL INTO THAT STATUS

As you use Joomla! 3 and want to use extensions or install new ones, you might notice that they aren't available for use. The system displays a message telling you what the issue is—this is a key to how to fix it.

Usually, all you need to do is to go to the correct Extension manager, find the extension, and click a box with a red X to make it a green checkmark. The extension will then be activated.

Step 1. If you're not already there, log in to the Administrator backend of the website.

Step 2. Open the Redirect Manager via the Components tab in the top menu (Figure 13-1). This action will result in an error message appearing on the screen (Figure 13-2).

Figure 13-1 *As with all components, redirects are accessed via the Components menu. The* **[A]** *Redirect link opens its manager.*

Figure 13-2 *Occasionally, there will be times when the extension you need is not enabled. The Redirect plug-in is one of those, as indicated by the* **[B]** *message.*

Step 3. Choose Extensions and then open the **[C]** Plugin Manager (Figure 13-3).

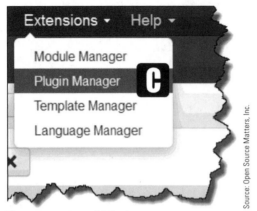

Figure 13-3 *The* **[C]** *Plugin Manager is accessed via the Extensions menu.*

Step 4. Enter **[D] redirect** in the Search area and click on the **[E]** magnifying glass (Figure 13-4).

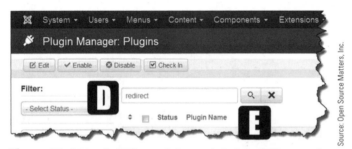

Figure 13-4 *Use the* **[D]** *search box and click the* **[E]** *magnifying glass icon to quickly access an extension within the manager.*

The action in Step 4 lists all plug-ins having *redirect* in the name; in this case, there is only one.

Step 5. Click the red X status button, which should change to a green checkmark (Figure 13-5).

The Redirect plug-in is now enabled and available to be used to create redirects using the component. Now you can move on to creating a actual redirect.

Figure 13-5 *This screen has the results visually embedded. They are two separate screens. Click the* **[F]** *red X so that it changes to a* **[G]** *green checkmark, which indicates that the item is enabled.*

Is the Site Configuration Correct?

At some point earlier in the book, we mentioned the global configuration. To get the Redirect component working properly, you need to set the Site Search Engine Optimization (SEO) setting, which you'll do in the next exercise.

EXERCISE 13-2: SETTING THE SEO CONFIGURATION

Objective: This exercise configures the SEO so that a redirect function will trigger the Redirect plug-in, based on what sort of redirect you determine.

Step 1. Go to the Control Panel and access the global configuration in the Admin Left Menu. It should open to the Site tab (Figure 13-6).

Figure 13-6 *Once in the* **[H]** *Global Configuration and on the* **[I]** *Site tab, the remaining settings are set as outlined in Step 2.*

Step 2. In the SEO Settings section, set the options settings to the following:

> **[J]** Search Engine Friendly URLs - Yes
>
> **[K]** Use URL Rewriting - Yes
>
> **[L]** Adds Suffix to URL - Yes
>
> **[M]** Unicode Alias - No

No other settings need to be changed or adjusted.

Step 3. Click the Save & Close button to save the configuration site settings and close the screen.

Website Users Can't Access the Web Page

The scenario is that a user has bookmarked a web page on your website. The web page has been deleted or archived and is no longer available. At some point in the future, the user clicks his bookmark link and gets the infamous "404 error" page, meaning the web page cannot be found. This is all correct. The web page is gone, so it can't be found. Fine. Perfect.

No, not perfect! You don't want your users to be hanging around in limbo, so you should set up a redirect to the replacement web page, or to another web page that is published and available. The redirect identifies the inactive URL and replaces it with a current URL.

THERE IS NO REDIRECT UNTIL AFTER THE BOOKMARK 404 ERROR

It would be nice for the super user to be able set up a redirect for any web pages that have been deleted or archived. This isn't the case. The website user must actually execute a bookmark to a web page on your site and fail with a 404 error. This triggers the Redirect component to list the attempt to access the nonexistent page. Remember this about plug-ins—they do something when triggered into action. This is a perfect example.

The bottom line of redirects is that they cannot be created until after a user has attempted to access a missing web page or content item. Something needs to "trigger" the redirect into action and that action is to display a list of the web pages that are no longer accessible when a user attempts to access them.

Setting Up a Redirect

All you need at this point is the "dead" URL and the desired URL to which the redirect will point. Easy enough.

EXERCISE 13-3: CREATING A REDIRECT

Objective: The goal of this exercise is to create a redirect by instructing the system to send users who request a page that's no longer available to the replacement page.

Part 1: Setting Up a Bookmark

It is suggested that you set up the following bookmark in a different browser. If you are using Internet Explorer to administer the website, set up the bookmark in Firefox, Chrome, or Safari, or any other browser other than IE.

Step 1.   Go to your website front-end in a different browser and bookmark the article called Upgraders, which should be a featured article on the Home web page. Open the article, and then set the bookmark. Note that the URL in the browser location bar is a complete link to the respective article.

Step 2.   Click the Home menu link item. Then go to your bookmarks and click on the Upgraders bookmark to make sure it opens the page.

Next, to continue to set up the testing part of the Redirect component. The article must no longer be available to users.

Part 2: Making the Article Unavailable

Go back to the browser that you're using to administer the website.

Step 1.   Go to Article Manager: Articles via the Admin Left Menu or via Content > Articles to display a list of articles.

Step 2.   Enter **upgraders** into the Search box and execute the action.

Step 3.   Select the article by clicking in the checkbox and clicking the Unpublish button in the top menu, or click the green checkmark next to the article's name. This essentially makes the article unavailable.

Step 4.   Go to the website front-end, refresh the screen, and confirm that the Upgraders article is no long available.

Step 5.   In the second browser, execute the bookmark to the web page. The web page should not appear. In its place, a page called "The requested page cannot be found" appears, which is a 404 error.

Part 3: Setting Up the Redirect

Go back to the browser that you're using to administer the website.

Step 1.   Go to the Redirect Manager: Links via the Components menu.

Step 2.   Click the link/name of the unpublished article in the Expired URL column. This action will open the individual Redirect Manager screen (Figure 13-7).

Important! The article that was unpublished will appear on the list *only if* an attempt was made to access it via a bookmarked web page (you did this in the last few steps).

Step 3.   The list should display the URL of the article that was just unpublished (Figure 13-7).

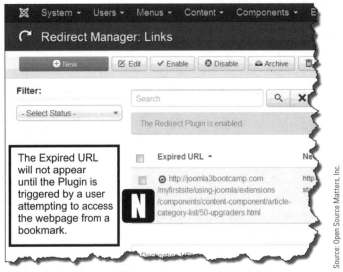

Figure 13-7 *After the* **[N]** *article name is clicked, the content item is available to establish a redirect.*

Step 4. Click on the name of the content item, which opens the screen where the destination URL should be entered. This also creates an Edit Link # tab.

Step 5. Go to the website front-end and click the Getting Started menu link item in the About Joomla! menu.

Step 6. Go to the location bar of the browser and copy the link location. It should be http://joomla3bootcamp.com/myfirstsite/getting-started.html.

Step 7. Copy the link into the Destination URL textbox (Figure 13-8).

Step 8. Change the status to Enabled.

Step 9. Click the Save & Close button to save the information and close the screen.

Step 10. Go back to the website front-end and refresh the browser window.

The success message should appear, and the screen should list the redirect links.

Go back to the browser that you're using to access the bookmarked web page.

Step 11. Go to the front-end and execute the old bookmark again. The Redirect function should now display the "Getting Started" article as a result of the bookmark triggering the Redirect plug-in.

While you did need to do some extra steps to bookmark the URL of an article before it was unpublished, this likely won't happen in real-life when you're using the Redirect component. After a while, you will know what the URL is for content items and simply type them into the appropriate boxes.

Figure 13-8 *When the content item is clicked, the Edit Link screen opens with the* **[O]** *source URL information already inserted. Enter the* **[P]** *destination URL information and* **[Q]** *enable the redirect.*

Remember to Check for Broken Links!

If you unpublish content items that you think website visitors may have bookmarked, by all means, take a few minutes every once in a while to check for failed web pages and be prepared to set up redirects.

There is no way for users to avoid getting a 404 error page (although there should be), but you can fix the issue once you are aware of it by using the Redirect component. Therefore, be sure to monitor the Redirect component frequently when logging in to the backend.

Summary

In this chapter, you learned:

◆ The purpose and function of redirects.

◆ How to enable the Redirect plug-in.

◆ How to modify the SEO settings to use redirects.

◆ How to simulate a failed bookmark to an article.

◆ An unpublished article can need a redirect.

◆ How to create the redirect from the unpublished article to one that is published.

◆ How to determine if a redirect is working properly.

Chapter 14

Components: Search and Smart Search

Learning Objectives

What's included in this chapter:

◆ Introduction to the Search component.

◆ Is a Search feature necessary?

◆ How to implement the basic Search feature.

◆ Creating and positioning the Search module.

◆ Understanding the Smart Search component.

◆ Activating the Smart Search plug-in.

◆ Indexing the website content for Smart Search.

◆ Adding the Smart Search module.

◆ Associating the Smart Search module with a menu link item.

Understanding the Search Component

This component allows users to search your website for terms or keywords and display the results. The Search component can be easily implemented. If you have a small site with very little content, the Search component may not be useful or necessary.

The Joomla! Search module has been available in most past versions. However, the Smart Search, which is relatively new, is discussed in this chapter as well. You'll also find exercises that teach you how to implement both the Search and the Smart Search components.

Basically, all that is required to implement a Search feature on your website is to create the Search module and place it into a module position. After that, users can enter search terms and obtain a list of the content items that contain the term.

Do You Really Need a Search Feature?

This is an important question. If your website is small and contains information for friends and family, you probably don't need a full-blown Search feature. If the website does not have a lot of content, or the content spread out among a number of categories, the Search function is probably not necessary.

However, if you are managing a large commercial or corporate site, with a lot of content and the need for website users to find information, then adding a Search option is a good idea. After all, the last thing you want to do is make your users hunt through dozens of pages and chase links all over the place to find information. You can solve that problem with Smart Search.

Implementing the Basic Search Feature

By default, Joomla! 3 has a built-in Search module, and the Protostar template has a built-in Search module position. Joomla! 3 has saved you the trouble of creating and activating a Search feature by publishing the module and assigning it to a module position. In the case of this template, it is position-0, located at the top of the page banner area.

Normally, there are two steps involved in adding a Search feature to your website. They are:

Action 1. Create the Search module.

Action 2. Place it into a search module position.

When those two steps are completed, a Search module will display in the module position you designated.

Let's go through the process of creating a Search module and assigning it to another module position. This will show you how to add this feature when you use a template that does not have the feature included during the installation of the template.

EXERCISE 14-1: CREATING/DISPLAYING THE SEARCH MODULE

Objective: This exercise explains how to implement the basic Search feature on a website and to create the Search module and place it into a module position. Because the steps involved are basic Joomla! 3 admin actions, no screenshots are included in this exercise.

A Search module already exists at module position-0 on the Protostar template. Because of this, the following steps will provide instruction on placing a new Search module in another position. The CSS for the Search module for any position other than 0 will not be correct. This exercise is only to instruct you on creation and placement options.

CAN YOU DO THIS WITHOUT SCREENSHOTS?

While performing this exercise, we are not going to present a screenshot to follow. At this point, you should be able to complete these tasks with basic instructions. If you have any problems, go to **joomla3bootcamp.com** and search for more information about this function.

Step 1. If you're not already there, log in to the Administrator backend of the website.

Step 2. Open the Module Manager via the Admin Left Menu in the Control Panel.

Step 3. When the Module Manager opens, click the green New button in the top menu.

Step 4. On the Select a Module Type screen, scroll down the page and click the Search Selector link.

Step 5. Name the Module **My Search Module**.

Step 6. Assign the module to the Protostar template right position-7 location.

Step 7. Check to make sure the status of the module is Published.

Step 8. Click the green Save button to save the information and remain on the same screen. The green success message panel should display.

Step 9. Go to the website front-end and verify that the My Search Module is in the right column on the screen. It should be the very top module shown on that side.

SEARCH BOX APPEARANCE

Note that the Search text input box is too wide for the column. This happens when a module has preset parameters and Cascading Style Sheet (CSS) settings that control the width. In this case, the module's parameters were set assuming it would be displayed in position-0 on the template. You will likely not run into this issue when using other templates besides the ones installed by default. This is because the CSS is likely to be different or allow you to make parameter settings for the module.

On the front-end, notice that there is no button that executes the search. The search can be triggered by pressing the Enter or Return key. However, this might not be intuitive to some website users, so there is the option to add a Search button.

Step 10. Open the Module tab for the module you just created.

Step 11. Select the Yes option for the Search Button parameter. The selector should change from red to green.

Step 12. For the Button Position, select the bottom location.

Step 13. Click the green Save button to save the information and remain on the screen. The green success message panel should display.

Step 14. Go to the website front-end, refresh the browser window, and verify the button has been added and that it is located below the Search text input box.

At this point, this particular Search module is not needed for the remainder of the book, so Unpublish it by doing this:

Step 15. Under the Module tab for the Module, change the status to Unpublished.

Step 16. Execute the Save & Close action. The list of modules should display.

Keep in mind that modules can be configured to display in any available position on a template and that some templates have a default location and the CSS that associates with it.

The Smart Search Component

Another useful component is the Smart Search feature, which allows website content to be indexed. When users type words into the search, a list of options appears based on the words being input. Users can then click on an option and the search becomes automatic based on the website's indexed content.

Implementing Smart Search

You need to perform several administrative tasks before you can use the Smart Search feature:

Action 1. Enable the Smart Search content plug-in.

Action 2. Index the content of the website.

Action 3. Create and publish the Smart Search module.

Exercise 14-2 shows you how to begin the process.

EXERCISE 14-2: ACTIVATING THE SMART SEARCH FEATURE

Objective: This exercise illustrates how the Smart Search feature is enabled and readied for use on the website.

Step 1. If you're not already there, log in to the Administrator backend of the website.

Step 2. Under the Extensions menu, open the **[A]** Plug-in Manager (Figure 14-1).

Figure 14-1 *The Smart Search feature must have its plug-in enabled to work on the website. Open the Plug-in Manager via the Extensions menu drop-down* **[A]**.

Step 3. In the **[B]** Search box, enter **smart search**, and then click the Magnifying Glass icon next to it, or press the Enter/Return key on your keyboard (Figure 14-2).

Step 4. A list of plug-ins used in conjunction with Smart Search will display.

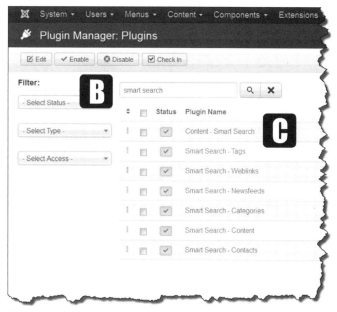

Figure 14-2 *An easy way to find any content item on any list display is to enter a search term. The search for* **[B]** *"smart search" returned a* **[C]** *list of all the plug-ins that have "smart search" in their names.*

Step 5. Enable the **[C]** Content-Smart Search plug-in by either clicking on the name and when the next screen opens, toggling the status to Enabled or by simply clicking on the red X next to the name, which enables it (a green checkmark will display). The plug-in is now ready for use.

Step 6. Go to the Smart Search component by accessing it via the Components menu.

At this point, it is necessary to index the content of the website, which then allows Smart Search to function properly. It is suggested that only content that is actually published be indexed.

Step 7. Change the Filter option from **[D]** Any Published State to Published Only (Figure 14-3).

Step 8. Execute the index action by clicking the **[E]** Index button in the menu bar.

Figure 14-3 *There is no searching content available initially. The* **[E]** *Index action must be triggered to generate a list. It is also a good idea to index only the website's active content, or only the content that is* **[D]** *published. You do this by filtering the content items to be indexed.*

DO NOT INTERRUPT THE INDEXING PROCESS!

The Smart Search's indexer will open a pop-up window and will display the status of the indexing process. Allow the indexing to complete, which may take a few minutes if your website has a great amount of content. When the Indexing Complete message displays, you can close the pop-up by clicking the X in the top-right corner.

When the results are displayed, all of the indexed content is shown in alphabetical order by both category and content types. This means that content of all available types has been indexed.

ARE ADDED EXTENSIONS INDEXED?

Yes, they are. If you added an extension that creates and manages content, and then execute the Indexing action, that content will also be included in the results. Which brings up another point: Indexing can be executed at any time. After an extension has been installed and content is added to the extension, a new indexing action will grab that information and include it in the content that's accessible via Smart Search.

Narrowing the List

Once an indexing action is completed and the list is displayed—which includes all indexed items and can easily be very long—you can narrow the number of items to determine exactly what content has been indexed.

Use the Any Type of Content filter to select the content areas to view. If you select Articles Only, indexed content from the articles will display.

If there are content items in the index that you do not want included in the Smart Search activity, change their status from Published to Unpublished using the checkbox to make the change.

Putting Smart Search into Action

Two of the three action steps for enabling Smart Search have now been completed. The plug-in was enabled and the content of the website has been indexed. A list of content items has been viewed and verified, and the option to remove some of those items is available.

The next action is to publish a Smart Search module to allow users to find content easier and quicker. You'll learn how to do that in Exercise 14-3.

EXERCISE 14-3: CREATING THE SMART SEARCH MODULE

Objective: In order to use the Smart Search feature, you must include a Smart Search module somewhere on one of the website's pages. This exercise adds the module and associates it with a menu link item.

Step 1. Assuming you are already logged in to the Admin backend, open the Module Manager.

Step 2. Make sure you are in the Site area to view the list of modules. This is shown on the top left, under the New button. The list can also be toggled between Site and Administrator using the top drop-down in the Filter area.

Step 3. Enter **[F] smart search** into the Search text box and click on the magnifying glass icon. It should display the **[G]** Smart Search module with the status of **[H]** published (a green checkmark). The type **[I]** is also shown (Figure 14-4).

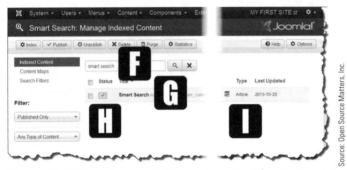

Source: Open Source Matters, Inc.

Figure 14-4 *The actions needed to create and publish the Smart Search module are not unlike the procedure that is followed for any other content module.*

If you recall in previous exercises, there is a function available to determine where module positions are located on a template. Execute the ?tp=1 feature now by adding it to the end of the URL in the front-end browser location bar. In the center of the page, there is a module position called position-3. This is where the Smart Search module will be positioned.

Step 4. Go back to the Smart Search module in admin, click on the name to open it, and select the **[J]** top center position-3 location (Figure 14-5). Make sure you are selecting that location under the Protostar template.

Step 5. Click the **[K]** green Save button to save the information and remain on the screen. The green success message panel should display.

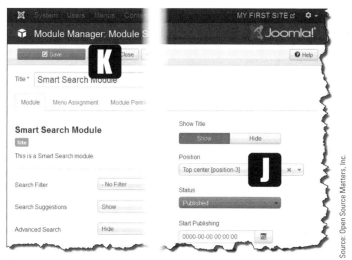

Figure 14-5 *After you have designated the module position, click Save to lock the settings.*

Before the next step, go to the front-end and remove the ?tp=1 from the URL location bar.

Step 6. In the Smart Search module, open the Menu Assignment tab. When it's open, no menu link items should be selected, which means the module will not display anywhere on the website. Remember that modules *must* be associated with a menu link item to display.

Step 7. Verify that the module assignment location is Only on the Pages Selected. The goal is to have the module display only with a designated menu link item.

Step 8. Because tags are closely related to searching, the module will be assigned to the Show All Tags menu link item. Scroll down the list of menu link items and find Show All Tags near the bottom of the list. Check the checkbox.

Step 9. Click the green Save button to save the information. This will take you back to the module's Details tab.

Step 10. Go to the website front-end and refresh the browser window.

Step 11. Click the Show All Tags menu link item in the top menu. The Smart Search module should display. Note that the text input box is part of the tagging feature, not the Smart Search function.

Step 12. In the Smart Search module text input box, enter **orch** (stop typing after the *h*). Notice what happens. A list of terms that contain "orch" appears. This is Smart Search in action. Not only does it find content that contains that search term, but it also attempts to complete the search query based on the indexed content.

Step 13. Select Orchard We Grow on the list. The result should be links to the articles that contain the term.

Experiment with more search terms to get a better understanding of what is displayed on the Results list.

Advanced Search Option

When the Smart Search has been activated, the results also show the actual term used and include an option to use the Advanced Search feature. This allows you to combine the search criteria to narrow search results. The Advanced Search criteria consists of the following:

◆ Search by author
◆ Search by category
◆ Search by country
◆ Search by language
◆ Search by region
◆ Search by type

Summary

In this chapter, you learned:

◆ About the basic Search component.
◆ How to determine if a Search feature is needed.
◆ How to implement the basic Search feature.
◆ How to create and position the Search module.
◆ About the Smart Search component.
◆ How to activate the Smart Search plug-in.
◆ How to index the website content for Smart Search.
◆ How to create and add the Smart Search module.
◆ How to associate the Smart Search module with a menu link item.

Chapter 15

Components: Tags

Learning Objectives

What's included in this chapter:

◆ What tags are and how they are used.

◆ What tags are not.

◆ The purpose of the Tags component.

◆ How to implement tagging.

◆ What's involved in tagging.

◆ Best practices for tagging.

◆ Using tags for content.

◆ Other tagging options.

Understanding the Tags Component

One of the newer features found in Joomla! 3 is the Tags component, which offers website administrators the opportunity to classify content using a method separate from the category assignment to which most content adheres. If you recall, just about every type of content must be assigned to a category within its own classification areas.

Tagging breaks the mold by allowing content items to be tagged with one or more words, which then can be used to search for, retrieve, and display the content.

No, Joomla! 3 tags are not hash tags that most of us are familiar with via Twitter and other social media communications platforms. The tags found in Joomla! 3 are pseudo-categories—sort of, maybe!

To put it simply, tags allow content to be grouped for display, but with more flexibility than just adding items to categories. However, keep in mind that there is no specific relationship between tags and categories. They are distinctly different and should not be confused with each other.

You can think of categories as being somewhat linear in nature—they have shape and structure and must be ordered in a certain way. Tags allow another method of grouping content, but it does not physically organize it like categories would do.

The bottom line for tags is that they allow you to organize content, and allow website visitors to find information by using a tag search to bring up a list of results. Recall the rule that a content item can be assigned to only one category. Well, tags do just the opposite in that you can have many, many content items tagged with the same word.

So there you have it—tags are nothing more than a label that is attached to a content item.

How to Implement Tagging

Content structure consists of categories and items, and then a menu link item. This chapter limits the discussion to only using articles for tagging examples.

Here are the three standard ways that articles can be accessed:

◆ Categories
◆ Articles
◆ Menu link items

Now, here is the fourth way they can be accessed:

◆ Tags

To use tags effectively on a Joomla! 3 website, there are several requirements:

Requirement 1: Tags must exist. Tags cannot be assigned to content unless the tag is already in the backend system.

Requirement 2: Some sort of content must also exist. For the purposes of this chapter and its exercises, the assumption will be based on the existence of articles, although web links, newsfeeds, categories, and contacts can also be tagging candidates. For the most part, if it is a content item, it can be tagged.

Requirement 3: The content items should have some sort of logical relationship to each other. For example, cats and dogs are both animals. So a category of Animals could have many articles that can be tagged as cat, dog, or both cat and dog.

Requirement 4: The individual content items need to be tagged either at the time they are created, or at any time thereafter. In other words, as the need for a tag is noted, the item can be tagged and then it becomes accessible via tag links.

Once all that is done, the tags can reference a content item or provide a method of accessing content items from a menu link item.

Best Practices for Tags

When used properly, tags can be an asset to any website that has an abundance of content, when the content is interrelated. When used incorrectly, tags can interfere with content access and create confusion.

So, let's define some best practices for tagging:

Rule 1. Never use tags as a substitute for assigning content into categories. Yes, you can use tags to separate content that is in one category, but it is not the best way to keep it all organized.

Rule 2. Plan the use of tags when you plan content. Determine if tags even fit the content needs of your website.

Rule 3. Don't over-tag content. Having too many tags assigned to items, while it might create some complex cross-navigation, may not serve the purpose of your website.

Rule 4. Make sure the tags are descriptive enough to accurately define the tag purpose.

Implementing Tags

The easiest way to learn about tags is to actually implement the feature in some articles and then create the link mechanism to display the articles based on how the items have been tagged in the process. Exercises 15-1 and 15-2 take you through that process.

EXERCISE 15-1: CREATING TAGS

Objective: This exercise demonstrates how tags are created within the Joomla! 3 backend.

Step 1. If you're not already there, log in to the Administrator backend of the website.

Step 2. Open the Tags component from the Components menu at the top.

Step 3. Click the green New button at the top left of the screen.

Step 4. Create a **[A]** tag named **Orange**.

Step 5. Execute the Save & New action. The tag should appear on the list view.

Step 6. Click the green New button at the top left of the screen.

Step 7. Create a **[B]** tag named **Green**.

Step 8. Execute the Save & New action. Both tags should now appear in the list view.

Step 9. Create a **[C]** tag named **Farm Products**.

Step 10. Execute the Save & Close action. All three tags should now appear in the list view (Figure 15-1).

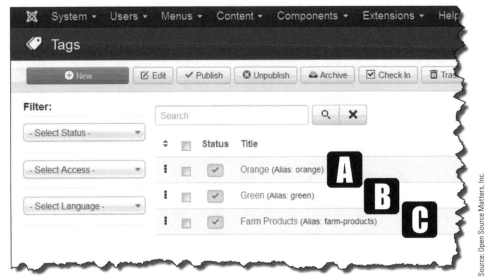

Figure 15-1 *Three tags were created and appear in the list display.*

EXERCISE 15-2: ASSIGNING TAGS TO ARTICLES

Objective: In this exercise, you assign the tags you just created to articles or other content items.

Step 1. If you're not already there, log in to the Administrator backend of the website.

Step 2. Open the Article Manager via the Admin Left Menu in the Control Panel.

CHANGING THE NUMBER OF ITEMS DISPLAYED IN LIST VIEW

By default, the number of items displayed in a list view is 20. You can change that value in the Global Configuration settings by changing the Default List Limit to a higher value and executing the Save & Close action. The highest value option is 100.

Step 3. Filter the category to Fruit Shop Site and Growers to narrow the list (Figure 15-2).

Step 4. Open the **[D]** article entitled "Happy Orange Orchard."

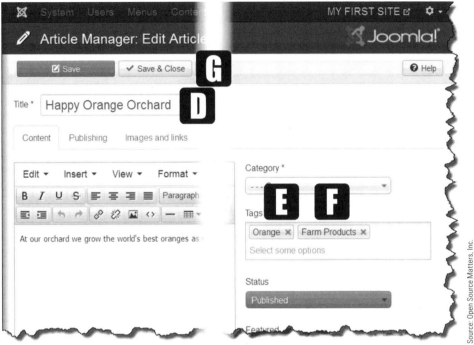

Figure 15-2 *The Tags area of the Article Manager allows you to add tags that apply to specific content items.*

Step 5. At the bottom right, in the Tags text field, begin typing **[E] Orange**. When enough letters have been typed, the word "Orange" will appear. Select the word in the blue box.

Step 6. Remaining in the same location, begin typing **[F] Farm Products**. Click on the word to include it with the previous tag. Two tags should now appear in the text area.

Step 7. Execute the **[G]** Save & Close action, which returns you to the previous article list (Figure 15-3).

Step 8. Open the **[H]** article called "Wonderful Watermelon."

Figure 15-3 *Tags assigned to content items can also be assigned to other items, including new tags, as long as the tags have been previously created.*

Step 9. At the bottom right, in the Tags text field, begin typing **[I] Green**. When enough letters have been typed, the word "Green" will appear. Select the word in the blue box.

Step 10. In the same location, begin typing **[J] Farm Products**. Click on the word to include it with the previous tag. Two tags should now appear in the text area.

Step 11. Execute the **[K]** Save & Close action, which returns you to the previous article list.

At this point, you have created three tags. Then you gave two different articles tag attributes, as follows:

Article Name	Tags Assigned
Happy Orange Orchard	Orange Farm Products
Wonderful Watermelon	Green Farm Products

Source: 200mph Media Group, LLC.

Making Use of the Tags

Now that you've tagged the content, you can put it to work. First, let's verify that the tags have, in fact, been applied to the two articles. Go to the website front-end and check the articles, which can be found here:

Top menu: Sample Sites link

Fruit Shop menu (right):   Growers link; click on the article's title to see the tags

Happy Orange Orchard: Tags at bottom

Wonderful Watermelon: Tags at bottom

With both articles showing both tags, you can now use the Tagging feature.

TAGS DON'T SHOW IN CATEGORY BLOG

One of the places where tags do not display is in the Category Blog layout. You need to open the individual articles in order to view any assigned tags.

EXERCISE 15-3: SHOWING A LIST OF ALL TAGS

Objective: This exercise illustrates using tags in a practical way, where you create a menu link item to display a list of the tags.

Step 1.   If you're not already there, log in to the Administrator backend of the website.

Step 2.   Open the Menu Manager via the Admin Left Menu in the Control Panel.

Step 3.   Open the top menu.

Step 4.   Click the green New button at the top left of the screen.

Step 5.   For the **[L]** Menu Item Type, select Tags > List of All Tags in the selection areas (Figure 15-4).

Step 6.   Name the **[M]** menu title **Show All Tags**.

Step 7.   Execute the Save & Close action, which returns you to the Menu Link Item list.

Step 8.   Go to the website front-end and refresh the browser window. The menu link item called Show All Tags should display in the top menu. Click it. The list of the three tags you created should display. Click on each item and view the results.

For **Farm Products**, links to both articles display.

For **Green**, the Wonderful Watermelon article link displays.

For **Orange**, the Happy Orange Orchard article link displays.

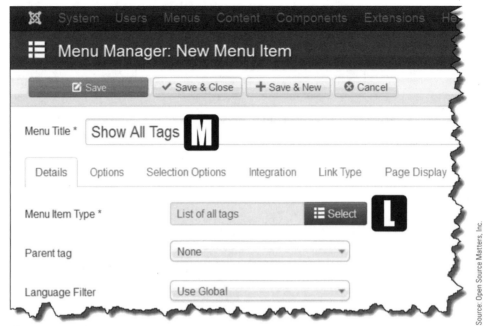

Figure 15-4 *The list of all tags is one of three choices for displaying content items that are common among the listed tags.*

Other Tag Display Options

There are two other menu item type options, which display the tagged items in different ways. The choice is dictated by how many results are expected. For a short list, use Tagged Items. For larger numbers of results, use the Compact List of Tagged Items as the display option.

Tagged Items—Displays content that has the same Tag attribute, which means that content from an unlimited number of categories can be displayed, even those with different content types—articles, web links, and so on, would all display. Multiple tags may be selected to display a wider range of items.

Compact List of Tagged Items—Same as Tagged Items, but the display is visually compact. Tagged Items displays the article head in a larger font size. With this choice, the list is displayed in a smaller font, more suitable for long lists of content items. Multiple tags may also be used for this display type.

> ### TAGS DO NOT REPLACE CATEGORY ASSIGNMENT
>
> Don't be tempted! Tags are useful and good to use. But don't use tags as an alternative to good category structuring of website content. The best practice is to use both—use categories to formally organize content, and use tags to make content accessible as if it were assigned to multiple categories.

Summary

In this chapter, you learned:

◆ What tags are and how they are used.

◆ That tags are not substitutes for categories.

◆ The purpose of the Tags component.

◆ How to implement tagging.

◆ What it takes to use tagging.

◆ Best practices for tagging.

◆ How to add tags to content.

◆ Options for using tagging.

The "Options" settings for Articles will control exactly what system-generated content is displayed at the top or bottom of the Article on the front-end view.

Chapter 16

Components: Weblinks

Learning Objectives

What's included in this chapter:

- What weblinks are and how they are used.
- The purpose of the Weblinks component.
- How weblinks are organized.
- How to create a Weblinks category.
- Different ways to display weblinks on a website.
- How to capture user weblink submissions.
- How to manage submitted weblinks.

Understanding the Weblinks Component

If you take the Contacts component and change a few words here and there, you have the Weblinks component, more or less. The Weblinks component allows you to add a collection of links to other websites, and to categorize those links.

Administrators of company websites often have a number of companion websites or useful locations for their users to visit. To help organize such sites, Joomla! 3 has included a Weblinks Manager.

The Weblinks component operates in such a way that categories of weblinks are created and then individual weblink information is added and categorized for display. The Weblinks Manager is relatively easy to use.

This chapter covers the Weblinks Manager so that, when you're called upon, you can create a list of weblinks for your website. It's a powerful component and can be used in many different ways.

How Weblinks Are Organized

As with most areas of content, weblinks are organized in categories. No surprise there, as almost every type of content has some type of Category Manager to help organize the individual pieces of content. For the Weblinks Manager the categories are key, especially when you have a large number of weblinks to list and display.

If you are going to list many weblinks, the task can become complicated. You simply need to follow the instructions in this chapter and use a little organizational imagination to create the structure for the weblinks and the categories to manage them. You access the Weblinks component via the Components drop-down, as shown in Figure 16-1.

Figure 16-1 *The Weblinks component is accessed via the* **[A]** *Components drop-down. There is no Weblinks Manager link in the Quick Icons of the Control Panel.*

Accessing the Weblinks Manager

You can begin to learn about the Weblinks Manager by accessing it in the Components menu. Choose Components > Weblinks. This opens the Weblinks list, which shows the weblinks that the Joomla! 3 installer added.

If you switch to the Categories tab on the left, the list displays the categories that were installed as part of the default configuration.

To help you master the use of the Weblinks Manager, there are three important parts you need to familiarize yourself with:

Create Categories—All weblinks must be assigned to a category, and if there is not a suitable one already created, you must create one.

Create Weblinks—A weblink must be created to display, and this weblink must be assigned to a category. A URL must be included to create the actual weblink.

Manage the Appearance—You can control the look of the weblink, and the weblink's lists, using options, which allow you also to control the actual information displayed for each weblink. This operates in a similar way as the Contact Manager, except the weblinks allow you to monitor the number of clicks each link receives.

Let's begin by creating a Weblinks category in Exercise 16-1.

EXERCISE 16-1: CREATING A WEBLINKS CATEGORY

Objective: The objective of this exercise is to demonstrate how to create a category into which weblinks can be assigned.

Step 1.   If you're not already there, log in to the Administrator backend of the website.

Step 2.   Open the Weblinks Manager: Weblinks via the Components tab in the top menu.

Step 3.   Click on the **[B]** Categories link in the left column, which opens the Weblinks Category Manager (Figure 16-2).

Figure 16-2 *When the* **[B]** *Categories area is open, clicking the* **[C]** *green New button will open the individual Category Manager.*

Step 4. Click the green **[C]** New button at the top left of the screen.

Step 5. Enter **[D] Weblinks Group A** in the Title field (Figure 16-3).

Step 6. Click the **[E]** Save & Close button to save the information and close the screen.

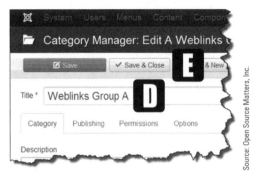

Figure 16-3 *For Weblinks categories, only a title is needed to create a category.*

At this point, when returning to the Categories tab view, ensure that the Weblinks category was actually created.

Step 7. In the Weblinks Categories screen view (Categories link on the left is highlighted blue), click on the column head "Title," which will sort the list alphabetically. The Weblinks category should appear as the last item on the list, in alphabetical order following the Uncategorised category. The status should also be active, showing a green checkmark to the left of the name.

There is now an active Weblinks category into which you can assign a website URL.

EXERCISE 16-2: CREATING A WEBLINK

Objective: This exercise shows you how to create an actual weblink and assign it to a category.

Step 1. Make sure the Web Links tab is active in the left column. It should be highlighted blue.

Step 2. Click the green New button at the top left of the screen.

Step 3. You should have opened the Web Links Manager for creating a new weblink, which is indicated by the **[F]** Edit Web Link tab at the upper left part of the screen (Figure 16-4).

Figure 16-4 *When creating a new* **[F]** *weblink, you must specify* **[G]** *the title,* **[H]** *a URL, and the previously created* **[I]** *category.*

Step 4.   Enter **[G] Joomla! 3 Documentation** in the Title field.

Step 5.   Enter the **[H]** URL **http://docs.joomla.org/**.

Step 6.   In the **[I]** Category drop-down, select the Weblinks Group A, which is likely at the very bottom of the list. Scroll down and select it.

Step 7.   Click the **[J]** Save & Close button to save the information and close the screen.

On the resulting weblinks list display, the "Joomla! 3 Documentation" item is listed about half way down the list.

LOOK AT THE END OF THE LIST

When you're viewing list displays in the backend, new items may be shown in its alphabetical order, or may be at the bottom of the list. If you can't readily find an item, look at the end of the list. Make sure you open the next page of the list if it is a long one and the system has broken them down into multiple pages. This happens often with websites that have a large number of content items within categories.

Weblink Manager Options

As with other managers in Joomla! 3, the Weblinks Component has an abundance of configurable options that allow you to customize it. You can control how information is displayed on the front-end. You can also collect the number of clicks, which tells you how many times each weblink has been followed by users.

The options are accessible via the Options tab in the top menu when the Weblinks Manager is open to either the Weblinks or the Categories sections.

The parameter settings, which affect both the backend management and the front-end display on a global basis, consist of these areas:

Weblink—Allows you to set the target window for the link. If you choose Open in Parent Window, the new website replaces your website in the browser window. The three other options—Open in New Window, Open in Popup, and Modal—are better choices, because they keep users on your website while they view the weblink destination. You also set the Count Clicks option here, as well as the option to use an icon, text, or a weblink only for displaying the actual link. Other items found here are more display related.

Category—Deals with how a Weblinks category is displayed on the front-end. Review the options. Menu link item types have some settings that may override the default settings.

Categories—Deals with how the categories are displayed with respect to sub-categories and empty categories, and other settings.

List Layouts—When there are many weblinks on a list of weblinks, the list can be very wide on the screen. These controls allow you to hide or show list columns, many of which are not necessary to display. Simply toggle the item's settings.

Integration—Some extensions integrate with the Weblinks Manager. This allows integration with those extensions.

Permissions—Allows you to manage the Access Control List (ACL) aspects of Joomla! 3, to be invoked for the Weblinks Manager. This is a global setting. This feature is used in Exercise 16-5, when the Submit a Web Link feature is explained.

Displaying Weblinks on the Front-End

Now that you've created a Weblinks category and assigned a weblink to that category, the next challenge is to get this information to display on the front-end.

The same procedure used to display other content, such as articles, is employed in displaying a weblink, or a weblinks category list, which is accessible via a menu link item in a menu. In previous exercises, this process was used to display "My First Article," which you did by clicking the My Menu Item in the top menu.

Showing a Single Weblink Category

Generally, weblinks are shown on a website front-end as a content item that complements the website's content. A website can have only a few weblinks or it can have a great number of them, classified into different categories. How is this done?

Complete the following exercise to display the "Weblinks Group A" information on the front-end. You'll do this using a menu link item called My Weblinks.

EXERCISE 16-3: DISPLAYING A SINGLE WEBLINK CATEGORY

Objective: This exercise takes you through the process of creating a menu link item that will connect to a single weblink item in the Weblinks directory.

Step 1. If you're not already there, log in to the Administrator backend of the website.

Step 2. From the Admin Left Menu, click on the Menu Manager link.

Step 3. When the Menu Manager opens, click on the Top menu.

Step 4. Click the green New button at the top left of the screen. This will open the Menu Manager: New Menu Item screen.

Figure 16-5 *You create a menu link item for the Weblinks component the same way as most other menu link items. The type, the category, and a title must be assigned to create it. In this case, it is a list of weblinks in a category.*

Step 5. For the Menu Item Type option, click the blue **[K]** Select button to open the types that can be created from those installed.

Step 6. Select Weblinks in the pop-up window, then choose List Web Links in a Category from the list that drops down (Figure 16-5).

Step 7. In the Select a Category field, use the **[L]** drop-down to select Weblinks Group A, which was previously created, from among the list.

Step 8. The **[M]** menu title is required, so enter **My Weblinks**.

> **DON'T LOSE WEBSITE VISITORS**
>
> Whenever you're creating a link to an external website, it's always a good idea to make the target window open in a *new browser window,* or in a new tab. That way, the user remains on your website in one browser window/tab, and the link opens in another. There is usually a drop-down selector that offers three options. The New Browser with Navigation is the best choice.

Step 9. Click the **[N]** Save & Close button to save the information and close the screen.

Step 10. Go to the website front-end, refresh the screen, and check to see if the My Weblinks menu link item appears on the right of the Top Menu. Click the menu link item.

Step 11. Click the Joomla! 3 Documentation link in the main content area. The Joomla! Official Documentation page should display in a new browser tab or window.

In this case, there was only one weblink in that category, so this could be used to display a single URL link that is controlled by the Weblinks Manager. If there were more weblinks in the category, they would have been displayed (assuming they were enabled).

EXERCISE 16-4: DISPLAYING A WEBLINK CATEGORY LIST

Objective: This exercise takes you through the process of creating a menu link item that will connect to a categorized list of weblinks that were added or installed by the system.

Step 1. If you're not already there, log in to the Administrator backend of the website.

Step 2. From the Admin Left Menu, click on the Menu Manager link.

Step 3. When the Menu Manager opens, click on the Top menu.

Step 4. Click the green New button at the top left of the screen. This will open the Menu Manager: New Menu Item screen (Figure 16-6).

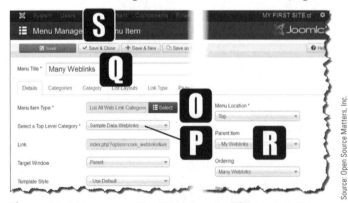

Figure 16-6 *To create a Menu Link Item for* **[O]** *List All Web Link Categories, the same information is required as for a single category, except in this instance, the menu link item is being assigned as a sub-item to the* **[R]** *My Weblinks main menu link item, so one more parameter must be set.*

Step 5.   For the menu item type, click the blue Select button to open the list of types that can be created from those installed.

Step 6.   Select Weblinks in the pop-up window, then choose **[O]** List All Web Link Categories from the list that drops down.

Step 7.   In the **[P]** Select a Top Level Category field, use the drop-down to open the list of weblink categories. Select Sample Data-Weblinks, which was created during the Joomla! 3 installation process.

Step 8.   The **[Q]** menu title is required, so enter **Many Weblinks.**

Step 9.   Assign the menu link item as a sub-item to the parent item in the drop-down to **[R]** My Weblinks.

Step 10.   Click the **[S]** Save & Close button to save the information and close the screen.

Step 11.   Go to the website front-end, refresh the screen, and check to see if the Many Weblinks menu link item appears under the My Weblinks item when the mouse is placed over it.

Step 12.   Click the Many Weblinks item, located under the My Weblinks menu link item.

The screen should display the park links and the Joomla! specific links, because those are the two sub-categories under the Sample Data-Weblinks main category.

Of course, your category structure might be quite different on your own site, with a main category and many sub-categories, as well as a good number of weblinks within each.

Collecting Weblinks from Users

Whenever weblinks are self-managed, it is usually a work in progress, with weblinks being continually added to the appropriate categories. You can save yourself some work by allowing users to submit weblinks for consideration to be added.

Toward that goal, Joomla! 3 has a weblinks option called Submit a Web Link, which is a form that is displayed where users can enter weblinks. These links are then stored in the system, and become part of the category that the user indicated on the submission form.

Once a user submits a weblink, the super user can approve or reject the link. You can imagine the kinds of weblinks that might be added by robots or hackers to legitimate websites. The feature of automatically unpublishing any submitted weblinks will help prevent unwanted links from appearing.

To add the Submit a Web Link feature to a Joomla! 3 website, several administrative actions are involved:

Action 1.   Create the Submit a Web Link menu link item.

Action 2.   Give users permission to submit a web link, because they are actually adding content to the website.

Action 3.   Approve and activate the submitted weblink, or alternatively, trash the submission.

EXERCISE 16-5: CREATING A SUBMIT A WEB LINK FEATURE

Objective: This exercise shows you how to enable users to submit links to your website. The first step is to create the Submit a Web Link item.

Step 1.   If you're not already there, log in to the Administrator backend of the website.

Step 2.   From the Admin Left Menu, click on the Menu Manager link.

Step 3.   When the Menu Manager opens, click on the Top menu.

Step 4.   Click the green New button at the top left of the screen. This will open the Menu Manager: New Menu Item screen (Figure 16-7).

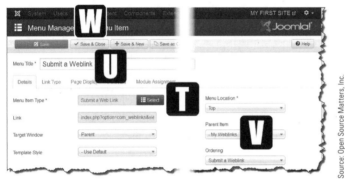

Figure 16-7 *Choose the* **[T]** *Submit a Web Link option from the Menu Item Type drop-down. In addition to the type, you must provide a* **[U]** *title and a* **[V]** *parent item.*

Step 5.   For the Menu Item Type, click the blue **[T]** Select button to open the list of types that can be created from those installed.

Step 6.   Select Weblinks in the pop-up window, then choose Submit a Web Link from the list that drops down.

Step 7.   For the menu title, enter **[U] Submit a Weblink**.

Step 8.   For the Parent Item drop-down, place the new menu link item under the **[V]** My Weblinks main menu link item. Note! Depending on your browser, you may have to fiddle with the browser's scroll bars to view the My Weblinks at the bottom of the screen.

Step 9.   Click the **[W]** Save & Close button to save the information and close the screen.

Step 10.   Go to the website front-end and refresh the browser window. The Submit a Weblink option should appear as the last item under the My Weblinks menu link item. If it does, click it now.

Did you get "the requested page cannot be found" error? Good, that is what was supposed to be displayed. Why? Because a user *per se*, does not have permission to add content to the website. Adding a weblink is adding content, so it was denied because there were no permissions granted.

Let's take care of the permissions issue:

Step 11.   Open the Web Links Manager: Web Links via the top menu bar.

Step 12.   Click the Options button in the Manager's menu bar (top-right side).

Step 13.   Click on the **[X]** Permissions tab (Figure 16-8). All website users who can view content without logging in are automatically in the Public group.

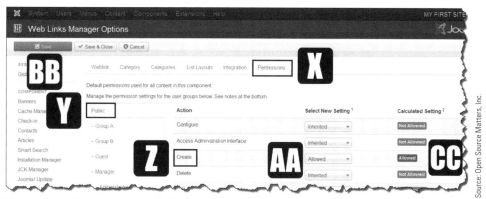

Figure 16-8 *You must grant the* **[Y]** *Public group permission to create a weblink URL via the front-end. If this permission is not set, the users will get an error page every time they attempt to submit a link.*

Step 14.   Click the **[Y]** Public tab to the left of the Permissions area.

Step 15.   For the **[Z]** Create action, open the Select New Setting drop-down, which should display Inherited, and change it to **[AA]** Allowed.

Step 16.   Click the **[BB]** Save button to save the information. This will display the success message and return to the Weblink tab.

Step 17.   Reopen the Permissions tab. The setting for the Create permission should now be set to **[CC]** Allowed. You'll see a green icon showing that effect.

Step 18.   Go back to the front-end and click the Home button to go back to the main page of the website. This will clear the error page.

Step 19.   Click the Submit a Weblink menu link item under My Weblinks.

The form for submitting a weblink should now display (Figure 16-9).

Step 20.   Give the weblink the name **[DD]** **View this Site**.

Step 21.   Select **[EE]** Sample Data-Weblinks in the Category drop-down.

Step 22.   For the URL, enter **[FF]** **http://joomla.org**.

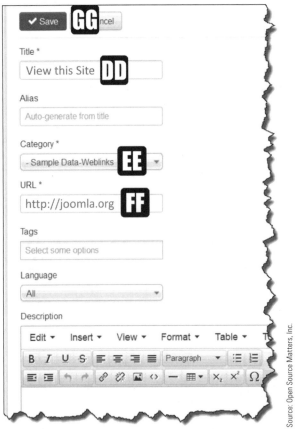

Source: Open Source Matters, Inc.

Figure 16-9 *To submit a link, three pieces of information are needed. You must give the weblink a* **[DD]** *title,
assign it to a* **[EE]** *category, and provide the website's*
[FF] *URL.*

IT'S CONTENT, SO IT CAN BE TAGGED

Because weblinks are in the content classification that can be tagged, there is a field on
the form for entering tags. But, remember, the tag must previously exist in order to tag
this content type.

Step 23. Click the blue **[GG]** Save button to save the weblink submission. A success
message will display and the website will return to the Home view.

Step 24. Go to the backend and open the Weblinks Manager again. Go to the bottom of
the list, where the View this Site link should be displayed in the disabled state
(the red X circle).

At this point, you can enable the weblink, which will allow it to appear in the list of links for the Sample Data-Weblinks category. If the link is not appropriate, you can delete it by selecting the checkbox and clicking the Trash button in the top menu bar.

Summary

In this chapter, you learned:

◆ What weblinks are and how they are used.

◆ The purpose of the Weblinks component.

◆ How to organize weblinks.

◆ How to create a Weblinks category.

◆ Different ways to display weblinks on a website.

◆ How to capture user weblink submissions.

◆ How to manage submitted weblinks.

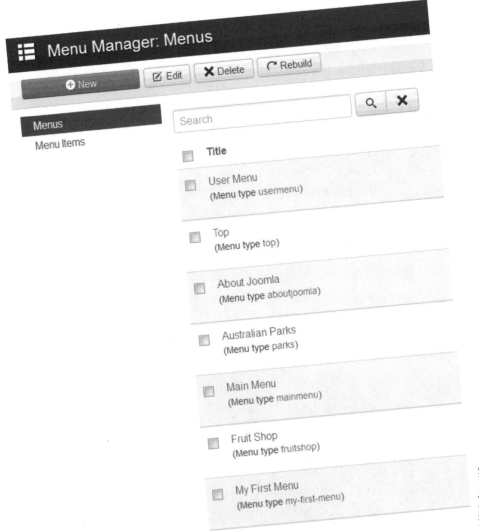

Website content is accessed via Menu Link Items, which are created within Menus. The Menu Module positions them on the page layout.

Chapter 17

Categories

Learning Objectives

What's included in this chapter:

- ◆ Categories and organizing content.
- ◆ Rules for category organization.
- ◆ How to create categories.
- ◆ Rearranging the order of categories.
- ◆ Rearranging category content items.

Organizing Content Using Categories

In previous chapters, categories were used to organize content. Categories are used throughout Joomla! 3 to keep content in some sort of logical order as compared to just having it scattered all over the backend and front-end, with no way to help website users find anything.

If you recall, in addition to article-related categories, categories also exist to help organize the content items in these areas:

◆ Banners

◆ Contacts

◆ Newsfeeds

◆ Weblinks

◆ Users (the categories are called Groups)

◆ Media (the categories are called Folders)

◆ Added extensions (almost all extensions that add content to the website have a category structure to help keep things organized)

Category Rules

Joomla! 3 has many fixed configuration rules that govern and manage how content is created and displayed. Here are some general rules pertaining to categories:

◆ Categories are the top level of content management.

◆ The top level category is sometimes referred to as the "parent."

◆ Sub-categories (child categories) can be created and be associated with any category above it (parent category).

◆ Content items may be assigned to the sub-categories.

◆ There is no specific limit to the number of categories that can be created.

◆ There is no specific limit to the number of child category levels that can be created within a parent category.

◆ Categories and sub-categories can have descriptive text, and this text may be displayed when using category-based page displays.

◆ There is no specific limit to the number of content items that can be assigned to a category.

As explained, Joomla! 3 structures content primarily as content items, which are assigned to categories. Categories can have sub-categories, and sub-categories can have sub-sub-categories built into the structure (Figure 17-1). Remember, a sub-category is simply the child of the category (parent), under which it is assigned.

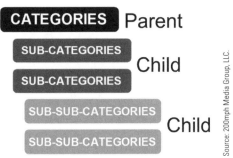

Source: 200mph Media Group, LLC.

Figure 17-1 *Categories contain the content items. The parent category can have any number of child sub-categories or sub-sub-categories. Although there is no limit to the number of Child categories, too many can complicate the organization of your content.*

Once you create a Category structure, you can assign content items to it. This process of structuring content is similar to a file cabinet that has drawers. Within those drawers there are hanging folders and within those are file folders. Within the file folders there are documents. This equals a category, with a sub-category that has a sub-sub-category and content items (Figure 17-2).

Source: 200mph Media Group, LLC.

Figure 17-2 *Content must be assigned to categories, and these can be parent or child categories at any level. There is no specific limit to the number of content items that can be assigned to a category, regardless of its level. However, the number of levels should be appropriate for the amount of content.*

Creating Categories

With each Content Manager, categories and sub-categories can be created. Creating a parent or top-level category is pretty straight forward. You use the green New button and then fill in the required information.

When creating a Child category, in addition to providing the required information, you must select the Parent category. This is usually accomplished in the Details area with a drop-down entitled Parent.

There are six steps involved in creating a category in any Content Manager. After opening the manager, the steps are as follows:

Step 1. Start the process by opening the Category or Categories tab for the Content Manager.

Step 2. Click the green New button.

Step 3. Enter a name or title for the category being created.

Step 4. Designate the category as a parent or child in the Details section, Parent drop-down.

Step 5. Select Published for the status of the category.

Step 6. Execute either a Save or Save & Close action.

DON'T OVERLOOK THE PUBLISHED STATUS

After creating a parent or child category, make sure to publish it. This vital step is often overlooked and can create problems when creating category list displays. Double-check to make sure the category that was created is, in fact, set to the Published status.

Rearranging the Categories

One recurring task that you must perform when creating categories is arranging their order of display. This issue also applies to the actual content items themselves. Yes, there are preset or predetermined order settings for displaying lists via menu link items, but within the Content Manager, the categories and items are added in a numerical Item ID hierarchy.

This item ID method actually translates to last added, last listed in the hierarchy. So when a category or content item is created, it simply goes to the bottom of the list of a parent item, or as the last child if it has a parent.

For convenience, the column headings in any Content Manager can be clicked to rearrange the items. This is simply an administrator convenience. It does not change the order of appearance on the actual website pages. The column heading functions allow the administrator to order the items in a more convenient way for editing, or setting the actual display order on the website pages.

To rearrange the order of content items on lists, complete Exercise 17-1.

EXERCISE 17-1: ORDERING CONTENT ITEMS

Objective: This exercise details the method to be used to change the order of content items such as categories, articles, contacts, weblinks, and so on. The changes made to the order will change the manner in which the content items are displayed on the website pages.

Step 1. If you're not already there, log in to the Administrator backend of the website.

Step 2. Open the Category Manager in the Admin Left Menu in the Control Panel. This displays the list of categories for articles (Figure 17-3).

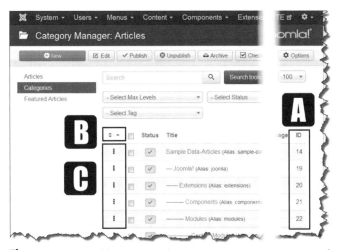

Figure 17-3 *In addition to a title, every content item is assigned an* **[A]** *ID. Item ID numbers can be used to designate ordering or to specify content items, or groups of items to be displayed, often in specialized extensions that may be installed.*

Step 3. Click on the **[B]** arrows column heading to the left of the item selector box. This step is necessary to enable ordering. If you don't do this, when attempting the next step, a tooltip reminder message will appear. If ordering has been enabled, the **[C]** three square dots underneath will change from grey to black.

Step 4. Scroll to the bottom portion of the list and find the **[D]** parent category called Fruit Shop Site (Figure 17-4). The order of its child categories will be changed in the next steps.

Figure 17-4 *The parent category has two child categories, which will be reordered within the parent. The parent of a child cannot be changed by the reordering method.*

Step 5. Place the mouse cursor over the three black square dots to the left of the **[E]** child category called Recipes. The mouse cursor should change to a four-directional arrow.

Step 6. Click and hold the left mouse button and move it slightly upward, which will highlight the child category with a green color across the screen. This color indicates that the content item will be reordered. The screen will also change, with some items hidden under a grey color, and the Growers Child category remaining with a white background. This is happening because the items being reordered are under a parent category. In this case, Growers and Recipes are under the parent category called Fruit Shop Site. In this way, Joomla! 3 helps in reordering the items by showing the administrator only the essential elements involved in the move.

Step 7. While holding the left mouse key down, slide the Recipes item just above the Growers item. If done correctly, the Growers item will relocate itself under the Recipes item. Make sure the entire green bar is above the Growers item when performing this step. This may take a little practice to make it work.

Step 8. Release the left mouse button. The two items have now changed position. No Save action is required. Releasing the left mouse button automatically saves the new ordering.

Step 9. Confirm that the order of the two items has changed, with Recipes as the first and Growers as the second child category under Fruit Shop Site.

MOVING CANNOT CHANGE PARENT

The process of changing the order of the content items *cannot* be used to change a parent or child assignment. You must do this by opening the item, changing its parent or category assignment, and then saving the new designation. Reordering only changes the order of appearance on the website front-end displays.

Exercise 17-2: Rearranging Category Content Items

Objective: In this exercise, you learn how to rearrange category content items. Individual content items within a category are rearranged exactly the same way as categories are, by following these steps:

Step 1. Open the Content Manager list view for the content items to be reordered.

Step 2. Activate the "enable ordering" feature by clicking the arrows at the top of the column.

Step 3. Click on the rearrange squares to the left of the item.

Step 4. Hold the mouse key down.

Step 5. Move the content item up or down to the desired order location.

Step 6. Release the mouse button to place the content item in that location.

The reordering method applies to all content items that are installed, including those for extensions that may be installed in the future. All extension developers must follow the content item reordering method for lists within their extension. If the content is displayed in a list view, the items can be reordered.

Sorting via Column Headings

When you're in the backend, clicking the column headings on list views rearranges the display by the column value only for your viewing purposes. That action does not change the actual order of how content items are displayed on the website. Only the actual reordering process will accomplish that task.

Summary

In this chapter, you learned:

◆ The content and content items are organized using categories.

◆ There are fixed rules for categories.

◆ How to create categories.

◆ How to rearrange the order of categories.

◆ How to rearrange category content items.

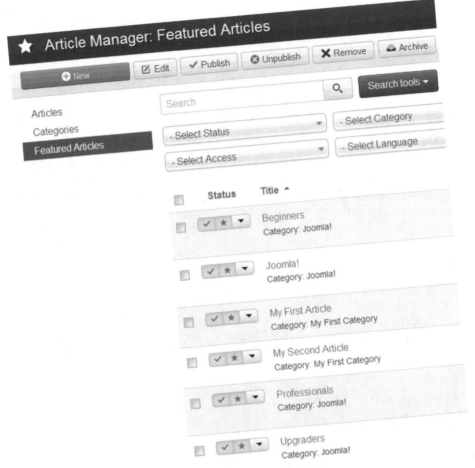

If the opening page of the website is a Category-Blog Layout, Articles can be designated as "Featured" so they automatically appear on the website front-end's first page.

Chapter 18

Articles

Learning Objectives

What's included in this chapter:

◆ Where articles display on the screen.

◆ How to assign an article to a category.

◆ How to designate an article as "featured."

◆ How to create an article.

◆ How to create a menu link item to an article.

◆ How to control the article's Details settings.

◆ How to override the global settings for articles.

◆ How to use content management functions for articles.

◆ How to enhance articles.

◆ How to add links to other articles.

◆ How to add images to articles.

◆ Settings for margins and padding around images.

◆ How to break an article into smaller parts using page breaks.

◆ Understanding the Intro Text and Read More functions.

◆ How to add a Read More function.

◆ Learning more about other article parameters.

◆ Finding online resources.

Understanding Articles

Articles are the most common type of content that can be created in a Joomla! 3 website. They are connected to menu link items. They are not simply associated, as with other content items such as modules. Of course, contacts, weblinks, and others are opened directly with a menu link item.

Articles must be directly connected to a menu link item. The exception to this steadfast rule is the category list or the category blog content from a menu link item, through which articles may be accessed, but not directly without clicking a link or two to get there.

Articles Always Appear in the Content Area

When an article's menu link item is clicked, the article will always appear in the main content area of the web page. The main content area is not a module position. It is a fixed location on each template layout, specifically reserved to display articles and other content items.

While content items, such as modules, can be displayed in any location in which there is a defined module position, articles can only show up in one place: the main content area (Figure 18-1).

Figure 18-1 *The location on the web page template where articles appear is the* **[A]** *main content area. All other locations—the website banner, search, menu, right menu and login modules—are module positions.*

238

Articles Must Be Assigned to Categories

When you create an article, it must be assigned to a previously created category. This allows for a classification hierarchy to be created for articles. This isn't a big deal for smaller websites, but for website with a large number of articles, the structure should be arranged using categories.

Chapter 17, "Categories" discussed how categories are created and how they can be nested to have sub-categories to create a hierarchy of content management.

Once the categories exist, you can assign articles to them. Following that, you can create menu link items to allow access to articles in one of these ways:

Method 1:   A menu link item links directly to the individual article.

Method 2:   A menu link item for the individual category displays the list of articles in the respective category. This type is called a Category List.

Method 3:   A menu link item for a "list of categories," which when a category is clicked, will display the articles within the selected category.

Method 4:   A menu link item that is connected to a content display function of an extension that configures web pages for the display of categories and articles, or other combinations of content. There are many such extensions in the JED that display category or article content from a menu link item action.

THE "UNCATEGORIZED" EXCEPTION

When an article is created, it is automatically assigned to a category called "uncategorised" (note British spelling). Yes, that sounds unusual, but that's what happens. Articles can be moved from uncategorised to any other category at any time. Be aware that a category of uncategorised does exist, and it's not really a category for the purposes of organizing content.

Using the Featured Articles Category

The use of "featured articles" is the only time when an article can be assigned to two categories. The rule is that articles may only be assigned to a single category.

Featured articles is the exception because this category designates the articles to appear on the Home web page for the website if the Featured Articles category blog layout is the default. This means that when the website opens in the browser, the Home (generally the default) menu link item, which is designated to display a category blog layout, will display only articles that have been secondarily designated as "featured." This designation is in addition to the regular category assignment for the article, which could be the "uncategorised" category.

Let's take a quick look at this designation in Exercise 18-1.

EXERCISE 18-1: CHECKING FEATURED ARTICLES

Objective: This exercise will demonstrate how to check to see which articles are designated as featured.

Step 1.   If you're not already there, log in to the Administrator backend of the website.

Step 2.   Under the Content menu link item in the top menu, select **[B]** Featured Articles in the drop-down (Figure 18-2).

Figure 18-2 *The Featured Articles Manager may only be accessed via the content menu, and will display a list of all published articles that are, in addition to their respective category assignment, also designated to display on the front-end of the website, but only if the Home button is set as a Featured Articles type.*

Step 3.   When the list displays, there should be five articles, all of which have the status of Published (Figure 18-3).

Step 4.   Notice that each article is assigned to a category. This indicates the primary category assignment for the articles.

Step 5.   Go to the website front-end, and when it opens, ensure that the articles displayed on the Home page match the articles in the supplemental Featured Articles category. How is this double category assignment accomplished?

Step 6.   Open the "Joomla!" article by clicking on the article's name, or by selecting the checkbox next to the name and clicking the Edit button in the menu bar.

Step 7.   Under the Details section to the right, click the Featured drop-down. The choices are Yes and No.

Step 8.   Select No as the option.

Step 9.   Execute either a Save or Save & Close action.

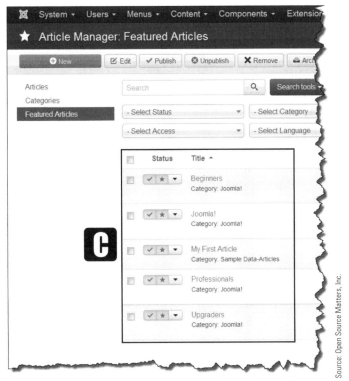

Figure 18-3 *This list displays the featured articles and their status. The gold star next to the published checkmark indicates it is a Featured Article.*

Step 10. Go to the website front-end, refresh the browser window, and notice that the "Joomla!" article no longer appears as a featured article. At this point, do not change the article back to its previous settings.

As a reverse process, when an article is created and assigned to its category, the "featured" selection can be made at that time, which will place the article in the featured category blog layout on the front-end, but only if the Home menu link item has been designated as a featured articles layout.

Step 11. Go to the Menu Manager via the Admin Left Menu and open the main menu.

Step 12. Open the Home menu link item. For the **[D]** Menu Item Type, Featured Articles has been selected. This sets the content type layout for the opening page on the front-end because it has also been designated the **[E]** default page in the right parameter area (Figure 18-4).

Figure 18-4 *The Featured Articles selection is performed within each respective article by invoking its designation and setting it as the default page.*

Creating Articles

Articles must be created individually, that is, each article is created one at a time. There is no internal method in Joomla! 3 to automatically create articles via any sort of "import" procedure. Article creation is a manual process, although some parts of article content are not and Joomla! 3 has provided mechanisms for doing that. For example, you can import some content from Microsoft Word documents, or import images to be added to articles.

Although creating articles might seem tedious, the process gets faster when you become more familiar with the action steps needed to bring it about.

There are two action steps involved in creating an article in the Article Manager, and they involve:

Action 1. Start the process, after admin login, by doing any of the following:

♦ Click Add New Article from the Admin Left Menu in the Control Panel to open the Article Manager: Add New Article screen.

♦ Click Article Manager from the Admin Left Menu in the Control Panel. Then click the green New button to open the Article Manager: Add New Article screen.

♦ Using the content menu at the top of the screen, mouse over the Article Manager, which will open the Add New Article fly-out. Click the name to open the Article Manager: Add New Article screen.

♦ Using the content menu at the top of the screen, click Article Manager to open it. Then click the green New button to open the Article Manager: Add New Article screen.

Action 2. When the Add New Article screen is open, you need to do the following:

◆ Enter a title for the article.

◆ Designate the Category into which the article is assigned.

◆ Designate the status of the article.

◆ Determine whether the article is to be featured.

◆ Add content, now or later.

◆ Execute the Save or Save & Close action.

These two action steps create the article, with or without content, which can be added later. You can also add or edit content at any time by simply opening the article via the Article Manager.

Article Actions in Common with Categories

Articles have some things in common with categories, for example:

◆ Articles must have a title.

◆ Articles must be assigned to a category.

◆ Articles must be set to Published to be displayed.

◆ Articles can be accessed only via a menu link item on the front-end.

◆ Articles may be indirectly accessed via the category list or the list of categories layouts.

◆ Articles cannot be nested, that is, they cannot be under another article, as is possible with categories. Articles may only be assigned to the same category.

◆ Article order within a category can be changed or reordered, which can affect how the articles display under certain other parameter settings, such as by author, by date, and so on.

◆ All of the rules pertaining to viewing and ordering categories also apply to articles.

EXERCISE 18-2: CREATING ARTICLES

Objective: This exercise will guide you through the article-creation process. An article must exist before a menu link item can be created to display it on the front-end.

Step 1. Open the Add New Article Manager via any of the methods described previously.

Step 2. Enter for the title, **My Second Article**.

Step 3. Add the article to the My First Category in the Category drop-down.

Step 4. Add a few lines of text in the text area of the JCK Editor. Here is what we have added:

This is some sample text for my second article.

This article is assigned to My First Category.

It is also being designated as a featured article, so it will appear on the front-end of the website, provided the Home menu link item type is Featured Articles.

Step 5. At the right, designate the article as Featured on the right side of the screen.

Step 6. Execute either a Save or Save & Close action.

The article has now been created and assigned to a category. The next set of actions to be taken involve the creation of a menu link item, which will allow the article to be accessed.

EXERCISE 18-3: CREATING A MENU LINK ITEM TO AN ARTICLE

Objective: Now that an article has been created, this exercise will create the menu link item that will appear on the front-end. When the link is clicked, the article will open for viewing.

Step 1. In the Admin Left Menu in the Control Panel, open the Menu Manager.

Step 2. Open the top menu.

Step 3. Click the green New button at the top left of the screen.

Steps 1, 2, and 3 can be combined by opening Menus in the top menu, and then mousing over the main menu and clicking the Add New Menu Item from the fly-out.

Step 4. Select Articles > Single Article for the menu item type.

Step 5. Select My Second Article in the Select Article area by clicking Select. Scroll down the list of articles, which should be in alphabetical order, and click on the article's name to select it.

Step 6. For the menu's title, enter **My Second Article**.

Step 7. For the menu location, select Top (right side of screen).

Step 8. Check the status choices to make sure the menu link item is set to Published.

This will be a menu link item without a parent, so make sure that parent item is showing Menu Item Root for that parameter.

Step 9. No other parameters need to be set at this time, so execute the Save & Close action.

Step 10. Go to the website front-end and refresh the browser window. The menu link item should appear at the end of the top menu. Click it to verify that the article will display.

Cleaning Up the Article

The article you just created, when viewed via the front-end, has a section at the top called "Details," which provides information about the article. These settings are controlled via the article's Options parameters. Unless there is a compelling need to do so, these details can be removed from all articles. (In some cases, particularly websites with an abundance of articles and authors, having information like this is helpful, especially for bylines and the like.)

In Exercise 18-4, you'll see how to disable all of the article's details display options.

EXERCISE 18-4: CONTROLLING THE DETAILS SETTINGS

Objective: This exercise illustrates how to set the global parameters for articles and defines what the parameters do.

Step 1.   Reopen the Article Manager via the Admin Left Menu.

Step 2.   In the top menu, click on the Options button.

These options, which apply globally to all articles when they are created, control virtually every aspect of individual articles, as well as individual categories, multiple categories, and with blog/featured layout and list layouts. View each of those parameter areas to familiarize yourself with the setting options. Remember, these are global settings and will apply to every action that creates a content item that involves articles, including the categories into which they are assigned, along with other types of layouts.

Step 3.   Under the Articles tab, scroll down the list to review the settings. Change the individual parameter settings as shown in the following table:

Parameter	Setting	What It Does
Choose a Layout	Default	If you have created custom layouts for articles, they are displayed here and can be selected via the drop-down. This is the Alternative Layout option under the article's Options tab.
Show Title	Show	This shows/hides the title of the article, which can be replaced by adding a custom title.
Linked Titles	No	Set the article title as a link to a single article menu link item for the article. This simply makes the article title open the article when in a list view of articles.
Show Intro Text	Show	Intro text is short text that appears before the rest of the article text. When an intro text teaser is used, the teaser text usually isn't displayed again when opening the article. This gives the option to do so.
Position of Article Info	Above	This defines where the details will appear when the article is opened, such as having the author's name below the article text rather than above it.
Show Category	Hide	Displays the name of the category into which the article is assigned.
Link Category	No	If the category is shown, make it an active link to the category.
Show Parent	Hide	If the category has a parent, show its name.
Link Parent	No	If the parent is shown, make it an active link to the category.
Show Author	Hide	Show or hide author.

continued

Parameter	Setting	What It Does
Show Create Date	Hide	Show or hide the date the article was created. Articles can be created in advance of publishing, which is the created date.
Show Publish Date	Hide	Show or hide the date article was published.
Show Navigation	Hide	Navigation on article displays are links to additional articles in the category in layouts that accesses those content items not displayed on the current screen. This is the familiar Next and Previous links displayed underneath content.
Show Voting	Hide	If article voting is used, show or hide it.
Show Read More	Hide	Read More is a break in a long article. The text is broken at a point with a link to read more. The term "Read More" can be replaced with text of your choice. Intro texts are displayed for Category Blog and Featured Articles layouts. This can also be used to tease readers and only allow registered users to view the full article.
Show Title with Read More	Hide	If Read More is used, the title of the article can be displayed, in the format *Read More – Article Title*.
Read More Limit	100	If the title of the article is shown with Read More, this limits the number of characters from the title that are shown. Helpful for very long article titles.
Show Tags	Hide	When tagging is used, show or hide the tags for this article.
Show Icons	Hide	Icons can be displayed for printing, emails, and so on, or can be set to not show.
Show Print Icon	Hide	Shows or hides the Print icon.
Show Email Icon	Hide	Shows or hides the Email icon.
Show Hits	Hide	Shows or hides the Number of Hits value.
Show Unauthorised Links	No	Intro text for restricted articles will display if set to Yes. If users click the Read More link, they will be required to log in to view the full article. If they are logged in, the article will open.
Positioning of the Links	Above	This positions the links with respect to the content.

Source: 200mph Media Group, LLC.

Step 4. Execute the Save & Close action.

Step 5. Go to the website front-end. If the article is displayed, refresh the browser. If not, refresh the browser and click the My Second Article menu link item.

The article should now display without any of the details showing above the content.

Overriding Global Options Settings

The ability to override or change settings for individual content items allows website administrators to display some content one way, some content another, and so on. With the global parameters set one way, you can modify the individual content items as you see fit, even if the setting is different than those in the global options.

THIS IS IMPORTANT: READ IT CLOSELY!

Within an article, there is a tab called Options, which has a list of the same parameter settings as listed in the global Options settings. Instinct would tell you that you could override the global settings for the content item under this tab, which is at the item level.

This does not work! Changing the settings here will do nothing. Go ahead and change a couple, save and then see if the changes show up on the front-end. They will not!

To override the global Options settings at the article level, you must go to the menu link item that accesses the article. In the case of this chapter, this would be My Second Article in the top menu.

When do the overrides work?

The override settings under the Article Options tab apply only when articles are being displayed via the Featured Articles category or the Category Blog layout. This means that you *must* use either of those two options for creating a menu link item to the respective category. If the parameters are set, and any other menu link item type is being used to display the article, the settings will not apply.

Step 6.   Open the Menu Manager for the top menu, and choose the My Second Article menu link item.

Step 7.   Open the Options tab. It will display the same list of settings as is shown for global options, and the article options tabs in the article. *The only difference between them—these options work to change the settings as an override!*

Step 8.   Go to Show Author and set it to Show.

Step 9.   Execute the Save action.

Step 10. Go to the front-end and click the My Second Article menu link item. The article should show "Written by Super User." The global parameter for this has now been overridden at the article level. It applies only to this individual article content item and no others.

Step 11. Return to the menu link item and reverse the override, changing the setting back to use the global one.

Step 12. Execute the Save & Close action.

The overrides via the article menu link item apply only to the particular article and no others. If you desire the same configuration for all your articles, go back and set those in the global options, not for each individual article.

Managing Article Content

In addition to the many parameters that control how articles are displayed—which are configured in global options, article options, and in the menu link item that opens the article—there are other parameters that are often set and not usually overridden.

There are five more controls that are used when creating the article details. This not only includes the text itself, but some content elements as well (Figure 18-5).

Figure 18-5 *Within the individual article manager, there are some action options shown below the content-editing screen.*

The buttons below the editing screen within an article are simply shortcuts for adding content other than text. Several of these are also used in the Custom HTML module type.

◆ **Insert Module**—This is a button from an extension that was added in a previous exercise and is not part of the default installation.

◆ **Article**—Allows a link to be added that connects to another article. Can be used to direct users to other content that is relevant or related to the current text.

◆ **Image**—Provides a method to upload images to the Media Manager and insert images into the article. Images can be placed anywhere in relationship to the text. Images may also be sized and adjusted for best fit.

◆ **Page Break**—Extremely long articles can be broken into smaller sections. This will automatically create a submenu of links to the different parts of the article.

◆ **Read More**—When inserted, it breaks the article text at that point and creates a link to read the rest of the article. Can also be used to tease readers and to limit access to registered users only.

◆ **Toggle Editor**—This switches the editor from WYSIWYG viewing mode to CODE viewing, which you might use in the future as you get familiar with HTML coding.

Using the Article Enhancement Features

Using the features described previously can be confusing if you have never been exposed to them. Exercises 18-5 and 18-6 explain the basics of the functions. Here are a couple of points to keep in mind:

◆ The **Read More** function is best used in conjunction with the Category Blog and the Featured Articles layouts, in order to show teaser text rather than display the entire article. This also can be used to save screen space when there are many articles in a category, or many designated as featured.

◆ The **Page Break** and **Read More** functions work best with very long articles. Generally, text that can be displayed on one screen is not broken into parts.

◆ The **Page Break** function creates an additional within-article menu of the parts of the article that have been broken into pages.

EXERCISE 18-5: ADDING LINKS TO ARTICLES

Objective: This exercise illustrates how to add a link to another article as a link within the current article. This is done in the Article Editor text area, using the Article link button below the editing window.

Step 1. If you're not already there, log in to the Administrator backend of the website.

Step 2. Open the Article Manager and then open My Second Article.

Step 3. After the last line of text, add **SEE THIS ARTICLE:**.

Step 4. Add a Return or Enter to create a line break after the new text and click the Article button below the text editing area. This will open a list of all articles that have been created for the website.

Step 5. Filter the list by going to the -Select Category- drop-down above the list. Select Sample Data-Articles.

Step 6. Click on the Administrator Components title. This returns you to the text editor window, with the title of the article displayed in blue, indicating it is a link.

Step 7. Execute a Save & Close action.

Step 8. Go to the website front-end, refresh the browser window, and open the menu link item to My Second Article, which is in the top menu.

Step 9. Click the Administrator Components link. The article should open in the main content area. Notice the Prev and Next Page buttons at the bottom. This allows backward and forward navigation within an article.

If you have many articles to which you want to create links, simply repeat this process. This way, you can create a unique cross-referencing system within an article.

Articles can be made visually attractive by adding relevant images. Images that relate to, or illustrate something in relation to the article, can be easily added. There is no limit to the number of images that you can add to an article, but usually a few are sufficient. If you want to display a large number of images, consider using a photo or image gallery extension from the JED.

EXERCISE 18-6: ADDING IMAGES TO ARTICLES

Objective: This exercise illustrates how to add an image with an article and position it to the left side. This is done in the Article Editor text area, using the Image link button below the editing window.

Step 1. If you're not already there, log in to the Administrator backend of the website.

Step 2. Open the Article Manager and then open My Second Article.

Step 3. Insert the mouse cursor before the first word at the beginning of the text.

Step 4. Click the Image button below the text editing window. This will open the Media Manager.

You can use any image on your computer for the next step. Use one that isn't any larger than 450×600 pixels; something like a face portrait shot or a small picture of a pet for example.

Step 5. Use the scroll bar on the far right and move to the bottom of the Media Manager window. This is easy to miss. Not doing so will block the upload file area of the manager.

Step 6. Click the Browse button, which opens the file structure of your computer.

BROWSER NAMING VARIATIONS

When you're executing browser actions such as Browse (in Firefox), note that your browser might call them something slightly different. In the Chrome browser, the button is called Choose Files. Be aware of the differences in terminology and naming conventions between different website browsers.

Step 7. Go to the location where the image to be uploaded is located and click on its name. The Media Manager window should reappear with the image name displayed next to the Browse button.

Step 8. Click the blue Start Upload button to add the image to the Media Manager images.

Step 9. With the image displaying in the Media Manager, click on it to make the selection. The name of the image will appear in the Image URL box to the lower left of the window.

Step 10. Use the scroll bar on the right to move to the bottom of the Media Manager window.

Step 11. Complete these actions:

Align—Select Left

Image Title—Enter **My First Image** in the text box

Caption—Select Yes to display the image title with the image

Step 12.   Use the scroll bar on the right and move to the top of the Media Manager window.

Step 13.   Click the blue Insert button to the top right of the window. This inserts the image into the article, and it is probably way too large to look good. If you save and then take a look at the article in the website front-end, you can see that it doesn't look very good.

Step 14.   Back in the Article editing window, click on the image. There will be handles displayed around the edges of the image. These handles can be used to resize the image, but it is better to use a manager to do this.

Step 15.   With the image still selected, click on the image icon in the editor control bars. It is in the middle row, about halfway across and is a small image with a + mark. This will open an image properties manager for this image. Each image in an article has a similar manager to control how it appears.

Step 16.   Next to the Width/Height boxes, there is an icon to lock the image proportions, so that when one value is changed, the other value will change proportionally. This ensures that the image won't be distorted. Make sure the icon is showing a locked image.

Step 17.   Change with width of the image to **150**. The height value will also change.

Step 18.   Click OK and then execute a Save action. The image should now be smaller.

Step 19.   View it on the website front-end. Remember to refresh the browser window.

   The image should appear smaller, with the article text to the right. But notice how close the text is to the image. This needs to be adjusted.

   The image's properties, which are accessed via the Article Editor, have settings that allow borders, horizontal space, and vertical space to be set for the image. This is how the image is separated from the text. Let's fix this issue now.

Step 20.   Click on the image so the handles appear, then click on the Image button in the editor menu—it is a small green image icon with a + mark. This opens the image's properties.

Step 21.   At the bottom left of the properties window, change these settings:

   Border—Set this parameter to the value of **4**

   HSpace—Enter **10** for the horizontal space

   VSpace—Enter **10** for the vertical space

   As those values are entered, the images in the small window change based on the entered values.

Step 22.   Click OK to apply the changes. If there is a confirmation message, click OK again.

Step 23.   If needed, click OK again and then execute a Save action.

Step 24.   Go to the website front-end and refresh the browser window. If the article is not displayed, click the My Second Article menu link item in the top menu.

Notice that there is space all around the image. In addition to the spacing between the image and the text, there is space at the top and left of the image. This isn't good visually. This happens because the HSpace and VSpace settings apply to both sides of the image. That can be changed.

Step 25. Go back to the Admin backend and continue. Adjusting the top and left spacing values involves changing some code, which isn't difficult to do. *Just follow these instructions closely.*

Step 26. At the top left of the menus for the JCK editor, click the Source button. If not using JCK, use the Toggle editor button at the bottom right. This will open the window to show the source code (HTML) for the article.

Step 27. Look at the first couple of lines of code for this line:

```
margin: 10px;
```

This is what was generated by the HSpace and VSpace settings for the image property. The px stands for pixels, which is the unit of measurement for web page displays.

Step 28. Change the code to read as follows:

```
margin: 0 10px 10px 0;
```

Step 29. Execute a Save action.

Step 30. Go to the website front-end and refresh the browser window. The image should now have moved up with no margin at the top, and moved left with no margin on that side. The text should still be pushed away from the image. If there was a lot of text and it went below the image, there would be a 10px space below, or typically one line of text.

PADDING AND MARGIN VALUES

Padding adjusts space between an object *inside* a given box area, whereas margin adjusts space *outside* of the given object box area. In this case, **margin 0 10px 10px 0;** sets the outside margin parameters this way:

```
margin: top right bottom left;
```

Every time you see a padding or margin value with more than one number, keep the clockwise rotation in mind—top, right, bottom, left.

Look up "CSS margin" and "CSS padding" in Google or any search engine and read some of the tutorials about these settings. It's not a bad idea to become familiar with some basic CSS coding.

After you have more experience with HTML code and CSS, you will be able to adjust any awkward looking layout involving images so they look good on the screen in relation to other page elements.

If you are going to work extensively on Joomla! 3 website projects, you should learn about HTML and CSS in order to obtain a fundamental working knowledge of how these things work. It will also be extremely helpful when creating or changing template layouts, which are comprised of HTML and CSS, along with some PHP code. That's a horse of a different color that we are not going to delve into in this book. It is somewhat complicated to understand and implement.

Using the Page Breaks Feature

Page breaks are a feature in Joomla! 3 that allows long articles to be broken into smaller parts to make it easier to read. No one likes scrolling and scrolling down a website screen to read content. This can be fixed using the Page Break feature.

Before starting this exercise, make sure you have at least three paragraphs of text in My Second Article, so there is something to break into pages.

EXERCISE 18-7: ADDING PAGE BREAKS TO ARTICLES

Objective: The objective of this exercise is to demonstrate the use of Page Breaks to convert long articles into a series of smaller parts that are easier to read.

Step 1. Open My Second Article with the Article Editor back in normal view (non-source).

Step 2. Place the editing cursor at the *end of the first line of text*.

Step 3. Click the Page Break button, which will open a parameter settings window.

Step 4. Enter this information:

For the page title, enter **First Page**.

For the table of contents alias, enter **Part One** into the text box. The menu link item can be given any name.

Step 5. Click the Insert Page Break button. The Article Manager will open and there will be a faint line after the first sentence.

Step 6. Execute a Save action.

Step 7. Go to the article in the front-end. The **[F]** image and only one line of text should display, along with the **[G]** Prev and Next Page buttons. There should be a **[H]** mini-menu to the right side, which shows the link to the pages. The first section of the mini-menu defaults to the first part of the article before the first page break has been inserted (Figure 18-6).

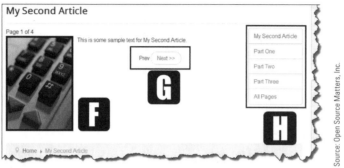

Figure 18-6 *Whenever the Page Break function is used, the article is broken into parts and a Prev/Next navigation is inserted at the breakpoint. A mini-menu is also created and it appears on the right side of the article window by default.*

Step 8. Repeat Step 4 for the remaining paragraphs, naming them progressively, such as **Second Page** and **Part Two**, and so on.

Step 9. Execute a Save action.

Step 10. View the article on the front-end.

Step 11. Click on the items in the mini-menu on the right side. Because the image is associated with only the first paragraph (also known as the "intro text"), it will only display for the My Second Article link in the mini-menu, and not for any of the other pages.

If you click the All Pages link in the navigation block, it will cause the entire text to be displayed, ignoring any Page Break settings.

You can visualize how this Page Break would work with articles that have a large amount of content. This can help tremendously for long articles and actually allows the creation of mini-articles when needed.

Using the Intro Text and Read More Functions

There will be many times, to save space or to organize content such as in the Category Blog or Featured Articles layouts, that only a small amount of text is displayed. In those cases, users must click a Read More link to see the full article.

Read More also allows you to show users only the intro or teaser, and then restrict the main part of the article to authorized users only.

In Exercise 18-8, you learn how to add the Read More function to My First Article. The article is displayed via the Home link in the top menu, which is a Featured Article link.

EXERCISE 18-8: ADDING THE READ MORE FUNCTION

Objective: The following steps guide you through the creation of a Read More link within an article to show intro or teaser text, and then show the entire article when the button is clicked.

Step 1.   Go to the website front-end and click the Home in the top menu, which should display the featured articles, with My First Article listed. The article should have two paragraphs. If it does not, add some text during Step 3.

Step 2.   In the Admin backend, open My First Article via the Content – Article Manager. Remember, this article is assigned to a category and is a featured article.

Step 3.   If there are not at least two paragraphs, add another one now.

Step 4.   Place the editing cursor at the end of the first paragraph of text.

Step 5.   Click the **[I]** Read More button below the editing window. This inserts a **[J]** visible line after paragraph one and before paragraph two (Figure 18-7).

Step 6.   Execute a Save action.

Step 7.   Go back to the front-end and refresh the browser window. Instead of displaying two paragraphs of the article in the main content area, only one should appear, with the Read More button below the text.

Source: Open Source Matters, Inc.

Figure 18-7 *Whenever a page break is inserted, it appears as a dotted line in the editor area, but it is not visible when viewing the article via the front-end.*

Step 8.   Click the Read More button. This opens the article to show the full text. The Newsfeeds module content that appears before the two paragraphs of text was created in Chapter 12, "Components: Newsfeeds," to associate with the Articles menu link item (My Menu Item), so the newsfeed should also display.

More Article Parameters

As you may have noticed on the Article Manager pages of My Second Article, there are a host of other settings that you can apply to your articles. These settings are described next.

In addition to the Content tab, there are five additional tabs with these options:

Publishing tab—Setting for publishing start/finish and other settings, along with an area to enter meta-content for search engines that pick up the keywords.

Images and links tab—Allows several images to be assigned to articles, such as the intro image (shows only in the intro text area), and the full article image. In addition, there are three text links that you can add.

Options tab—On this tab, there is a replication of the global options for articles. However, these do not function as overrides if the article is assigned to a menu link item. They would apply if this article is not associated with a menu link item, but is called within an article as an insert using the Article button at the bottom of the editing screen.

Configure Edit tab—These options simply turn off the display of the content items in the backend so that non-administrators cannot make overrides at the content item level. This is just another level of content management for larger websites that have many content editors who should not be able to alter anything but the actual content.

Permissions tab—Sets the ability for content editors to delete or edit the publishing state of a content item.

The article's optional parameters can be set at any time after the article is created.

More About Articles Online

As you probably know, this book has a companion website (joomla3bootcamp.com), which has updates and changes to book content. You will also find additional and more detailed information about the many different parts of Joomla! 3, along with additional exercises on the finer points of managing the website and its content items.

Additionally, you will find information about useful extensions, including exercises, that provide more options for administrators to manage content and set up a robust personal or corporate website.

Don't forget about the Joomla! wiki and help screens. Remember, when you're reading wiki text and other Joomla! resource material, make sure you are looking at the information for this version of Joomla! The wiki and information resources sometimes make the search for information difficult with text mixed from different versions, or incomplete or empty help pages. Just be aware of that when you visit those pages.

Summary

In this chapter, you learned:

◆ Articles always display in the main content area.
◆ How to assign an article to a category.
◆ How to designate an article as featured.
◆ How to create an article.
◆ How to create a menu link item to an article.
◆ How to control the article's Details settings.
◆ How to override the global settings for articles.

◆ How to use content management functions for articles.

◆ How to enhance articles.

◆ How to add links to other articles.

◆ How to add images to articles.

◆ About the settings for margins and padding around images.

◆ How to break an article into smaller parts using page breaks.

◆ What the Intro Text and Read More features do.

◆ How to add a Read More function.

◆ Where to find online resources.

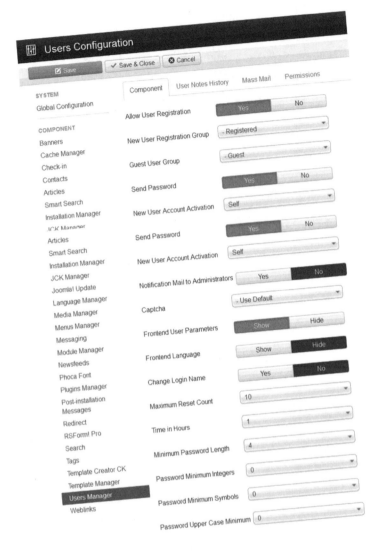

In the User Configuration Manager, all parameter settings relative to the way Users register on the website. If you are using ACL, this Manager will help you configure registrations.

Source: Open Source Matters, Inc. / 200mph Media Group, LLC.

Chapter 19

Modules

Learning Objectives

What's included in this chapter:

◆ What are modules and what they do.

◆ Modules in the default installation.

◆ Types of content that modules can display.

◆ Rules that apply to modules.

◆ How to name modules.

◆ Where modules can be located on a web page.

◆ Content within modules.

◆ How to download modules via the JED.

◆ How to install modules.

◆ How to configure a specialized module.

◆ How to display a module within an article.

◆ Modules can be stacked in the same module position.

◆ Modules can be reordered within module positions.

◆ Modules can be selectively displayed using menu link items.

Understanding Modules

Modules are the movable parts of Joomla! 3. Essentially, modules are content items (of many types) that can be added to a website and their location designated. Unlike articles, which appear only in the main content area, modules can be placed in any position on a template where a module position has been added. Thus, they are movable.

Many templates have a large number of module positions into which you can assign modules. Some have vertical and horizontal locations. Also, some have horizontal locations of two or more horizontal module positions on the same visual row.

The neat part about those module positions is that the assigned module can be set to spread to fill the entire area. If two modules are assigned, each shares half the space. If three are assigned, they all get one third of the space. This allows for some very nice looking layouts for displaying content generated through modules.

Modules are powerful. You can use them creatively to display many different types of content, using the default installation modules, and those added as extensions for specialized content.

Modules in the Default Installation

Modules are extensions. This means that modules can be added at any time via the Extension Installer. There are literally thousands of extensions available, many of them modules, or modules that are part of a component. Here are the module types that are available via the default installation (the [C] indicates that the module is part of a component):

Archived Articles—When articles have been archived, this module can be used to show a list of the archives by calendar months in which the action was taken.

Articles, Newsflash—Allows display of articles from a specific category. This is similar to a Category Blog display, but allows the placement of the module anywhere. The number of articles to be displayed can be fixed.

Articles, Related Articles—Using meta keywords, articles can be related to one another. If the current article has keywords, the module will display all other articles with the same keyword. Allows for a cross-referencing articles from within other articles.

Articles Categories—This module allows the display of a list of categories from within a single parent category. If the parent has five child categories, it will display those five based on the designation of the parent.

Articles Category—More selective than article categories, this module allows the display of articles from within one or more categories. This is done on a category-selective basis.

Banners [C]—If banners are created and categorized in the Banners component, the individual banner can be displayed in this module. More than one Banners module may be placed on a web page.

Breadcrumbs—This is also called the *pathway*, which simply shows the current location with the links or content location used to get there. Helpful on large websites with many areas of content; not so much on smaller, limited content websites.

Custom CSS—This is a nifty module wherein CSS code can be placed and the module assigned to a specific menu link item web page, which results in the CSS being applied to only the content of that web page. See the online companion to this book at joomla3bootcamp.com for details on how to implement custom CSS on website pages. This module should only be implemented by advanced users who have a working knowledge of CSS coding.

Custom HTML—HTML is code that can be displayed on web pages with a module or many modules on the same web page. Special images can be included, along with text, and it can be visually styled using CSS coding. This module functions differently than the custom CSS module, in that all the content in this module is displayed as is and does not affect any content on the web page.

Feed Display—If you want syndicated feeds from another website to appear on yours, then the Feed Display module can be used to collect and display the feeds.

Footer—By default, the Footer module shows the Joomla! copyright information at the bottom of the page. It can be set to not display by setting its status to Unpublished.

Language Switcher—If your website is configured in several languages, this module offers users the opportunity to change from the current language to any other available language.

Latest News—This displays a list of the Most recently published and current articles in a module position. As new articles are created, they display on the list in the module.

Latest Users—If your website has registered users and a feature to sign up, this module allows the display of the latest users added to the website.

Login—Displays the Login module on the web page.

Menu—A website can have many, many menus. This module allows the designation of which menu will appear in which module position and associate with which menu link item. A Menu module can be set to display after a menu link item in another menu is clicked.

Most Read Content—As users view content, this module displays the content that has been most accessed by them. Of course, it can't really tell if they read the content. It simply just shows articles that have the highest number of actual page views.

Popular Tags—The most commonly used tags, within specific time periods, can be displayed using this module.

Search [C]—By default, most templates have a Search module published in a specific module position. If not, this module can be added to create a search box anywhere on the web page.

Similar Tags—If content items have similar tags, the closeness of which can be specified, the module will display links to the other content items.

Smart Search Module [C]—Using the Smart Search functions, the module allows users to execute searches using advanced searching features.

Statistics—This module shows information about your server, website users, number of articles, and the number of weblinks included in the website.

Syndication Feeds—If you want to create an outbound feed for other websites to use to display your content, this module, if displayed on a web page, allows you to do so.

Weblinks [C]—From the Weblinks component, this module allows the display of weblinks selectively in a module position. Only one category of weblinks can be displayed in each module, but several modules may be used on a web page.

Who's Online—Displays the registered users (if logged in) and guests who are currently on the website. Can be displayed by number of, by usernames, or both.

Wrapper—Perhaps the most misunderstood and misused module in Joomla! The Wrapper is an iFrame window that displays a URL. It can display an entire website within the wrapper. However, the link functionalities of the displayed URL can go awry very easily because they are not intended for your wrapper display, but for that particular website. Before using the Wrapper Module, lower your expectations of what it can do and display.

Module Rules

Modules have their own set of peculiarities that govern how they function and display. Here are a few rules that apply to modules:

Rule 1. A module must exist via the default installation, or be installed as an extension.

Rule 2. A module position must exist in order to place a module on a template page.

Rule 3. A module must be published or enabled in order for it to display.

Rule 4. A menu link item generally cannot be created that specifically opens a module, but there are extensions that allow it.

Rule 5. Modules typically are associated with menu link items. That is, when a menu link item is clicked, the module will display only under that condition.

Rule 6. Specialized menu link item types can be created that open special modules directly.

Rule 7. A module may associate with more than one menu link item. In fact, a module could associate with every menu link item on a website.

Rule 8. More than one module of the same type can appear in module positions, either in separate locations on the web page or in the same position location. Each duplicate module may associate with different menu link items.

Naming Modules

When you create modules, you can give them a title and then choose to use it or not. For example, a categories display can be named something specific to what is being displayed. In other words, make the title of the modules relate to the content display it offers. Of course, if the title is set to not show, the module will appear without a title or header to identify it. Only the actual content displayed by the module will appear on the web page.

Locating Modules Anywhere on Template

If a template has a module position, a module can be located there. However, some caution must be used. For example, let's assume that a module is designed to display content that is visually wide and high. It's not a good idea to display that module in a position that is narrow and short. It will not display properly.

One example of this is the Breadcrumbs module. It is designed to be displayed on one line horizontally, so it displays a path to the current content from start to destination. It is not designed to be displayed in a module position in a left or right narrow column format. There are many such situations with display considerations for modules.

Many module types have layouts that are designated with their parameters—and often can be changed—or are controlled by the use of CSS specific to that module. If you run into the display "train wreck" caused by this wide-narrow disparity, seek an alternative location on the template to display the module.

Content of Modules

Many module types allow you to enter content or information using the standard Content Editor that is installed as the default, or the one selected by individual editors.

The Content Editor operates the same as with articles. It allows you to insert article links and images. Content capabilities vary widely between module types, so check each one before deciding to use the module on your website.

Most modules are content-type specific, which means that the module is designed to display certain content in a certain way. Modules are pretty much specialized in that regard, so keep that in mind also when searching the JED for a certain content display or functionality.

Use the Advanced Search functions on the JED, because it makes searching for extensions much easier and you can even search on a Joomla! version number.

Obtaining and Installing a Specialized Module

Modules are extensions, and extensions are obtained via the JED or directly from developer websites. One extension has always impressed us for its ability to display article content and to configure how it is displayed, and that is the Global News module extension.

WHAT ARE SECTIONS?

In earlier Joomla! versions, content was categorized in sections and categories with sections being the equivalent of a parent category in the current version. So, if you happen to run across "sections" in some extensions or its documentation, don't panic. They are just using older terminology. If the extension is marked as "3.2 compatible," and you see the word "Sections," you can ignore it. The extension should install and work properly.

The use of the Global News module requires three actions, which is typical of most all extensions that are added to a Joomla! 3 website, as follows:

Action 1. Download the extension.

Action 2. Install the extension.

Action 3. Configure the extension.

Some extensions have several additional actions, such as enabling a plug-in or using the extension as a component with a module, and so on.

Although downloading and installing an extension was covered in previous chapters, it is being covered again to help you master the tasks involved.

Downloading the Extension in the JED

Most all extensions are sourced via the JED, although you will occasionally find others, templates for example, that are not. These usually are obtained via the developer's website. The following exercise will download an extension via the JED and then via the developer's website, and save it to your computer.

EXERCISE 19-1: DOWNLOADING THE GLOBAL NEWS EXTENSION MODULE

Objective: This exercise guides you through the process of finding and downloading the Global News extension via the JED.

Step 1. Go to joomla.org and open the Extend tab in the top menu bar. In the drop-down, select the Extension Directory link.

Step 2. Click on the Advanced Search link in the menu just below the page title.

Step 3. In the Extension Name field, enter **Global News**.

Step 4. For compatibility, check the Joomla 3.x item.

Step 5. Click the blue Search button. After initiating the search, a new screen will display and there may be a short delay before the results populate the screen (Figure 19-1).

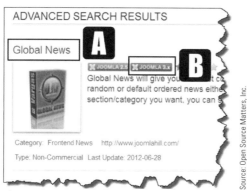

Figure 19-1 *The* **[A]** *name of the extension is a link that opens the next page for downloading. Note the* **[B]** *icons that indicate which version of Joomla! the extension is compatible with, which is 2.5 and 3.x in this case.*

Step 6. Click on the name of the extension. This opens the next JED screen with more information about the extension. This screen allows you to demo the extension, but don't expect that for every extension. Some developers do not have demos set up.

Step 7. Click the **[C]** Download button (Figure 19-2). This opens the extension download page. Developers often use one page for downloading their extensions, as is the case here.

Figure 19-2 *The Extension Information screen allows you to view a demo, if available, and provides other information about the extension, including a link to the developer's website and documentation for the extension.*

Step 8. Click the mod_globalnews.zip with the 3.x icon at the left (Figure 19-3).

Figure 19-3 *Note the extension is available for many Joomla! versions. You can also see some other extensions written by this developer.*

Step 9. Allow the download by selecting Save and OK. Make sure you know where your computer is downloading these files.

Installing the Extension

At this point, the extension has been downloaded to your machine. Now you need to install it on your website.

EXERCISE 19-2: INSTALLING THE GLOBAL NEWS EXTENSION MODULE

Objective: This exercise helps you through the steps involved to install the module and ready it for use.

Step 1. If you're not already there, log in to the Administrator backend of the website.

Step 2. Open the Extension Manager from the Admin Left Menu in the Control Panel. This displays the install screen.

Step 3. Open the Upload Package File tab.

Step 4. Click on the grey **[E]** Browse button to locate the downloaded extension. Find the extension on your computer and click on the name to select it, then execute the Open button. The screen should return and the **[F]** name of the extension will appear to the right of the Browse button—there may be a slight delay before this happens (Figure 19-4).

Reminder! There may be differences in how browsers display their file seeking access and other features, so bear that in mind when following these instructions.

Step 5. Click the blue **[G]** Upload & Install button.

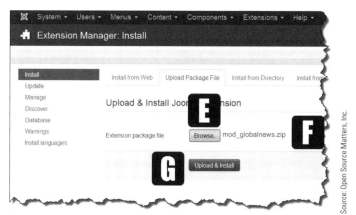

Source: Open Source Matters, Inc.

Figure 19-4 *Installing extensions involves finding the proper file that has been downloaded, selecting it, and then executing the installation. The name of the extension should appear next to the Browse button when it's ready to install. There might be a slight delay before the name appears, so be patient.*

Step 6.   After a few seconds, the green success message should display if the extension installation was successful. This specific extension installs as Unpublished by default.

You can now use the extension. Most extensions will need some configuration before actually displaying content on your website.

What Type of Content Does Global News Display?

The Global News extension allows you to display articles and associated information in a highly customizable manner. There are many ways to use the extension to display lists of articles. It allows you to display articles from several categories and configure exactly how the list appears, including the information and the size and colors.

The best way to learn how this extension functions is to actually set a version of it up to display articles. *Note:* More than one version of this extension can exist on a web page. Simply create additional versions of it using the New function in the Module Manager.

Follow the steps in Exercise 19-3 to activate the Global News module to display some selected articles and control how the results appear.

EXERCISE 19-3: CONFIGURING THE GLOBAL NEWS EXTENSION MODULE

Objective: This exercise illustrates the configuration and use of the Global News module by selecting where the article list will come from and how it will be displayed, including location, size, and color.

Step 1. Go to the Module Manager and click on the Global News module title. This will open the default version of the module. Scroll down the screen as there are many parameters that can be set for this extension.

Step 2. On the Module screen, add the following:

Title: **My Articles Module**

Position: Protostar Temple, Right [Position-7]

Status: Published

Step 3. Execute a Save action.

Step 4. On the Options screen, add the following by clicking in the Categories box, then scrolling the list to find the category to display:

Article List Layout: Plain List

Categories: My First Category

Step 5. Execute a Save action again.

Step 6. On the Menu Assignment screen, select On All Pages as the module assignment. *Remember:*—Modules must be associated with a menu link item.

Step 7. Execute a Save action again.

Step 8. Go to the website front-end, refresh the screen if it is already open, and view the module.

If these steps have been completed properly, the module should display at the top of the right column on the web page with the name of the category and the two articles that were assigned to that category (Figure 19-5).

How to fix it! If you do not get this display, make sure that the two articles: My First Article and My Second Article, are assigned to My First Category.

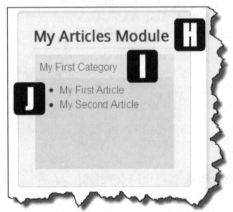

Figure 19-5 *Each of the module's items can display in a different manner using the many parameter settings for the module.* **[H]** *is the title of the module,* **[I]** *is the content category, and* **[J]** *are the two articles within the category.*

Step 9.   Before proceeding to the next step, change the module to a different Article List Layout option, called Static Content.

Step 10.   Execute a Save action.

Step 11.   View the resulting format on the website front-end (Figure 19-6).

Source: Open Source Matters, Inc.

Figure 19-6 *The entire display of content generated through this module can be changed and adjusted, making it a highly customized module.*

Step 12.   Near the bottom of the Module tab, find the HTML Supported Code for Content Layouts box (Figure 19-7).

Step 13.   Study the GN codes to get a basic understanding of which one does what.

Step 14.   In the box with the codes, remove **[K]** <small>GN_title</small>
.

Step 15.   Execute a Save action.

Step 16.   View the results on the website front-end. The date line should no longer display.

Figure 19-7 *The code key on the left indicates the codes that can be used to customize the actual content items that this module displays.*

Step 17. Again in the Modules tab, above the HTML code area, there are parameters that can be set to change how the module displays content.

Step 18. For the Content Area Bgcolor, enter **#FFEBCD**.

Step 19. Execute a Save action. View the results on the website front-end. The background color of the article text area should be light tan.

If you want to, play with some other settings in the Options and view the results. More information about using the Global News module can be found at the companion website for this book at joomla3bootcamp.com.

Step 20. So that this module can be used in the next exercise, in the Position drop-down box, type **inarticle1** (Figure 19-8). Make sure you press Enter after entering the text. Otherwise, the position will revert back to position-7. Entering a module position manually does not create a module position in the template. It simply assigns the module to a nonexistent location.

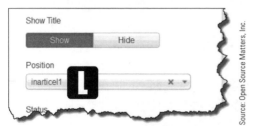

Figure 19-8 *A module position can be manually typed into the Position drop-down by inserting the cursor and entering the name of the position—which is not part of the template being used.*

Step 21. Execute a Save & Close action. View the results on the website front-end. The background color of the article text area should be light tan.

Many Modules, Many Configurations

There are many modules available in the JED for Joomla! 3. Modules are movable parts of a website and can display a wide range of content types. You should take some time and explore modules in the JED by viewing the demos available for them. It is often well worth the time when you want a certain functionality to be added to your website to find the proper and correct extension to accomplish that goal.

Keep in mind, also, that extensions can be free, but often you'll need to pay for them or subscribe to a developer's website. Look beyond the commercial and non-commercial designations for the extensions.

If there is a special layout for content that you want, chances are that there a several modules that will do the job.

Displaying Modules in Articles

Modules can be displayed in articles. Modules do not need to be assigned to a module position as a strict rule—although the position would be within the article rather than one designated as part of the template being used. In other words, in addition to module positions in a template, modules can be assigned to other location using two methods: one native to the Joomla! 3 installation, and the other by adding an extension that performs that action.

Here are two ways of inserting modules into articles:

Method 1. By using the built-in {loadposition} feature of Joomla! 3.

Method 2. By using a Modules Anywhere extension, which was installed on the website in an earlier exercise.

Method 2 is relatively easy to implement. You use the Insert Module button under the Content Editor when an Article Manager is open. By placing the cursor after the last text of the article and clicking on the button, that opens the list of modules. You simply click on one to select it. The module insertion code will appear within the article text on the backend. The module will then appear with the text of the article when it's viewed on the front-end.

MODULES WITHIN MODULES

It is possible, using the techniques described in Exercise 19-4, to configure a module within another module. Simply take the same steps as explained for configuring modules into articles.

Method 1 requires a bit more fiddling, and is explained in the following exercise.

EXERCISE 19-4: USING {LOADPOSITION} FOR INSERTING MODULES INTO ARTICLES

Objective: The objective of this exercise is to demonstrate how a module assigned to a unique module position can be inserted into an article by entering a predetermined code value with the name of the unique module position name.

Step 1. Go to Extensions, Plug-In Manager and make sure the Content—Load Modules plug-in is set to the status of Enabled.

Step 2. Go to the article (My First Article should be selected) in which the module is to appear. Place the cursor on a blank line where it is to be inserted.

Step 3. Enter **{loadposition inarticle1}** at the beginning of the article. Make sure you include the opening and closing braces.

It is important to assign the module to a unique location that does not actually exist in the template. That way, there will be no confusion about the module and where/how it is to display.

Step 4. Execute a Save action.

Step 5. Go to the front-end and click the Home button. Then, click the Read More button under the text for My First Article to open it.

Step 6. The My Articles module should appear underneath the text of the article. You should see the title of the Module, the My First Category name, and the two articles. The coloring is the same as the right side module and can be changed to match any website colorization.

MENU LINK ITEM TO DISPLAY MODULE

Another point about the **{loadposition}** function. It is possible to create an article, with no text content other than the **{loadposition}** code to connect to a Module. Then, you can create a menu link item to the article. The net result is that when the menu link item is clicked, it opens an article, but displays a module. It's a sneaky workaround to display modules in the main content area via a menu link item.

Stacking Modules

Modules can be assigned only to locations on a template wherever a module position is located or designated with the appropriate code. The exception, of course, is when a module is inserted into another type of content.

Here are some rules for modules in terms of their location on a web page:

Rule 1. Usually, more than one module of the same module type can be located on a web page. A duplicate module can be created using the New function in the Module Manager and selecting the type of module to be created, then assigning it to a module position.

Rule 2. More than one module can be assigned to the same module position. Many templates have only the left and right module positions. Multiple modules can be assigned to the left or the right. Of course, some templates have other module positions that display modules in the main content area, and do so with a horizontal layout. Each template has its own set of module sub-rules for those layouts.

Rule 3. If multiple modules are assigned to the same module position, they can be rearranged on the web page. You reorder modules the same way as any other list item. See Exercise 17-1 as an example of reordering a list item.

Rule 4. Unless the module opens from a menu link item, modules must be associated with one or more menu link items.

Rule 5. By using the menu link item assignments, modules can be set to hide or show when the menu link item is clicked. This allows modules to appear on certain web pages, but not appear on others.

Summary

In this chapter, you learned:

◆ What are modules and what they do.

◆ Which modules are included in the default installation.

◆ The types of content modules can display.

◆ Which rules apply to modules.

◆ How to name modules.

◆ How to locate a module on a web page.

◆ The type of content within modules.

◆ How to download modules via the JED.

◆ How to install modules.

◆ How to configure a specialized module.

◆ How to display a module in an article.

◆ Modules can be stacked in the same module position.

◆ Modules can be reordered within module positions.

◆ Modules can be selectively displayed using menu link items.

Any template can be "previewed" to show the front-end and the module positions that are available on the respective Template layout.

Chapter 20

Plug-Ins

Learning Objectives

What's included in this chapter:

◆ What plug-ins are and what they do.

◆ How plug-ins work.

◆ Types of plug-ins in the default installation.

◆ Setting plug-in parameters.

◆ Where to find plug-ins.

◆ Extension file prefixes.

◆ Actions to take when plug-ins do not work.

Understanding Plug-Ins

Plug-ins are the parts of Joomla! 3 that make things happen. Plug-ins don't get the credit or attention they deserve. This is because once a plug-in is installed, there isn't much to be done to it to make it work, other than to enable it.

Regardless of the limited need to administer plug-ins, they are very powerful and allow certain functions to exist on a website powered by Joomla! 3.

How Plug-Ins Work

Plug-ins don't do anything until they are "triggered" into action. A *trigger* is some kind of event that takes place, such as executing a menu link item, loading a web page, or displaying a module.

You saw an example of a plug-in function in Chapter 19, "Modules," where a module was set to display within an article using the {loadposition} feature. When the article was called to display via a menu link item, it was loaded into the main content area. During that process, a plug-in that controls {loadposition} was "triggered" into action. That's how plug-ins work. Something happens, the plug-in is "triggered," and then something else happens.

Plug-ins are no more complicated than that. They do stuff, but don't need a lot of configuration or attention by the website super user.

More examples of plug-ins that do something when triggered are the Read More and Page Break functions, which were explained in Chapter 18, "Articles."

Types of Plug-Ins

Just as components and modules have different types, so do plug-ins. By default, Joomla! 3 added a bunch of plug-ins during the installation process. Here are the types of plug-ins installed:

◆ Authentication
◆ Captcha
◆ Content
◆ Editors
◆ Editors-xtd
◆ Extension
◆ Finder
◆ Quickicon
◆ Search
◆ System
◆ User

Each plug-in plays a distinct role in the operation of the website. But most importantly, other than checking to make sure the plug-in is enabled, there is nothing to do to make them function.

Each plug-in type also has several different functional plug-ins that control various content or are triggered by some actions.

Some Plug-Ins Have Parameters

Some plug-ins have settings as part of their configuration, but on the other hand, some do not. If a plug-in has parameters that can be set, the administrators need to configure the plug-in so that it will function.

To get an idea of possible parameters that might need to be set for a plug-in, try the following exercise.

EXERCISE 20-1: EXPLORING PLUG-IN PARAMETERS

Objective: This exercise demonstrates the parameter settings for the Editor - JoomlaCK plug-in. Not all parameters will be defined, but several will be discussed as the plug-in is examined.

Step 1. If you're not already there, log in to the Administrator backend of the website.

Step 2. Under the Extensions menu link item in the top menu, select Plug-in Manager in the drop-down. There is no link in the Admin Left Menu in the Control Panel to open the Plug-In Manager.

In a previous exercise, the default content editor was replaced by the Editor - JoomlaCK , and it was designated as the default. When the component was installed, it also installed a plug-in for it.

Step 3. Find and open the plug-in called Editor - JoomlaCK.

Aside from the Plugin tab, this plug-in also has a Description and Advanced parameter settings. Within the Plugin tab, there are several settings.

Look at the many different parameters that can be configured. As you gain more skills as a Joomla! 3 administrator, you may need to change some of these parameters, especially the FrontEnd Toolbar Mode, which can limit some toolbar icons based on the user's role.

Step 4. Open the Advanced tab.

Step 5. Look at the different parameters that can be configured.

One parameter setting that comes in handy is the background color for the Editor window. If your website has a white background (hex #FFFFFF), the default setting is good. However, if your website has a black or different color background, it is convenient to have the Editor show the entered content as it would appear on the website pages. As an example, if the background of your website is black, the background color setting should be #000000, which is the hex code for black.

The other Advanced options deal with other elements of the Editor and how it is configured for entering content. As you learn more about Joomla! 3 by using it on a regular basis, and gain a better understanding of HTML and CSS, these parameter settings will make more sense.

You can also find information about this, and other Editors for Joomla! 3, on the companion website to this book at joomla3bootcamp.com.

Plug-Ins Support Components and Modules

It is very possible that when a component or module extension is installed, a plug-in might be installed with it. That was the case when the Component JCK Manager was installed. The companion Editor-JoomlaCK was added to the plug-ins at the same time. This is probably the way the large majority of plug-ins are installed.

Finding and Obtaining Plug-Ins

You must first define what the plug-in is to do on the website. Once that question has been answered, and there is no component or module to perform that function, plug-ins are the next consideration.

Plug-ins are extensions. Extensions are obtained via the JED. Because they are extensions, they install exactly the same way as components, modules, and templates.

When looking for plug-ins in the JED, using the Advanced Search is probably best so the results can be filtered by Joomla! version. Check the Joomla! 3.X icon to search for those that apply only to this version. Also, check the Plug-in icon and search by Joomla! version.

CATEGORIES AREN'T FOR PLUG-INS ONLY

When obtaining the search results in the JED, the Categories listed on the left of the page are not applicable just to plug-ins. They include all extensions within the particular category. Unfortunately, there is no way to fine-tune the actual results of the search to narrow the plug-ins by their functionality.

Extension Prefix for Plug-Ins

Joomla! 3 extensions usually have a prefix designating their type. It is possible that some developers do not use the prefix, so there might be an exception here or there. Here are the typical prefix uses for extensions:

> **com_** is used for components.
>
> **mod_** is used for modules.
>
> **plg_** is used for plug-ins.
>
> **pkg_** is used for extensions that are packages of extensions.

If the downloaded file has UNZIP FIRST at the end, it means the extension has many parts and needs to be uncompressed before installing via the Extension Manager. If there are many parts to an extension, make sure you install all of them.

What to Do When a Plug-In Doesn't Work

If you install a plug-in, but it is not working, investigate immediately to make sure the extension is enabled. This is particularly true for plug-ins, which are often installed in the disabled mode.

If that doesn't work, uninstall the extension and reinstall it.

If that doesn't work, contact the extension's developers and ask for their assistance.

Summary

In this chapter, you learned:

◆ What plug-ins are and what they do.

◆ How plug-ins work.

◆ The types of plug-ins in the default installation.

◆ How to set plug-in parameters if needed.

◆ Where to find plug-ins in the JED.

◆ What extension file prefixes are used.

◆ What to do if a plug-in doesn't work.

Template Manager: Customise Te...

Copy Template | Template Preview | Manage Fol...

Editor | Create Overrides | Template Description

- 📁 css
- 📁 html
- 📁 images
- 📁 language
- 📁 library
- 📄 ReadMe.txt
- 📄 component.php
- 📄 template_thumbnail.png
- 📄 functions.php
- 📄 index.php
- 📄 jquery.js
- 📄 modules.js
- 📄 script.js
- 📄 script.responsive.js
- 📄 templateDetails.xml
- 📄 template_preview.png

All of the files that make up the Template can be accessed for customization.

If you are not familiar with HTML and CSS coding, you should not make changes to these files.

If you are familiar, the files can be modified to further customize the page layouts.

Chapter 21

Templates

Learning Objectives

What's included in this chapter:

- ◆ Overview of templates.
- ◆ How templates work.
- ◆ Obtaining templates.
- ◆ Responsive design templates.
- ◆ Types of template acquisitions.
- ◆ Template frameworks by developers.
- ◆ Downloading templates.
- ◆ Installing templates.
- ◆ Designating the "default" template.
- ◆ Assigning templates to menu link items.
- ◆ Using template-creation software.
- ◆ Introduction to template overrides.

Understanding Templates

What a user sees in the browser window is generated by content entered by the administrator or others via the backend. But "how" they see it is accomplished by something completely different: Templates.

A *template* is an extension that has been designed to display web pages on a Joomla! 3–based website. Almost every website, regardless of operating platform, uses a template to display the content. Websites that do not use templates are becoming extinct, as it is much easier to use a template than to code each individual page manually.

However, the templates used among different website platforms are not the same. Joomla! 3 has its own template requirements to display content.

A CMS is a website that separates content from design and layout. This way, content administrators can enter content, and not be concerned about the details of color, page arrangement, appearance, and other factors. Content administrators are generally not very good at website design, so the CMS is perfect for their use. They enter the content and save it, and it appears on the website within the template's parameters, which come from the website designer.

How Templates Work

Templates work by being designated as the default for the website. There are a number of coded files that comprise the template, along with folders and the all-important Cascading Style Sheet (CSS).

When a user visits a website that has a template assigned to it, the template is fired up and the page displays. Then, based on the visual architecture of the template and the CSS associated with it, the content appears.

Here are some bits of knowledge you should know about templates:

◆ Templates are extensions.

◆ Templates are generally not available in the JED.

◆ Template enhancements are available in the JED.

◆ Templates are typically obtained from private developers.

◆ Templates install exactly the same way as other extensions.

◆ One template must be designated as the default.

◆ More than one template can be used on a website.

◆ Each template used can be different than the "default."

◆ Templates can be assigned to different web pages via the Menus assignment configuration settings.

◆ Most templates are built upon a custom "framework" different from Joomla! 3.

◆ If a template uses a framework, it is installed along with the template.

◆ There are programs available that create templates that can be installed on Joomla! 3 websites.

◆ There are extensions that allow changes in templates without changing any template files.

◆ Templates can have overrides that change the template configuration and display.

Where to Get Templates

Templates are not generally available via the JED, so they must be obtained directly from developers or from websites that sell or distribute them. If you search Google or any other search engine for "Joomla! 3 Templates," you will get a bunch of results. You will find both free and not-free template websites.

The best way to approach the template-shopping experience is to have in mind the kind of template and the "look and feel" you want from it. Then, visit the websites offering templates, look for Joomla! 3 types, and view the demo. If you like it, download and install it.

SOMETIMES FREE ISN'T FREE

When seeking free templates, you may find a few that are full-featured, but probably limited in that regard. Very often, the free version is a limited version of the commercial offering, in that some of the modification parameters have been disabled. If you find a free template that works for you, and you need all the features, your only choice is to purchase it from the developer. Keep in mind that free might not be totally free when it comes to template features and ability to set parameters.

Quite often, the free templates have a fixed link to the developers in the footer area of the web page. The only way the link can be removed is to purchase the premium version of the template.

Templates, Free or Otherwise

Templates are available from websites under these typical scenarios:

Free to Download and Use—This is a template that you can download and use on any Joomla! 3 website without any associated cost.

Free to Download, Pay for Full Version—A good number of quality templates can be downloaded in a stripped-down version. The full-featured template can be obtained via a fee.

Pay per Template—The individual template must be purchased *a la carte*. The templates may be able to be used on any number of websites, or be restricted to only one.

Membership Required—This requires a paid membership to a website or a club and allows downloading the templates. This is one of the most popular methods developers use to give access to their templates. If the membership includes unlimited downloads and use of the templates, the membership fee might just be well worth it.

Restricted Use—From among the paid template sources, you may find that some individual templates can be purchased *a la carte* or as part of a membership or club, whereas with others, you have to specify the domain on which the template is going to be used. Be aware of that possible restriction before purchasing a template with the intent to use it on one or more websites. You may need to pay for the template for each domain on which it will be used.

When you find a template that is appropriate for your website, decide whether you want to pay for it or not, and then obtain and download it for use.

Desktop and Mobile Templates

If you have a mobile device, and have accessed websites with it, you already know that some websites simply do not display very well on anything other than a desktop browser.

The latest in template design is to make the template responsive. That means the template displays equally well on desktop browsers and mobile device browsers, which typically implies the Apple Safari and the Android Chrome browsers.

When you're selecting a template to use on your website, and if you think that it might be accessed via mobile devices, search for one that claims to have a responsive design.

CHECK THE VERSION COMPATIBILITY

While embarking on a template hunt, make absolutely sure that the template is compatible with Joomla! 3. It should be a native template, one that was produced specifically for this version of Joomla.

Do not attempt to use a template that is not Joomla! 3 compatible.

Some developers deliver their templates so you can use them with different versions of Joomla! The template files are usually marked for each version. The downloaded files will generally have **UNZIP FIRST** as part of the filename.

Template Frameworks

Joomla! 3 has a template framework that is installed by default. The framework is coded to support the default templates for the front-end and the backend that were included during the installation process. Independent template developers often build their templates based on their framework and not the Joomla! 3 framework. Why? They do so to be able to add features and functionalities to the templates to make them work better or display content in unique ways.

It is not coincidental that the template developers mentioned here also have their own template frameworks, but some do not. Here are some of the developers who, for the most part, use their own specialized framework for their templates:

- ◆ T-3 Framework
- ◆ YJ Simple Grid
- ◆ Vertex
- ◆ XTC
- ◆ Expose
- ◆ Wright
- ◆ HD

- ◆ Gantry
- ◆ Gavick
- ◆ YooTheme
- ◆ Shape 5
- ◆ JV Framework
- ◆ Warp
- ◆ EF3

If we missed identification of any specific framework, we extend apologies.

Because of the complex and advanced coding required for template frameworks, we will not cover that subject in this book. Figure 21-1 displays how a framework integrates with Joomla! 3.

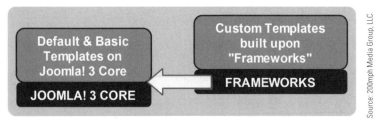

Figure 21-1 *The frameworks are added to the Joomla! 3 core as an additional method of programming templates. The templates then operate on both the Joomla! 3 core and the framework, which offers many more options for administrators to customize a template for a website.*

Using Bootstrap

Twitter has given the web designer world a program called *Bootstrap*, which is freely available to use. Bootstrap is a set of interface elements, layouts and JavaScript code, none of which you need to know anything about when using templates created by developers.

Essentially, Bootstrap consists of a foundation of HTML and CSS for use in building forms, buttons, labels, layout grids, navigation, and typography within a template. Most current templates use the bootstrap code within its general framework, which allows the template to be easier for you to use and customize.

If you search the Internet for "Twitter Bootstrap," you will get plenty of results that explain what it is, how it is used, and other similar topics.

Obtaining and Downloading Templates

As is done with all other extensions, templates, being extensions themselves, must be obtained and downloaded, and then installed into a Joomla! 3 website via the Extension Manager.

For demonstration purposes, you will download and install two templates that were generated by the template-building software called Artisteer. The templates that were chosen have module positions that match the default Joomla! 3 naming convention.

The goal is to replace the default Protostar template with a different one, and then configure the new template. Additionally, leaving Protostar as the default template, you'll assign a different template to content via its assignment to a menu link item.

For the following exercises, two templates will be located, downloaded, and installed. Then, each template will be applied to the website and some of the features will be discussed and put into effect.

EXERCISE 21-1: OBTAINING AND DOWNLOADING THE DEMOTEMPLATEA

Objective: This exercise will download the DemoTemplateA template from http://joomla3 bootcamp.com/demotemplates/.

Step 1. Open a browser window and go to the URL http://joomla3bootcamp.com/demotemplates/.

Step 2. Click on the DemoTemplateA.zip filename.

Step 3. Save the file to your computer downloads location.

Two different templates are going to be used for demonstration purposes, so complete Exercise 21-2 to download the second template.

EXERCISE 21-2: OBTAINING AND DOWNLOADING THE DEMOTEMPLATEB TEMPLATE

Objective: This exercise will download the DemoTemplateB template from http://joomla3 bootcamp.com/demotemplates/.

Step 1. Open a browser window and go to the URL http://joomla3bootcamp.com/demotemplates/.

Step 2. Click on the DemoTemplateB.zip filename.

Step 3. Save the file to your computer downloads location.

Installing Templates

Templates are extensions. Therefore, they install just like any other extension. Joomla! 3 makes no distinction in this regard, although templates are most likely only installed via the file download method.

EXERCISE 21-3: INSTALLING THE TEMPLATES

Objective: This exercise will install the two templates, downloaded in the previous exercises, into your working website.

Step 1. Open Extensions > Extension Manager in the top menu, or in the Admin Left Menu section of the Control Panel, under the Extensions heading. Click on the Install link in the left menu and then the Upload Package file.

Step 2. Browse to the file download location on your computer that has the DemoTemplateA file. Click on the zip filename. If you're using the Chrome browser, the Browse reads Choose File. Be aware of verbiage differences between browsers.

Step 3. If the zip filename displays next to the Browse button, execute the Upload & Install action. The name may take a few seconds to appear next to the button. The template, or any extension in fact, cannot be installed unless the filename appears next to the Browse button.

Step 4. When the installation is completed, the success message with the green background should display.

Step 5. Repeat these steps to install the DemoTemplateB template.

Step 6. Go back to the Control Panel by clicking the Joomla! logo at the top-left corner of the screen.

Step 7. Open the Template Manager via the Admin Left Menu under the Configuration heading.

Step 8. Verify the two templates are installed and available for use (Figure 21-2).

Source: 200mph Media Group, LLC.

Figure 21-2 *If the* **[A] [B]** *templates have been successfully installed, they will appear on the list of templates. The* **[C]** *eyeball icon indicates a preview of the template that can be viewed without making the template active. Click on one of the previews icons and check it. This preview also displays the template's module positions.*

This completes the download activities. You may have noted that downloading and installing templates is rather easy to do, and the process is the same as when you downloaded and installed either a component or a module.

Using Templates on a Website

Once templates are installed, they can be used. In the next exercise, one of the templates that was installed will be designated as the default for the website. Templates are used in two ways: (1) as the default or the main template, and (2) as templates that are assigned to a menu link item and display only when that item is clicked.

EXERCISE 21-4: DESIGNATING THE DEFAULT TEMPLATE

Objective: This exercise will demonstrate how the website's default template can be changed to another one that has been installed. If a template has been purchased (or was free) and downloaded, it can be used as the primary template for the website by assignment. The process is divided into three parts with consecutive action steps.

Step 1. With the Template Manager open, note the default templates for both the administrator and the site. The gold star should appear in the Default column and in the default installation they should be "isis - Default for the Administrator" and "Protostar - Default for the Site."

Step 2. Click on the grey star in the Default column for the DemoTemplateA template. The gold star should then display, indicating that template is now the default for the website.

Step 3. Go to the website front-end via another Browser tab. Refresh the screen.

The screen should display the website content with a menu at the top, although it does not appear the same as the Protostar template. This is because of the variations between the two templates. You will run into this situation frequently if you have installed the sample content into the website and use another template.

Step 4. When you're done viewing the front-end showing the DemoTemplateA, reset the default template back to Protostar.

Default or Assigned Templates

Templates can be either designated as the default or can be assigned to a menu link item, or a group of menu link items. In theory, every menu link item could have a different template associated/assigned with it. In practicality, only two or three templates would suffice for even the most complex website, although the possibility exists that a website could be created with the more complex template configuration.

In the demonstration, the Fruit Shop part of the website has a different template assigned to its menu link items. The Beez3 - Fruit Shop is being used for the Fruit Shop.

The Australian Parks uses the Protostar template with different modules, which are assigned to menu link items. Although these modules are among the activated ones, they display only when certain menu link items are clicked within the Australian Parks menus.

Templates can be assigned to menu link items, either one only or several. The way this is done is via the individual Template Manager, using the Menu Assignment feature.

The best way to understand how this is done is to examine the template that has been assigned.

EXERCISE 21-5: CHECKING MENU ASSIGNMENTS FOR TEMPLATES

Objective: You'll sometimes need to determine which menu link item has an assigned template. This exercise illustrates how to accomplish that task.

Step 1. Go to the Template Manager and click on the Beez3 - Fruit Shop template to open it.

Step 2. Open the Menus assignment tab.

Step 3. View the different menus for the site and note the checkmarks next to those menu link items in the respective assigned menus. Only those for the Fruit Shop are selected, so this template will only be used when those menu link items are clicked.

As you can see, any menu link item can be selected, which then creates the menu assignment for the template. This process is unique because each menu is listed, along with the individual menu link items within it. By simply selecting the menu link items within a menu, the immediate template can be designated to display.

If you are responsible for the administration of a larger corporate website and each department has a different template, the assignments to menu link items can be configured via the template menu assignment tab area.

EXERCISE 21-6: ASSIGNING A TEMPLATE TO A MENU LINK ITEM

Objective: This exercise guides you through the process of assigning a template to a menu link item so when it is clicked, the web page will open with the non-default template used to display the content.

Step 1. From within the Admin area, go to the Menu Manager in the Admin Left Menu.

Step 2. Open the My First Menu option.

Step 3. Click the green New button on the top-left navigation bar.

Step 4. Name the menu link item **Template Two** in the menu title box.

Step 5. For the menu item type, select Articles > Category Blog.

Step 6. For the Choose a Category option, assign the menu link item to the My First Category.

Step 7. Execute a Save & Close action.

Step 8. Go to the Template Manager and click on the DemoTemplateB template to open it.

Step 9. Open the Menus assignment tab.

Step 10. In the My First Menu section, check the Template Two menu link item.

Step 11. Execute a Save action.

Step 12. Go to the website front-end and refresh the browser window.

Step 13. Click the Template Two menu link item from My First Menu in the right column. The DemoTemplateB template should appear with some content. Again, because of the differences between templates, module positions, module class suffixes, and other parameters, some items do not display. There are a myriad of settings and configurations to change when a different template arrives in the middle of the movie. The best practice is to install the template into a clean, content-free website, then build the content and configure the modules and other items to conform to the template's requirements.

Step 14. Go back to the Template Manager and execute a Save & Close action.

Template Parameter Settings

The default Joomla! 3 templates that were installed have some, but very limited, options for setting such things as colors, fonts, layout, and more. Open the Protostar template, Advanced tab, and note the different settings that can be applied to make alterations to the template.

Go into any one of the demo templates that were installed. Note there is no Advanced tab.

Why is this? Recall the discussion about frameworks? Frameworks allow all of those parameter settings to be available. The two demo templates that were installed have only a limited number of settings. They are not built on any particular framework so only the default Joomla! 3 framework is being used.

Template-Creation Software

At present, there are primarily four template-creation programs that create Joomla! 3 templates, generate the necessary files for installation, and allow administrators to add them via the conventional extension installation method.

Here are four of the most popular programs that install on your computer (PC only):

Artisteer ($130.00 US)—Easy to use, lots of features, most all parameters are configurable, lots of options across the design spectrum. Everything in the template must be configured here before installing it on the website. There are no advanced settings for these templates. Beginners can be proficient in a short time. This program works with Joomla! 3.x via developer's server-confirmation when generating template files, which prevents pirated software from being used. We agree.

Template Toaster ($99.00 US)—Also easy to use, lots of features, most all parameters are configurable, lots of options across the design spectrum. Beginners can also learn this platform in a short time with some experimenting. You see the design results immediately, just like Artisteer. Once you understand how templates work, you can knock them out rather quickly.

MAESTRO Creative Template Designer – ($125 US)—This is a pretty complicated and advanced package. Probably best for experienced template designers who appreciate the intricate actions involved in doing so. The learning curve on this one is pretty steep! You really must understand templates and layouts to use this software.

Template Creator (about $33.00 US)—Not as complicated as Artisteer or Template Toaster, but a worthy program nonetheless. It has features that others do not have. What makes this one unique it that it is a Joomla! 3 extension plug-in and is used directly within the Joomla! admin backend as a component. Very easy to use!

Did we miss a good one? Let us know about it at joomla3bootcamp.com.

No Frameworks Involved

Other than the Joomla! 3 core framework, the template creators that have been referenced do not have any special framework upon which the templates function. That means that many of the handy-dandy controls for setting template parameters may not be available in the final template that is installed on the website.

Make sure you confirm that the current version of any template-creator software does, in fact, create templates for Joomla! 3.x.

More about template-creation software can be found at joomla3bootcamp.com. There will be an ongoing addition of information about templates and the use of the programs listed above, as well any new ones that are made available.

Using Template Overrides

Let's assume you are using the Protostar template on your website and you have made modifications to something via changing the Joomla! 3 core code for the template. This, of course, is an advanced set of tasks that should only be undertaken by those skilled in HTML and CSS coding. These changes alter the default installation files.

Now then, let's assume that a little ways down the road an update is issued for your version of Joomla! 3 and you go ahead and do the update. This update likely will also install the Default files, which includes the templates, all over again. Guess what? Those changes that were made to the template via code changes now have vanished because the files have been automatically overwritten.

How do you make changes and prevent them from being nuked during updates? Joomla! 3 has a feature built-in called *template overrides*, which allows you to make changes in such a way so as not to have them destroyed during updates. Every Joomla! 3 template has the provision for creating these overrides and allowing serious customization of the templates and content components.

This is an advanced-skills topic, so there is limited discussion about it in this book. You should be aware of the possibility of doing overrides in Joomla! 3. The companion website for this book located at **joomla3bootcamp.com** has additional information and instructions on the use of template overrides.

Summary

In this chapter, you learned:

◆ What templates are.

◆ How templates work.

◆ Where to obtain templates.

◆ About responsive design templates.

◆ Different types of template acquisitions.

◆ About template frameworks by developers.

◆ How to download a template.

◆ How to install a template.

◆ How to designate a template as the default.

◆ Methods of assigning templates to menu link items.

◆ Template-creation software exists to build templates.

◆ Template overrides can be created to make changes.

Chapter 22

Images and Media

Learning Objectives

What's included in this chapter:

- Differences in media types.
- Understanding how images and media are placed on websites.
- What the Media Manager does.
- Examining the Media Manager.
- Types of files and images allowed.

Understanding Images and Media

Images and media are used extensively on websites to enhance content. Joomla! 3 accommodates the ability to place images and media into content. Images can be used on websites as icons, photos in articles, photos in modules, photo albums, photo galleries, and even as sliding image displays or image carousals.

Images are conceptually nothing more than icons and photos, or graphics that have been created for insertion into the website. Graphics (images) are abundant on most websites and are different from media.

Media is generally considered to be movies or videos, which can be found on YouTube and other feeder websites. Joomla! 3, unfortunately, doesn't have a built-in feature, plug-in, module, or any other way to place media into content. But there are many such extensions that accommodate that need. For example, if you want to include a YouTube video, install an extension from the JED, and then insert the video-viewing element onto the web page.

Using the Media Manager

Images included in Joomla! 3 websites are contained in the Media Manager. It is not necessary to create a special place to store images. That location is already there and is accessible via the Control Panel's Admin Left Menu under Content.

If you recall from Chapter 19, "Modules," there was no type of module that specifically allowed the placement of images or media into module positions on a web page. If you want to insert image galleries or media content, you must install and configure a specialized extension. There are plenty of them in the JED that will do the job. The Custom HTML module could be used, of course, to add an image for placement into a module position, but that's about the extent of what it can do.

By default, images added to articles and modules are stored in the Media Manager. Graphics that are uploaded for inclusion are also placed into the Media Manager.

Let's take a look at the Media Manager and learn a few things about the management of images.

EXERCISE 22-1: EXAMINING THE MEDIA MANAGER

Objective: This exercise provides a tour of the Media Manager, where images and graphics are stored after upload.

Step 1. Open Content > Media Manager from the top menu, or in the Admin Left Menu section of the Control Panel.

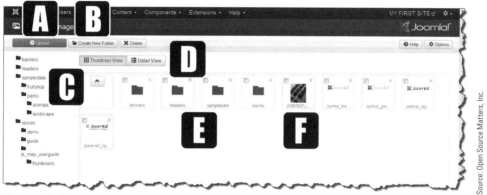

Source: Open Source Matters, Inc.

Figure 22-1 *The opening view of the Media Manager displays everything needed to manage your image files.*

The Media Manager contains the following features, as shown in Figure 22-1:

[A]—Images can be manually uploaded into the Media Manager using the green Upload button. The Upload process is not unlike the method used to add extensions to the website. This action places the uploaded image into the main area of the Media Manager, or into the folder that is open when the upload is initiated.

[B]—If the website content requires it, you can add folders to the Media Manager to store/classify your images in a more organized manner.

[C]—The left side of the Media Manager shows a standard tree view of the folders in use in the Media Manager. The left side mimics the main area display.

[D]—The Media Manager main area can be viewed graphically, such as when the Media Manager is opened. However, you can view a list view by clicking the Detail View button. This is similar to the left list but here, the actual image names are displayed.

[E]—The main area shows the actual images that are located in the Media Manager and the folders that have been created.

[F]—These are image thumbnails that help you select the image when placing it into an article or module.

Step 2. Click on the Detail View button and observe how the image folders are arranged.

Step 3. Return to the regular view by clicking the Thumbnail View button.

Step 4. Click on the Sampledata folder. Two sub-folders should display for the Fruit Shop and Parks areas.

Step 5. Open the Fruit Shop folder, which will display the images used in articles for that part of the website.

Step 6. Use the ^ (the up arrow icon) in the left box to return to the main area. It takes two clicks to get back to that location.

You can browse around the Media Manager and view the images and graphics within the different folders. When the image selection is used in an article or module, the system automatically looks there for previously installed images and graphics.

Types of Images Allowed

Images have many different formats that dictate the clarity and physical size of the actual image or graphics files. Only the file, image, or graphics formats that are set to be allowed can be uploaded to the Media Manager.

For the most part, this ensures that only images are uploaded and that harmful files are not uploaded to the website.

The legal file types are .bmp, .csv, .doc, .gif, .ico, .jpg, .jpeg, .odg, .odp, .ods, .odt, .pdf, .png, .ppt, .swf, .txt, .xcf, .xls, .BMP, .CSV, .DOC, .GIF, .ICO, .JPG, .JPEG, .ODG, .ODP, .ODS, .ODT, .PDF, .PNG, .PPT, .SWF, .TXT, .XCF, and .XLS.

Note that both the lowercase and uppercase versions are included, and that .jpg and .jpeg are both allowed.

You can restrict file uploads by editing the types for both files and images via the Options button in the Media Manager's upper menu. For example, if you do not want other administrators to use the excessively large .bmp image files, remove that extension from Legal Extensions (File Types) and the Legal Image Extensions (File Types).

Using Media, Videos, and More

Media (movies and similar files) is not normally added to a Joomla! 3 website without using an extension dedicated to that task. There are many such extensions in the JED that allow you to insert videos, Flash files, and third-party video library files.

If you want to include media on your website, you should use an extension that will do exactly what you want it to do. There are extensions to add all of the file types, including image galleries and more.

Most of these extensions come as components with modules, and some also have plug-ins. This type of extension configuration allows you to administrate the images and determine how/where they are displayed on the website. Plug-ins affect how some of the extensions function. Be sure to read the user instructions for these extensions when you download and install them.

If you install a media extension and don't like the way it works, by all means, uninstall the extension as soon as possible. There is no need to keep them installed if they are not going to be used. It's good extensions management policy.

> **SCROLL THE MEDIA UPLOADER**
>
> When you're in an article or module manager, and you click the Image button to insert something, make sure you scroll down to access the Browse button to find the images on your computer. The window isn't initially big enough, so make sure you scroll down a bit to find what you need.

Summary

In this chapter, you learned:

◆ The differences in media types.

◆ What the Media Manager does and how it's used.

◆ The different sections of the Media Manager.

◆ Which types of files and images are allowed.

The Media Manager allows full control and management of all the images used on the website.

When images are added to a content item via the Article's Manager or the Custom HTML Module, the images are added to the "stories" folder in the Media Manager.

Images can be manually added to the Media Manager and inserted via the Article's Manager.

Chapter 23

Access Control List and Permissions

Learning Objectives

What's included in this chapter:

- Overview of ACL.
- Where to administer ACL in the backend.
- Actions required to implement ACL.
- Overview of ACL permissions.
- ACL actions that can be set.
- How to view existing permissions.
- Overview of access levels.
- Rules that apply to ACL.
- Understanding ACL configuration.
- How to create a user group.
- How to define access levels for a group.
- How to set allowed action permissions.
- How to assign a user to a group.
- Controlling access to components.
- Controlling access to content items.
- Differences between global- and item-level ACL.

Understanding Users, Access Control List, and Permissions

One of the more recent features that has been added to Joomla! 3 is the very powerful method to control users' access to your website, called ACL (Access Control List). These are the users responsible for adding and editing content, not simply website visitors.

If you have a small, personal website, you probably won't use ACL, so you can skip this chapter for the time being. ACL is relevant only when there is a large number of content managers who need certain permissions and restrictions on what content they can manage, edit, or change. ACL is used globally in Joomla! 3 to reference access control and the access control list.

If you have a large or corporate website to administer, and it requires that you control who can edit the site, then ACL is something you want to learn and master. A good example of the need for ACL is a newspaper website where there are many content managers, many of them at remote locations. The actual content they can individually access will likely be controlled and limited to their own topic areas. Sports editors only edit the sports section, social editors can edit the social section, and so on.

Where to Administer ACL

There isn't any sort of dedicated manager in the backend that is used for controlling access and permissions. They are controlled at the user group and content item level. You can give individual users permissions via their group assignments, which determine what a group can and cannot do to content.

The best way to learn how to use ACL is to step through the process. However, it will be useful to you to understand the basics involved in Joomla! 3 ACL first. When you first encounter ACL, it might be confusing. By the end of this chapter, you will have performed all of the necessary tasks to have an understanding of how to implement any type of ACL on a website, should you need to do so.

How to Administer ACL

There are several major steps involved on the part of the administrator, including the following:

Action 1. Manually create users or allow users to self-register via a user registration function. This puts the users into the system, so to speak. Users become registered after completing the process. Administrators then must manually assign them to other user groups.

Action 2. Create user groups and assign users to those groups. Users can have many roles via their assignment to different groups, which have different permissions.

Action 3. Set the specific viewing access for groups to view content items.

Action 4. Set the specific action permissions for the groups (into which users are assigned).

> ### Don't Confuse Doing and Viewing
>
> Within the ACL there are two different functions—*doing* and *viewing*. The latter sets permissions on who can view content. The doing part addresses which users can create, edit, or modify the content. Please keep in mind that these two functions are separate and distinctly different in the ACL scheme of things.

Understanding General ACL Permissions

By default, there are five groups of users, some of which have sub-groups, as illustrated (Figure 23-1). The Public, Guest, Manager, Registered, and Super Users groups, as well as their respective sub-groups, are all created by default during installation.

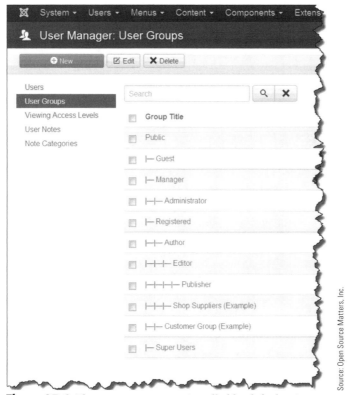

Figure 23-1 *These user groups are installed by default using example content during the installation process.*

In the default installation, there are two other groups containing example content—Shop Suppliers and Customer Group. These are part of the sample data from the Fruit Shop part of the website.

If you look into the User Manager: User Groups, and open any one of the groups, you can see how an individual group is assigned within the hierarchy. By default, all groups are assigned to the parent group called "Public."

Setting the Seven User Actions

Within the ACL structure, there are seven user actions for which you can set permissions, and they are based on the public permissions.

Configure—User can edit her own user options, which include the actual editor she uses and other user-specific settings. These settings apply individually to the user.

Access Administration Interface—User can log in to the Admin backend, but not as a super user. He can log in and access only those components and content items that he has affirmative permissions for. Users must be assigned to the Special group, along with any other user group in which they are also assigned.

Create—User can create a content item.

Delete—User can delete a content item.

Edit—User can edit any content she created, or anything she has the permission to edit.

Edit State—User can change the state of a content item such as published or unpublished.

Edit Own—User can only edit the categories or content items he created. This action is limited to content in certain managers, such as the Article Manager and the Contact Manager.

EXERCISE 23-1: VIEWING THE GROUP PERMISSIONS

Objective: This exercise introduces the permissions that are assigned to the different user groups for managing website content.

Step 1. If you're not already there, log in to the Administrator backend of the website.

Step 2. Open the User Manager in the Admin Left Menu or via the top menu under Users.

Step 3. On the far-right side of the top menu, open the Options button to view ACL configuration. It's on the Component tab.

Step 4. Open the Permissions tab. This screen shows all of the user groups and their respective group permissions, which are limited to six. Remember that these are user-level permissions. The Public group is obviously not allowed to do anything actionable with regard to content.

Step 5. Click on the Manager to observe the permissions for that group. The users in that group are not allowed to configure anything nor access the Admin backend.

Step 6. Next, click on the Super Users group and note that the Configure and Access Administration interfaces are now allowed for this group.

Step 7. Click through the Registered, Author, Editor, and Publisher groups and note how the permissions change based on the users in the group's content responsibilities.

Step 8. Note the Select New Setting column. Open one of the drop-downs and view the parameter settings, which are Inherited, Allowed, and Denied. Also note that the default setting is Inherited, which comes from the next higher level of a sub-group—and all of these are based on the Public group, which has no specifically allowed actions that can be performed by users.

Access Levels

When you set up a login module, you can set access for users who register by default. For the most part, these users are assigned to the Registered group, which simply means they can view any content that has been designated to be read-only by users who have logged in to the front-end.

The Registered group has no access whatsoever to the backend of the website. These same users can also be assigned to another group following registration, which could allow them to log in to the website backend, but it must be done manually by the administrator.

There are four possible default group assignments for users who go through the Registration process:

Guest—Any user who views any part of your website is, in fact, a guest user.

Public—This isn't any different from the guest user. This group allows all website visitors to view everything on the front-end, except restricted content, which requires the user to log in.

Registered—Restricts user access to both public and registered content items that have been designated to require user login before viewing. This is the most basic ACL group permission setting. The registered content configuration/access permissions are assigned by the Joomla! 3 core features.

Special—This is a unique group, into which all levels of users may be assigned, and the function is to allow users to log in to the Admin backend of the website. That is all this group is allowed to do. To restrict user's actions in the backend, they must be assigned to another group that has controls for these actions, and the content items or components must be designated to that group. Remember, this is for simple backend login ability and does not relate to component or content item management action permissions.

All this boils down to doing and viewing, which is what the ACL system is all about. This amounts to splitting the website content into public and restricted parts. Then, in the content management part that's accessible via the Admin backend, you'll find the doing part. There, you can grant or deny permissions to users in designated groups.

Understanding the General ACL Rules

It is easier to understand the ACL rules if you understand the permissions and their assignments:

Rule 1. If a registration system is used, users are automatically assigned into the Registered group upon email verification or by administrator assignment actions.

You can assign users to any other group during registration. This is accomplished via the Options button at the top right. Select the desired assigned group in the drop-down for New User Registration group. Only one group can be designated. Assignment to multiple groups can be done only by the super user after the user has registered.

Rule 2. To access restricted content, users must be assigned to the Registered group. This group can only log in to the front-end of the website. In addition to public content, users can also view the content that has been designated as restricted to registered users.

Rule 3. To log in to the Admin backend, users *must* also be assigned to the Special group, in addition to any other group(s) into which they may be assigned. Not doing so will result in the user not being able to access the backend, regardless of ACL settings for the user's group.

Rule 4. Users must also have Action permissions to access the administration interface in the backend, which allows them to access components and content items that have been designated to allow access by a specific group.

Rule 5. Permissions for a group or sub-group are inherited from the group above it, or from the Public group if there is no sub-group. This is akin to the parent and child relationships discussed in earlier chapters.

Rule 6. Group or sub-group settings cannot override the parameters of the parent group. For example, if anything in the parent is set to denied, it cannot be set to allowed in a sub-group. This is important! The parent must have permissions that the child can inherit.

REGISTRATION INTO MULTIPLE GROUPS

Users who register on a Joomla! 3 website can, by default, be assigned to only one group. There is an extension in the JED that allows users to select the groups into which they would like to join when registering. It is an opt-in feature and not an automatic multi-group assignment method.

ACL Levels

You need to understand the levels of permissions that are assigned and at what point, and under which conditions, overrides can be assigned to groups. This is where the ACL shows its strengths—allowing overrides at various levels when managing content (Figure 23-2).

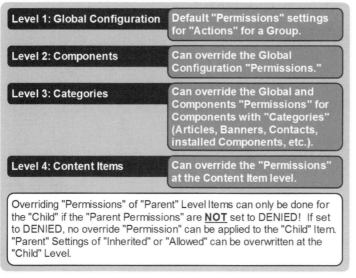

Figure 23-2 *The four levels work together, based on the permissions of the parent and the permissions of the child group level. The notable fact is that if the parent level is* denied permission *on something, it cannot be overridden at the child level.*

The ACL Configuration Process

Initially, the ACL configuration process might be a tad confusing, but if you follow a systematic approach to setting up the Groups, Access Levels, and Permissions for Users, you'll master it in no time.

After you've set the group and other permissions, you need to assign the users to their respective groups. Here are the steps involved:

Step 1. Create a group.

Step 2. Set the global viewing access levels for the group.

Step 3. Set the global actions permissions for the group.

Step 4. Create/assign a user to the group.

Step 5. Set the permissions at the component or content item level.

The following exercises address each part of the ACL Management process, so follow the steps exactly as outlined.

Creating a User Group

To establish the ACL, users must be assigned to groups. This is done as described in the following exercise (Figure 23-3).

EXERCISE 23-2: CREATING A USER GROUP

Objective: This exercise illustrates how a user group is created. Two user groups will be created, which will be used in later exercises.

Step 1. If you're not already there, log in to the Administrator backend of the website.

Step 2. In the Admin Left Menu, open the User Manager. Then choose User Groups in the Admin Menu below Users. This displays the website's user groups. Note the blue highlighted User Groups location in the left menu.

Step 3. In the top menu, click the green New button.

Step 4. For the group title, enter **Group A**.

Step 5. Leave Public as the group parent.

Step 6. Execute the Save & New button.

Step 7. Create a new **Group B**, using the previous steps.

Step 8. Execute the Save & Close button. The two groups should appear near the top of the User Groups list, under the Public group.

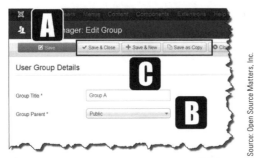

Source: Open Source Matters, Inc.

Figure 23-3 *Groups can be given any* **[C]** *group title and assigned to any* **[B]** *group parent. After you create a group, execute a* **[A]** *saving action.*

Defining the Viewing Access Levels

You've now created two separate user groups, both having the parent of Public. They will both inherit the actions and permissions from that group. If you recall, when viewing the individual groups earlier, the Public group has no permissions. The two other options for Public are Allowed and Denied.

The next step in the process is to set the viewing access levels for the groups you just created.

EXERCISE 23-3: SET VIEWING ACCESS LEVELS FOR A GROUP

Objective: This exercise illustrates how the viewing permissions are set for a group, which gives the groups the permissions necessary to view what they need to view.

Step 1.   Assuming you are still in the User Manager: User Groups area, click on Viewing Access Levels in the left menu.

Step 2.   Create a new viewing level named **Group Viewing Level**.

Step 3.   Execute a Save & Close action.

Step 4.   Open the Special level in the User Manager: Viewing Access Levels list.

Step 5.   Select Group A and Group B for the Special group. This will allow them to log in to the Admin backend (Figure 23-4).

Step 6.   Execute a Save & Close action.

Step 7.   Open the Registered level in the User Manager: Viewing Access Levels list.

Step 8.   Select Group A and Group B for the Registered group. This will allow them to log in to the website front-end to view content that's for registered users only.

Step 9.   Execute a Save & Close action.

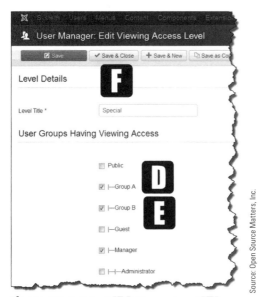

Figure 23-4 *Select* **[D]** *Group A and* **[E]** *Group B to assign them to the Special group. Then execute the* **[F]** *Save & Close action. You need to do this only for the user groups/users who will be permitted to log in to the backend. If this permission is not needed, do not assign the group to the special viewing access level.*

Setting the Allowed Actions for a Group

The next step is to set the actions that are associated with each group. Actions relate to the permissions the group has to perform tasks related to content.

EXERCISE 23-4: SETTING ACTION PERMISSIONS FOR A GROUP

Objective: This exercise demonstrates how action permissions are established for user groups, which determine what groups can do when accessing components or content items.

Step 1. Assuming you are still in the backend, click the Joomla! logo at the top left of the screen to open the Control Panel.

Step 2. Open the global configuration using the link in the left menu under Configuration.

Step 3. Open the Permissions tab for the global configuration.

Step 4. Click on Group A in the column under the Public group.

The display shows which action permissions are available for Group A and the settings that are applied by default. Review the list of action parameters. These are the global permission levels for this group.

Step 5. Set the new action permissions for Group A, as shown in Figure 23-5.

If you need to know the exact function of each action, mouse over the action name and view the pop-up message.

Step 6. Execute a Save action.

Step 7. Complete the same permissions settings for Group B.

Step 8. Execute a Save & Close action.

Step 9. Check the permissions for each group to make sure they have changed.

ADMIN LOGIN VS. ACCESS ADMINISTRATIVE INTERFACE

Within permission settings, there are two parameters that deal with the Admin access. Here is what happens for each:

Admin Login—If the user group is also assigned to the Special group, users will be able to access the Admin backend and manage components and content items. When the permissions are set to Not Allowed, though, they will be able to see everything, but will not be able to manage any component or content items.

Access Administration Interface—Allows the users in the group to access the full backend, with the exception of the website's global configuration. This should be reserved for highly privileged users, yet not to the level of having super user privileges.

Under both circumstances, the users must also be assigned to the Special group, which enables their access to the Admin backend.

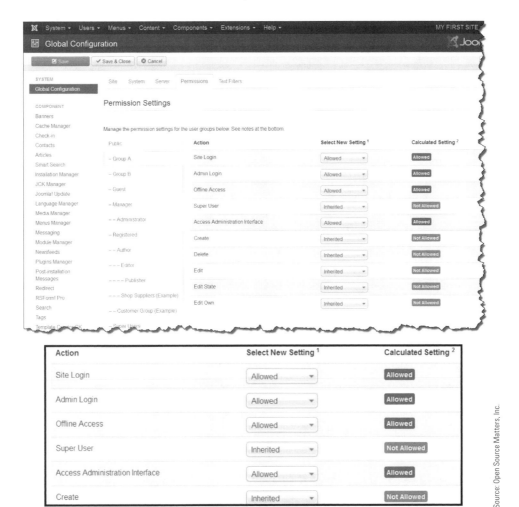

Figure 23-5 *This is a global setting where the user group automatically has the permissions on every component or content item in the backend. By* not *setting the ability to do anything but view the component or content item, the control of the actions has been transferred down to the item level. All of the items can be viewed, but cannot be edited or deleted.*

EXERCISE 23-5: CREATING USERS AND ASSIGNING THEM TO A GROUP

Objective: This exercise creates two users who will be assigned to a group and be able to log in and access the Admin backend.

Step 1.   Assuming you are still in the backend, click the Joomla! logo at the top left of the screen to open the Control Panel.

Step 2.   Open the User Manager from the Control Panel's Admin Left Menu or via the top menu, under Users.

Step 3. Create a user by clicking the green New button at the top left of the screen.

Step 4. Enter the following into the text fields to create this new user:

Name	**Test User 1**
Login Name	testuser1
Password	**-enter a password-**
Confirm Password	**-confirm the password-**
Email	noemail@noemail.com

Step 5. Execute a Save action.

Step 6. Open the Assigned User Groups tab in the User Manager: Edit User Manager for testuser1.

Step 7. Assign the testuser1 to Group A.

Step 8. Execute a Save & Close action.

Step 9. Click the green New button to create another user. The email cannot be the same as the previous user, so change that also.

Name	**Test User 2**
Login Name	testuser2
Password	**-enter a password-**
Confirm Password	**-confirm the password-**
Email	noemail2@noemail.com

Step 10. Execute a Save action.

Step 11. Open the Assigned User Groups tab in the User Manager: Edit User Manager for testuser2.

Step 12. Assign testuser2 to Group B.

Step 13. Execute a Save & Close action.

Step 14. Log out of the backend as the super user.

Step 15. Log in to the backend as the testuser1 with the password you assigned. You should be logged in to the Control Panel.

Step 16. Click on any of the managers in the Admin Left Menu area.

You should be able to click on the content managers, yet no Admin controls will display for creating, editing, or otherwise managing any of the backend. The managers can be viewed, but no management buttons appear at the top.

Notice that the Australian Parks article is accessible. Why? The default installation is allowing this article to be viewed, but you can't access the management buttons.

Why is this? There have been no Permissions for the user group to allow *actions* within components or content items. The permissions are limited to viewing only.

Step 17.   Log out of the backend as **testuser1**.

Step 18.   Log in to the backend as the **testuser2**. You should be logged in to the Control Panel.

Here again, you should be able to click on the content managers, but no Admin controls will display for creating, editing, or otherwise managing any of the backend.

This situations exists because no permissions have been granted on the component or content item level to allow the users in Group A or Group B to access them.

Controlling Component Access

Now that you've dealt with the assignments and permissions, the next step is to give the user group permissions to do something with a component. While components may generate content, there is a difference between the two. Content is generally considered to be categories and articles. Components are the mini-applications that run inside Joomla! 3 and can generate a wide range of content that can be used on the website and displayed via a menu link item.

In Exercise 23-6, you'll enable the Group A users to do the following within the Contact Manager:

◆ Access the administrative interface.

◆ Create contact categories.

◆ Create contacts and assign them to categories.

◆ Delete contacts.

◆ Edit contacts.

◆ Edit the state of the contacts.

EXERCISE 23-6: SETTING PERMISSIONS FOR THE CONTACTS COMPONENT

Objective: This exercise sets the necessary action permissions for Group A to manage the Contacts Manager via the Admin backend.

Step 1.   Assuming you are still in the backend and logged in as the super user, click the Joomla! logo at the top of the screen to open the Control Panel.

Step 2.   Open the Components > Contacts Manager.

Step 3.   Open the Options tab in the Contact Manager: Contacts menu at the top, far right.

Step 4.   Click on the Permissions tab to the far right.

Step 5.   When the screen opens, click on the Group A link under the Public group. Set the action permissions for this group, as shown in Figure 23-6.

Source: Open Source Matters, Inc.

Figure 23-6 *Because the users should have permissions to do all things* except *configure the component, the Configure setting must be set to Not Allowed.*

Step 6. Log out of the backend as the super user and log in as the **testuser1**.

Step 7. Click on any manager in the Admin Left Menu. Viewing is permitted, but you can't configure anything—the absence of the menu bars is the indicator.

Step 8. In the top menu, open the Components > Contacts Manager, which should result in the control menu bar being displayed at the top.

Step 9. Open the Components > Banner Manager and note that no menu appears. That's because there were no action permissions assigned in this manager's options control to allow this user group into the Banner Manager.

Controlling Content Item Access

In the previous exercise, viewing was allowed but the actions were not until the component's options were changed to allow the latter. This same kind of control can be implemented on the category and article, or content-item level.

The controls that can be implemented at this level can be global or item-specific. However, the Edit Own parameter has been added because you might want to limited users to only take actions on content items they specifically created. If Edit is also selected, that will allow the user to edit any content item.

Exercise 23-7 guides you through the user permissions for content items, such as categories and articles. The Group B users will be granted permissions relating to a content item and its category.

EXERCISE 23-7: SETTING PERMISSIONS FOR A CONTENT ITEM

Objective: This exercise shows you how to grant permissions to Group B in order to manage categories and articles.

Step 1. Log in to the backend as the super user. Click the Joomla! logo at the top of the screen to open the Control Panel.

Step 2. Open the Content > Article Manager.

Step 3.   Open the Options tab in the Article Manager: Articles menu at the top.

Step 4.   Click on the Permissions tab to the far right.

Step 5.   When the screen opens, click on the Group B link under the Public group. Set the action permissions for this group, as shown in Figure 23-7.

Figure 23-7 *Because the user should have permission to do all things* except *configure the component, edit it, and edit its state, the settings for these three options must be set to Not Allowed.*

Step 6.   Execute a Save & Close action.

Step 7.   Log out of the backend as the super user and log in as the testuser2.

Step 8.   Open the Content > Category Manager > Add New Category Manager.

Step 9.   Name the new category **Group B Category**.

Step 10.   The status of this item is automatically set to Published by default.

Step 11.   Execute a Save & Close action.

When the category list displays, note that this new category is the only one the user has access to—which is the correct result for the permissions for this user's group.

Step 12.   Open the Content > Article Manager > Add New Article Manager.

Step 13.   Create the article by naming it **Group B Article**, and assign it to the Group B category that you previous created. Enter some random text into the editor box.

Step 14.   Execute a Save & Close action.

When the article list displays, scroll down the screen and find the article. Note also that the only accessible article is the one created by this user, which is consistent with the permissions granted to the user's group.

However, because you set Edit State to Not Allowed, users in this group cannot change the Unpublished state of the article. This must be done by another user—for example—a managing editor.

GLOBAL VS. ITEM-LEVEL PERMISSIONS

If permissions are allowed for a group at the global level, all components and content items are accessible by the users in the group—and the actions are globally applied. That means, in order to deny any actions, you need to set the denials separately for every component or content item. That can be tedious. This is called a *grant-all, override-many* method of accomplishing permission limitations.

If the other method is employed, as you learned in the previous exercises, the permissions for the user group must be granted in the affirmative, which is likely the easier (and more secure) route. This is called the *deny-all, override-few* method.

Of course, if the Edit State was set to Allowed, the user would have been able to publish the content item. It is a good example on how fine-tuning the user groups and the permissions to take actions can make ACL a powerful tool for large, many-editor websites.

The Super User Controls All Permissions

The super user has administration-level permission to override any of the viewing access levels or actions permissions for any applicable component and content item. This kind of upper-level control allows the super user to maintain full control of the components and content items, regardless of previous settings. The super user can simply change the settings and configure everything in the backend.

If you have a small website with only one or two content managers, you won't likely need to use these ACL techniques. However, using these ACL techniques on large corporate websites is a highly important factor in maintaining control of who can access and manage what.

You can find more information about ACL on the book's website at joomla3bootcamp.com.

Summary

In this chapter, you learned:

◆ What ACL is and how it functions.

◆ Where to administer ACL in the backend.

◆ What actions are required to implement ACL.

◆ About the ACL permissions.

◆ Which ACL actions can be set.

◆ How to view existing ACL permissions.

◆ About different ACL access levels.

◆ Which rules apply to ACL.

◆ The general ACL configuration.

◆ How to create a user group.

◆ How to define access levels to a group.

◆ How to set allowed action permissions.

◆ How to assign a user to a group.

◆ How to control access to components.

◆ How to control access to content items.

◆ The differences between global and item-level ACL.

◆ The super user is in control of all permissions.

By default, and based on the language selection during the installation process, English (UK) is the language for the website.

There are spelling variations in UK English as comparted to US English.

Additional languages may be added to the website at any time. Additionally, the Google Language Translater can be added as an extension, allowing users to select their lanugage of choice.

Chapter 24

Using the Menu System

Learning Objectives

What's included in this chapter:

- ◆ How to create menus.
- ◆ Differences between templates.
- ◆ How to create a menu module.
- ◆ How to use a menu to display content.
- ◆ How to display content from categories and articles.
- ◆ How to display content from components.
- ◆ How to show or hide menus.
- ◆ Menu extensions are available.

Using the Menu System

Navigation on websites is generally accomplished through a system of menus and menu link items. Joomla! 3 is no different than any other website. In fact, it has a built-in system for creating and managing menus, where you can add menu link items to display website content, which are loosely termed "web pages."

Creating Menus

The process of creating menus is actually a backward process, in that the menu is created after the content has been added, or the menu exists through content that will be generated from a component. The content must exist in order to create a menu link item to it.

Here are the steps for creating a menu link item that opens as a web page:

Action 1. If the content is coming from a component, configure the component as needed. If there is a Contacts directory, for example, create the contact categories and add contacts to them.

Action 2. If the content is coming from articles, create the categories and then create/write the articles and distribute them within the categories.

Action 3. Create a menu in the menu manager, which automatically creates a link to "Add a Module for this Menu Type" in the Linked Modules column.

Action 4. Create a menu module in the module manager and connect it to the menu.

Action 5. Assign the Menu module to a module position for the template being used.

Action 6. Assign the Menu module to display on the website, such as on all pages or only on selected pages, or not certain pages, or a combination of pages.

Action 7. Implement any desired options that control how the menu displays and other similar parameters.

Action 8. Create menu link items to the items you want to display.

When those steps are completed, there will be a menu with a menu link item that will open some sort of content when it's clicked.

At this point, pages and pages of this book could be devoted to the general operation of menus, but that's not the goal of this book. Let's move directly into the menu-building process and create a new menu for the "My First Site" demonstration.

Big Differences Between Templates

Keep in mind, when performing the exercises, that Joomla!'s default built-in menu system is being used. No additional extensions need to be installed to create the menus. However, also keep in mind that the look-feel-function of the built-in menu system for templates may be—and should be—dramatically different.

If you might use a third-party template for future websites, especially those built upon the frameworks that various developers use, take heed. The template's menu system might be considerably different than the built-in ones, and may have many more features coded by the developers.

Adding and Using the Menu System

The best way to learn how to use the menu system is to create a menu and go through all the actions needed to create the menu link items connected to your content.

There is plenty of example content provided on the website, so you don't need to create any dummy text. The existing content listed in the components and categories/articles is used in the exercises in this chapter.

WHAT? NO SCREENSHOTS?

The steps involved in creating menus and making them work are actually pretty simple. By now, you should have enough experience in navigating around the Admin backend to do things pretty much on your own.

So, for this chapter, screenshots have been purposefully omitted so you can follow the instructions and determine what to do where, all on your own—well, with some guidance, of course.

The process for almost all Joomla! 3 backend tasks is so characteristically similar, that this chapter is a good one to try on your own. If you have successfully completed the exercises in the previous chapters, the next series of exercises should be a breeze.

Getting the Menu and Module Ready

The first two things that you must accomplish when creating menus are to create the menu and then create the Menu module and assign it to a module position on the template.

EXERCISE 24-1: CREATING A MENU

Objective: This exercise demonstrates how to create a menu.

Step 1. If you're not already there, log in to the Administrator backend of the website.

Step 2. Open the Menu Manager in the Admin Left Menu section of the Control Panel. This will display a list of the menus that have already been created.

Step 3. Click the green New button at the top left of the screen. This opens the Menu Manager: Add Menu screen.

Step 4. Two items of information are needed here. Enter **My First Menu** into the Title and the Menu Type text fields.

Step 5. Execute a Save & Close action, which will save the menu and open the Menu Manager: Menus screen with the addition displayed at the bottom of the list.

At this point, remain on this screen and move to the next exercise.

EXERCISE 24-2: CREATING THE MENU MODULE AND ASSIGNING IT TO MODULE POSITION

Objective: This exercise shows you how to create the menu module for the menu you created in the last exercise.

Step 1. In the Linked Modules column of the list, for the My First Menu item, click on "Add a Module for this Menu Type." This will switch over to the Module Manager: Module Menu screen.

Step 2. Give the module a title by entering **My First Menu** into the text field.

Step 3. Add the module to the position called Right [position-7] and make sure that you have selected this position for the Protostar template. There are other templates as part of the website, so be sure to select the correct one.

Step 4. Execute a Save action.

Step 5. Open the Menu Assignment tab and make sure the Module Assignment is set to On All Pages in the drop-down.

Step 6. Execute a Save & Close action.

At this point, you've created a menu and a menu module, and you've set the module to display in the right position on the Protostar template.

If you look at the website's front-end, the menu will not appear. Why not? *You haven't added any of the menu link items to the menu.* Once that is done, the menu will display.

Using the Menu to Display Content

Once you've created the infrastructure for the menu, you can create the menu link items, which will open the desired content in the main content area of the website.

Linking Single Articles

The most common menu link item type on Joomla! 3 websites is the one that opens a single article. Most menu link items open articles, so let's create a menu link item that does just that.

EXERCISE 24-3: ADDING A MENU LINK ITEM FOR AN ARTICLE

Objective: This exercise creates a menu link item to the My First Menu module that will open the My Second Article link, which was created in an earlier exercise.

Step 1. Either via the Admin Left Menu in the Control Panel, open the Menu Manager, or in the top admin menu, open My First Menu in the Menus drop-down. Both take you to the same location, the Menu Manager: Menu Items for this menu.

Step 2. Click the green New button at the top left of the screen. This opens the Menu Manager: New Menu Item screen.

Step 3. For the Menu Item Type, click the blue Select button, which opens a modal window with the Type options.

Step 4.   Open the Articles link, which opens the list of Types that can be selected, based on what kind of content display is desired.

Step 5.   Select the Single Article option. When selected, you're returned to the previous screen and a new option is displayed called Select an Article.

Step 6.   Click the grey Select button. This will open a modal window that displays all of the articles on the website, whether they are used/displayed elsewhere or not.

An easy way to find articles in long lists is to use one of the filters at the top.

Step 7.   In the -Select Category- drop-down, select My First Category, which will then display all the articles created within it. It will likely be at the bottom of the list since it was the last one created.

Step 8.   Select My Second Article.

Step 9.   Name the menu link item **My First Link Item**.

Step 10.   Execute a Save & Close action.

Step 11.   Go to the website front-end. The My First Menu should now display at the top of the right column with the My First Link item displayed. Click it! It should open My Second Article in the main content area of the web page.

Linking to Categories of Articles

Another frequently used menu link item type is the link to a category or a list of categories. There are several combinations of selections that can be made for this type of content display.

EXERCISE 24-4: ADDING A MENU LINK ITEM FOR A CATEGORY

Objective: The goal of this exercise is to demonstrate how to create a menu link item to a single, previously created category.

Step 1.   Within the same Menu Manager, add a new menu link item by clicking the green New button at the top left of the screen.

Step 2.   For the menu item type, select Articles > Category List as the choice in the drop-down.

Step 3.   For the Choose a Category, select My First Category as the choice in the drop-down, which will probably be at the bottom of the list of Categories available.

Step 4.   For the menu title, enter **My First Category**.

Step 5.   Execute a Save & Close action.

Step 6.   Go to the website's front-end and refresh the screen. The menu should now contain an additional menu link item. Click it! It should open a table view in the main content area that shows the two articles that are assigned to that category. Note that there are no sub-categories.

Another way of displaying similar content lists is to use List All Categories.

EXERCISE 24-5: ADDING A MENU LINK ITEM FOR A LIST OF CATEGORIES

Objective: This exercise creates a menu link item that will open an option called List All Categories, from which you can access content by drilling down into each individual category.

Step 1. Within the same Menu Manager, add a new menu link item by clicking the green New button at the top left of the screen.

Step 2. For the menu item type, select Articles > List All Categories as the choice in the drop-down.

It is necessary to designate the highest category level, under which there are sub-categories. Any top-level category that has at least one or more sub-categories can be selected. The default is Root, which will show all categories. All the sub-categories under the Root level will display. You'll do something more content-targeted in this exercise.

Step 3. Choose Sample Data-Articles for the top-level category.

Step 4. Name the menu title **My List of Categories**.

Step 5. Execute a Save & Close action.

Step 6. Go to the website front-end and refresh the screen. The menu should now contain the third menu link item. Click it! It should open a table view in the main content area that shows the list of all categories that are under the Sample Data-Articles category. Each will also show the number of articles within the category. Drill down through the Categories using the + and - icons to the right to explore the content.

Showing Content from Components

Components, the mini-applications that reside within and can be added to a Joomla! 3 website, can generate content other than simple categories and articles. While the default installation does not have that many components, there are hundreds of them in the JED that will display different content.

The menu item type selections include those components from which content can be selected and displayed. But remember, when you add a component to the website via the Extension Installer, that Component's content can be selected based on what the extension developer created for content display. An image gallery is a typical component that might have several type selection options. So would a shopping cart or a social media component.

The following exercise is typical of how to display content from a component.

EXERCISE 24-6: ADDING A MENU LINK ITEM FOR A LIST OF WEBLINKS

Objective: This exercise creates a menu link item that opens a list of weblinks from within the weblinks component.

Step 1. Within the same My First Menu Manager, add a new menu link item by clicking the green New button at the top left of the screen.

Step 2. For the menu item type, select Weblinks > List All Web Link Categories.

Step 3. Select Sample Data-Weblinks for the top-level category choice.

Step 4. Name the menu title **My List of Weblinks**.

Step 5. Execute a Save & Close action.

Step 6. Go to the website front-end and refresh the screen. The menu should now contain the fourth menu link item. Click it! It should open a table view in the main content area that shows the list of all weblinks categories that are under the Sample Data-Weblinks parent. Look at the Parks Links category. The links therein will display. The Joomla!-specific links will display when that category is opened.

Showing or Hiding a Menu

Because a Menu module is nothing more than a Module in itself, the same controls and options can be assigned to it via other menu link items. For example, say that when a certain menu link item is clicked, the My First Menu module should *not* display.

This is accomplished via the modules menu assignment feature. Let's set one of those conditions up now using this menu.

EXERCISE 24-7: HIDING THE MODULE FOR ONE MENU LINK ITEM

Objective: This exercise shows you how to display or hide a menu module (or any module of any type). You'll hide the My First Menu module when the Show All Tags menu link item is clicked in the top menu.

Step 1. Open the My First Menu module via the Module Manager in the Control Panel Admin Left Menu or via the Extensions > Modules access in the top menu.

Step 2. Click on the Menu Assignment tab.

Step 3. For the module assignment, you are going to do a reverse-selection for this task. Select the Only on the Pages Selected option, which unselects menu link items that the menu module should not display.

Step 4. Scroll down the list and find the Show All Tags menu link item. Uncheck it. It should be found near the bottom of the list in the top menu area. When it's unselected, it should be the only menu link item in that state—all others should be selected.

Step 5. Execute a Save & Close action.

Step 6. Go to the website front-end and refresh the screen.

Step 7. To make sure everything is in the proper state for display, click the Home menu link item in the top menu.

Step 8. Next, click the Show All Tags menu link item in the same top menu.

The My First Menu module should not display because it was disassociated with that specific menu link item. Click around the other menu link items. When you do so, the menu module should reappear.

You can apply this same method for hiding/showing a module of any type website-wide. Any module in any module position can have its visibility controlled in the same way.

You might notice that as you click around the menu link items for the example content, that some of the menu modules show and some don't show. They are controlled by the same menu assignment options used in this exercise.

Menu Extensions Are Available

In addition to the Joomla! 3 default menu system, there are many extensions in the JED that allow you to create good looking and highly functional menus. Spend some time in the JED and use the advanced search for menus filtered for version 3.2. Menus are usually found in the Structure & Navigation category of the JED.

FREE VERSUS NOT-SO-FREE EXTENSIONS: A REMINDER

When you search the JED, be aware of the paid and free availability of extensions, and the possible misrepresentation of the "free" label. Before you get too excited about a menu extension that appears to be free, follow the trail to the final destination to determine if there are membership fees or other charges associated with the "free" extension.

You can find more information about Joomla! 3 menus on the book's website at joomla3bootcamp.com.

Summary

In this chapter, you learned:

◆ How to create menus.

◆ How to create a menu module.

◆ How to use a menu to display content.

◆ How to display content from categories and articles.

◆ How to display content from components.

◆ How to show or hide a menu.

◆ That more menu extensions are available.

Chapter 25

Joomla! 3 Websites on Mobile Devices

Learning Objectives

What's included in this chapter:

- ◆ Viewing websites on mobile devices.
- ◆ Types of website layouts.
- ◆ Mobile app layouts and types.
- ◆ Responsive templates and layouts.
- ◆ Testing a template for responsiveness.
- ◆ Choices for website templates for mobile viewing.
- ◆ How websites are changing for mobile display.

Websites on Mobile Devices

Mobile devices are, to say the least, on the upswing for accessing the Internet. Most websites are not what is termed as "mobile compatible." Most websites can be viewed on a mobile device. But, what does the website look like? Does it conform to the many different screen sizes? Is the menu or navigation system logical and is it easy to navigate around the website on iPhones and iPads? Does the website display properly on all device operating systems?

Chances are that most of the answers to those questions is a resounding "no," unless, of course, the website has been configured for desktop browser display and for display on mobile devices.

Viewing on Mobile Devices

Given that most websites can be viewed on mobile devices, regardless of their layout, you should have an understanding of the different types of websites or mobile device compatible websites that can be viewed, which are:

Regular website with standard layout—This is a regular layout, with fixed or fluid width, as well as menus, modules, slideshows, and image galleries. This type of website viewed on a mobile device is usually difficult to navigate and requires a considerable amount of zooming and pinching to view the web pages. It is the type of website that is the least compatible with any mobile device, although it may view better on "pads" rather than the small-screen "phones."

Regular website with responsive layout—A website that has a template or layout that has been configured to be "responsive" is the most compatible with mobile devices. This website has a layout that adjusts to different screen sizes, especially the smaller sizes found on mobile devices. There are two types of responsive layouts:

> **Type 1**—This type of website responds to the screen size of the mobile devices and looks exactly like the website viewed in a desktop browser. The site can be zoomed and content viewed using menus, links and so on. The website is somewhat clumsy to navigate in that a lot of resizing of the viewing window is required. The website is adequate for viewing, but cumbersome in many ways, most dealing with the resizing of the screens.

> **Type 2**—This type of "responsive" website displays well on the mobile devices but has a different layout. Instead of showing the entire website on the screen, which requires the viewer to zoom the screen, the screen is laid out so that no zooming is required to navigate.

Many Joomla! 3 "responsive templates" also have a series of parameter configurations that allow the administrator to structure the actual layout of the web pages on the mobile devices.

Options for this kind of mobile-viewable website include responsive templates with mobile configurations, a template specifically for mobile viewing, automatic template switchers, and others, many of which are available as extensions in the JED.

Mobile Web App—This website has been designed specifically for mobile devices using the parameters for the smaller screen sizes. This type of website is accessed via the mobile device browser and is laid out for viewing in that manner, as are regular websites as described previously. The difference is that the layout has been purposefully created to display on the mobile devices, and does not display in a "responsive" manner on the desktop browser. The website displays in the smaller view on the desktop, or spreads itself wide and does not display correctly. If configured, the mobile web app may be "cached" on the devices and viewed without a Wi-Fi connection, with some limitations.

Mobile Native App—This is not a website. A native app may resemble a website in look, feel, and navigation, but it is not one. The native app is actually installed on the device and can be viewed whether there is a Wi-Fi connection or not. Native apps can usually only be obtained via a download from an app storing/download location, and not accessible via a web browser.

While Joomla! 3 can produce regular websites with both types of responsive layouts, it cannot produce a mobile web app, and it certainly cannot produce a mobile native app.

Responsive Templates Plus

Perhaps the best solution for any Joomla! 3 website is for the template to be both "responsive" and "mobile compatible." By mobile-compatible, this means the template should have parameter settings that optimize how the website displays will be viewed on mobile devices with different screens.

When you're looking for templates that will serve your website's display needs for both the desktop and on mobile devices, look for those that meet both of the requirements.

Most template providers are now labeling templates that are responsive (Figure 25-1). This means they will adjust to different screen sizes, but might not have settings that control the actual display/layout of the content on the mobile devices.

Figure 25-1 *The templates shown have been marked as being "responsive" for mobile devices.*

Looking at Some Demos

If you would like to look at some templates that are responsive and see how they display on mobile devices—assuming you have one or two of them, here are a few to look at:

Template Name	Source
Elastica, Puresite	joomlart.com
Lifestyle	joomlabamboo.com
Helion	shape5.com
Mj Newstar	bestofjoomla.com

Most of those template providers have a mobile device simulator view for their templates. This allows you to view the template in the manner it will display on the mobile device. This will give you a pretty good idea of how the template displays content for the different devices.

CROSS-BROWSER DOES NOT MEAN RESPONSIVE

Almost every available template touts "cross-browser compatibility." But make no mistake about it, this does *not* mean the template is "responsive" on mobile devices. The cross-browser thing simply means that it will show properly on all of the major desktop browsers, or mobile browsers as a regular website. When you're looking for mobile- responsive templates, look for the "responsive" label and ignore the "cross-browser" claim.

Here's a Trick...

If you want to visualize how a "responsive" template will look like on a smaller device or screen size, the following steps explain how to do so. This demo uses the ja_elastica template from http://www.joomlart.com/demo/#ja_elastica. Feel free to visit the link and then follow these steps:

Step 1. Access the Demo View or Live View of any responsive template on any Joomla! 3 template source website.

Step 2. Make sure you are viewing the Joomla! 3.x version of the template.

Step 3. Set the **[A]** browser resize to allow adjustment of the window size (Figure 25-2).

Step 4. Grab the right side of the browser window and begin to narrow it. Observe what happens to the layout. At the very minimum size, use the scroll bar to move up and down the page. It functions like scrolling a mobile browser window (Figure 25-3).

Step 5. Slowly make the browser window about twice as wide as in Step 4 and notice how the content reassembles for the wider view. That is how the template might look on a tablet (Figure 25-4).

Step 6. With the browser window at a minimum width, click the **[A]** icon again to enlarge the screen slowly. Pay close attention when it happens. You will notice how the page rebuilds itself, showing which items are being "responsive" to the change in size.

You can use this viewing trick to check any template to see if it is at least responsive to the size of the display window of the browser.

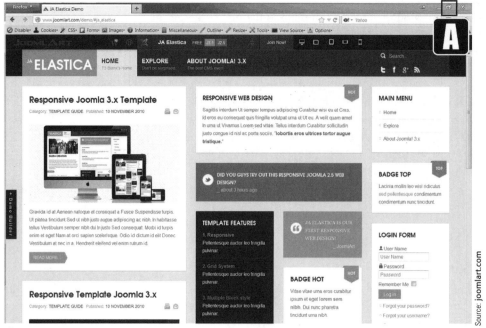

Figure 25-2 *Set the* **[A]** *browser resizer to allow the edge of the browser window to be adjusted. This screenshot shows the browser window at full size on the desktop.*

Figure 25-3 *The browser window is set to the minimum width, which emulates how the template will display on a phone-sized device.*

Figure 25-4 *The browser window is set to the minimum width, which emulates how the template will display on a tablet-sized device. Compare this display with the narrower version in Figure 25-3.*

More Responsiveness

Using the same template in the full browser width view, click the Explore link in the top menu. Then, under the 6 Responsive Layouts, view the Tablet Layout and Mobile Layout links.

The Tablet Layout indicates the different sizes for devices such as laptops, and the settings that apply for minimum and maximum widths (Figure 25-5). Minimum and maximum widths are usually specified to ensure that pages don't simply "break" when viewed on devices with smaller screens.

Figure 25-5 *This template has built-in display instructions for different screen sizes, which specifies a minimum and a maximum page width for the web pages when viewed on devices with smaller screens.*

The Mobile Layout explains how the template is set for the portrait and landscape layouts on the mobile devices. If you read the text, you will see there are a few pieces of CSS code here and there that you must insert. In time, you will learn all about this kind of customization for many different types of templates from different designers and developers. The nice part about this template is that the coding—which you might not understand right now—is already included in the template's files. When you install the template, the coded files are included and you really do not need to do anything to make it display correctly on mobile devices.

Choices for Mobile Websites

At this point, you should pretty much be convinced that any website you produce, either for yourself or for clients, should be mobile-device compatible. This means you need to make choices about how this compatibility will be implemented. Here are some of the choices and their solutions:

Choice 1—Use a responsive template from a developer, which might be of the "free" to "paid" type. You can pick a template, add it as an extension to your website, and make it the default. You can add more than one of these types of templates if you want the page layout and designs to be different for different menu link items.

Choice 2—Use a responsive template with additional parameter settings if a mobile device is detected. This means the regular browser template will be one type, but when a mobile device is detected, the settings and parameters you have set will control how the website is displayed. The "detection" aspect can be part of the template, or it can be an extension.

Choice 3—Use a responsive template for browser viewing, and a completely different template for the mobile devices. These additional templates would likely require additional actions when a new menu link item is added. You might need to add it, and some other content (modules, perhaps) to both templates. The advantage of the separate mobile template is the content can be trimmed and selected specifically for mobile viewing.

The choice you make depends upon the needs and content objective of your website. Heck, if your website isn't likely to be viewed on mobile devices, don't worry about it. This is especially applicable for small, personal websites.

However, if you are producing and managing business or corporate websites, these choices become very important and will be guided by the nature and amount of content on the website. Remember, you can always change templates and their configurations, so if the first choice you make doesn't work, you aren't locked in.

Everything Is Bigger

Have you noticed that there has been a shift in how websites are being designed? It wasn't long ago that the design trend was small, compact, neat-looking layouts with as much content on the screen as possible. Viewing websites on mobile devices has changed that.

The current trend is bigger, bigger, bigger in terms of page element sizing. Headings are bigger, menus have bigger buttons, and the text is bigger. Why is this shift happening?

Well, as you may have guessed, those nice compact website layouts simply don't display well on mobile devices. Larger elements display much better and do not require the mobile users to zoom in on the screens to view content. There is still some zooming required, but the dynamics of viewing a website on a mobile device have changed with the upsizing.

So, next time you visit a website on a desktop browser, and the elements seem a tad too large, you will know why. The website's layout has been "optimized" for viewing on mobile devices. This is very noticeable on "news" websites, which used to contain multi-column layouts with lots of content. They now have big blocks of content areas.

If you are a website designer or developer, this re-sizing thing simply means more work to convert existing sites to mobile-friendly optimization and responsive layouts.

Summary

In this chapter, you learned:

◆ About issues with viewing websites on mobile devices.
◆ About the different types of website layouts.
◆ Difference between mobile app layouts and types.
◆ What is a responsive template.
◆ How to test a template for responsiveness.
◆ Template options for mobile viewing.
◆ Changes being made to websites for mobile display.

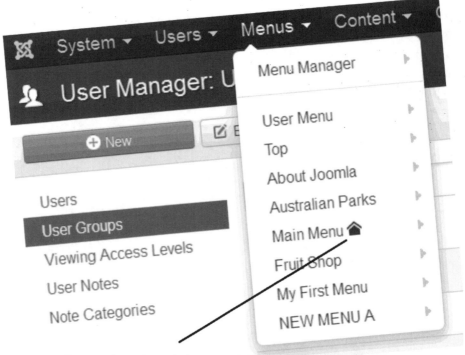

When in the Menu Manager,
the menu that controls the
front-end display is indicated
by the "home" icon.

The Menu Link Item within
the menu that has the "gold"
star, indicates that item controls
the format of the front-end.

Chapter 26

Using Forms

Learning Objectives

What's included in this chapter:

- ◆ Understanding the use of forms.
- ◆ Where to obtain form extensions.
- ◆ Determining form requirements for a website.
- ◆ Testing form extensions.
- ◆ How to use two different form extensions.
- ◆ Adding spam prevention to the forms.
- ◆ Using captcha for form spam prevention.
- ◆ Protecting email addresses from spiders.

Understanding Forms

If you administer any kind of Joomla! 3 website, chances are you will eventually need to add a form for some reason or other. Forms are used so website visitors can communicate with the website administrator, or to send messages to the personnel involved with the website, for whom a contact or message form has been created. If you're running a business website, your visitors may want to send messages to the people involved in managing the business. It is quite possible that a large number of forms are necessary on a large commercial website.

The most common form used on websites is the traditional "Contact Us" form. This form is usually very basic and is automatically sent to the intended recipient. In fact, the Joomla! 3 Contacts component is set up to do exactly that, and a bit more. This component is covered in Chapter 9, "Components: Contacts," where you learned how to classify contacts into categories and how to create a menu link item to open the form.

This chapter dives into forms a little deeper by discussing the use of customized forms that are available as extensions.

Where to Get Form Extensions

To add a form to your Joomla! 3 website, you need to obtain and install an extension. All extensions are sourced via the JED on the joomla.org website.

Use the Advanced search in the JED to search for forms in the Category field. Forms are listed under Contacts & Feedback in the extension directory area. You'll find about 30 or so extensions.

Form extensions fall under two categories—free and paid—which are the new designations for extensions formerly classified as non-commercial and commercial, depending upon where you obtain them.

If you combine search terms—"forms" in the Category field and "free" in the Type field—almost 20 are available. Mind you, some of the freebies are stripped down versions of the paid extension, but they will give you a good idea of how the extension works and what it takes to administer forms.

Determining Form Requirements

Before charging into the JED and pulling down extensions, it's probably a good idea to determine what sort of features the form extension should have as compared to what you want the forms to do on the website.

Here are some things you might want to consider when selecting a form extension. Of course, you need to compare the features to the needs of the form on the website.

Form fields—Can custom form fields be included, or must you use a "canned" form template?

Form field types—Does the extension have form fields that include drop-down selectors, choice buttons, radio buttons, text fields for more than one line, and other features your forms might require, such as date insertion, self-copy, and so on?

Multiple pages—Do your forms need more than one page? Employment applications, and forms along those lines often need several pages.

Easy-to-use interface—How easy is the extension to use? It should be intuitive and have easy-to-find controls.

Acknowledgments—Do the forms have an acknowledgment, either onscreen or in an email sent to the sender with a copy of the submission?

Security—Will the users need to prove they are "human" and not a robot that's sending spam forms when submitting a form?

Captcha—This is the security validation feature used to implement anti-spam on the form.

Email cloaking—This obscures actual email addresses from being scanned and harvested. Cloaking the email from the "bad guys" on the Internet is a good feature to employ when using forms.

Look and feel—Forms don't need to be ugly. Forms can/should have some sort of interactivity like field highlighting when the cursor is inserted, color-coding, and general ability to control the appearance of the forms.

Administration—Can multiple forms be created, enabled, or disabled, and is the admin interface for the forms extension easy to understand and use?

Multiple-purpose forms—Can the forms extension be used for a multitude of forms, such as opt-in for mailings, surveys, questionnaires, and similar special-use forms.

Database integration—Aside from the Joomla! database, can the form be used to populate a separate database or can the form submissions be exported into a spreadsheet for further use?

Form generation—Does the form extension generate its own forms that can be accessed with a menu link item, or must the form be created using special coding in an article or a module? Both of these tasks should be avoided in favor of automatic form generation.

There are, of course, many other considerations, especially when you're creating specialized forms, or forms that have dependent fields where the values of field #2 are determined by the selection in field #1. You must analyze your form needs before deciding which form extension to use. In fact, you might need to use more than one form extension, especially on larger websites.

Testing a Form Extension

One way to learn how to use a form extension is to install one. The following exercises will install a free (stripped-down version) of two different form extensions and quickly explain how to use them. Both extensions have a paid version, which has all the features.

These two extensions were chosen strictly as examples of different extensions and different approaches to accomplish the same task. Using them in the exercises does not imply an endorsement. Research and evaluate each form extension and make your own determination as to which one will suit the task the best.

Type of Installation

Form extensions are generally components and are therefore found under the Components menu after installation. Some form components may also include the installation of plug-ins and modules, so check to ensure the plug-ins have been enabled, and if modules must be used as part of the form display on the web page. This process is part of the administration of the forms component in Exercise 26-2.

EXERCISE 26-1: USING PROFORMS BASIC

Objective: This exercise will install the Proforms Basic extension and review some of the administrative features. A form template must be created to which the actual form fields are added. Then, a form is created and the template is applied.

Step 1. Go to the JED and find the Proforms Basic extension. Download and install it into your website. Make sure the download version is for Joomla! 3.x. You can use any method of your choice to obtain and install the extension. This extension installs as a component. The form is then configured. A menu link item is then created to link to the form.

Step 2. Open the Proforms Basic component in the Components menu. The component should open and display. There should be no forms listed.

Step 3. Create a Category by clicking on the **[A]** Category button in the menu bar. After the Category screen opens, click the **[B]** New Category button at the right of the menu bar. Name the category **Form Category 1** and enter an email address in the field below it (Figure 26-1).

Figure 26-1 *All form-creation activity takes place in the component's menu. The* **[A]** *Category icon opens the manager and* **[B]** *New Category icon is used to create the hierarchy for the forms.*

Step 4. Check to make sure the Access Level is set to Public and the Category is set to Active. The checkmark icon will display green.

Step 5. Click the green + Add button to the top right of the menu bar. If you are simply editing the category, click the Apply button. The result of this action will display a list showing the category.

Step 6.   Click on the **[C]** Templates icon in the top menu bar.

Step 7.   Click the **[D]** New Template button at the top right of the menu bar. The demo version allows only one template to be selected. Look at the other formats that can be created in the PRO version (Figure 26-2).

Figure 26-2 *The* **[C]** *Templates option holds the actual form elements, which are created after you click the* **[D]** *New Template icon.*

Step 8.   Name the template **My First Template**.

Step 9.   Click the Proceed button at the top right of the menu bar. This opens the screen that allows the creation of form elements, which are listed on the right side. The circular red X button at the top left cancels the current screen activity without saving.

TYPES OF FORM TEXT FIELDS

The fields that allow a form user to enter data are of two types:

Text Field—Usually a single line of text such as a name, address, or other type of text entry. This is the most common text-entry form field.

Text Area—A larger text area box that might allow entry of long text such as a question or text that consists of one or more paragraphs. Text areas can be controlled as to the visual size on the screen and the amount of text that can be entered.

Step 10.   Click the **[E]** + Textfield button. When the screen opens, look over the various settings that can be applied for this form element (Figure 26-3).

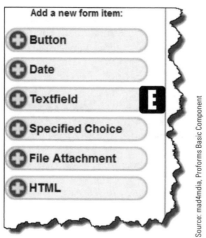

Source: mad4mdia, Proforms Basic Component

Figure 26-3 *All form elements are created by clicking one of the item options in the right menu of the Templates > Items Manager.*

Step 11. Enter **Your Full Name** into the Your Question field. None of the other parameters need to be set for this question.

Step 12. Click the green + Add button to the top right of the menu bar. This will take you back to the template screen, showing the item that was just added.

Step 13. This forms component allows you to preview how a form will look while it is being created. Click the **[F]** Preview button to the top right of the menu bar (Figure 26-4). This opens the front-end of the website with the form displayed in the main content area. Click the red X button to the top right to close the preview window.

Step 14. Click the green + button to the right of the screen, which will allow you to create a checkbox or a yes/no menu, usually called a "radio button."

Step 15. Enter **Did you enter your name above?** into the Your Question field.

Step 16. Make this a "Yes/No menu" type of button element.

Step 17. Click the green + Add button to the top right of the menu bar. This will take you back to the elements of the template screen, showing the element that was just added.

At this point, you have two form elements in this template. Now you need to create the actual form. The screen should have both items listed (Figure 26-5).

Figure 26-4 *As you add form elements to your template, you can evaluate them using the* **[F]** *Preview feature.*

Figure 26-5 *As form items are created and added, they will appear on the Elements of the Template screen. Items and elements are used interchangeably when discussing forms.*

Step 18. Return to the Proforms component control panel screen via the Components > Proforms Basic menu.

Step 19. Click on the **[H]** Forms button in the top menu bar (Figure 26-6).

Step 20. Click the green **[I]** + New Form button to the top right of the menu bar.

Figure 26-6 *After a category and a template is created for a form, you can configure the form.*

Step 21. When the screen opens, name the form **Proforms One**.

Step 22. Click on the **[J]** My First Template button in the "Add Form Template" column, which applies the previously created template to the form (Figure 26-7). The My First Template icon bar will move to the "Included Form Template(s)" column.

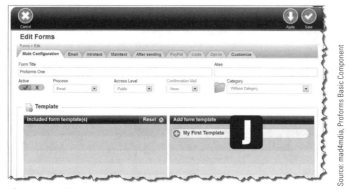

Figure 26-7 *To create a working form, you must assign a template to it, which contains the form elements.*

Step 23. Click the Add button to the top right of the menu bar. Remember that you can apply the change only if the item has been created and you're making changes to it.

Step 24. On the results screen, click the **[K]** form name (or the **[L]** pencil icon to the far right), and re-open the form (Figure 26-8).

Figure 26-8 *You can access your forms for editing by either of two methods.*

Step 25.   Open the Email tab.

Step 26.   Enter your email address in the Email field. This is where the form will be sent when the user submits it, so enter a legitimate email address where you can receive emails.

Step 27.   Enter **Proforms Test Email** in the Subject field.

Step 28.   Enter some text in the Email text area. Any text will suffice.

Step 29.   Click the Save button to the top right of the menu bar.

At this point, the form is complete and now requires an action item to access it, which is a menu link item.

Step 30.   Return to the main control panel by clicking the Joomla! icon to the top left of the screen.

Step 31.   Open the Menu Manager in the Admin Left Menu.

Step 32.   Open My First Menu by clicking in the title.

Step 33.   Click the New button at the top left to create a menu item in this menu.

Step 34.   Enter **Proforms One** as the menu title.

Step 35.   Click the blue Select button to select a menu item type (Figure 26-9).

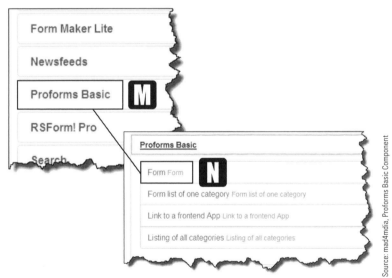

Figure 26-9 *The Type selector for this extension was added to the list of those available during the installation process.*

Step 36.   In the popup window, click the **[M]** Proforms Basic link item. When the component was installed, the menu type selector for the extensions was automatically added to this selector screen.

Step 37.   Select **[N]** Form as the choice, but note the other items that may be selected, depending upon how your forms strategy is being employed on the website.

Step 38. In the drop-down, select Proforms One as the choice of the form to open. If there is only one form, it will be selected automatically.

Step 39. Execute the Save & Close action.

Step 40. Click the website name at the top right of the Admin backend screen to view the front-end.

Step 41. In the My First Menu, the Proforms One link should display. Click it.

The form should show the two form elements that were created and the captcha security feature. The Send button should also display.

Step 42. Fill out the form and the captcha code, and then execute the Send action.

Step 43. If the action worked, the "Data Successfully Sent" message should appear. You can customize that message to display other information.

Step 44. Check your email account for the form message.

This exercise showed you how to create a very simple form; it shows how easy this component is to use. You can create forms with greater complexity by creating the template, assigning it to a form, and then setting the submission parameters for the form.

Next, you'll create a similar form using a different forms extension.

EXERCISE 26-2: USING FORM MAKER LITE

Objective: This exercise will install the Form Maker Lite extension and review some of its administrative features. This component's forms do not open directly with a menu link item. The form called Plugin Code is inserted into an article and the article can then be opened with a menu link item to display the form. This is a different approach than the form component in Exercise 26-1, which opens forms directly from menu link items.

Step 1. Go to the JED and find the Form Maker Lite extension. Download and install it into your website. Make sure the download version is for Joomla! 3.x. You can use any method of your choice to obtain and install the extension. This extension installs as a package, meaning a plug-in and/or module is also installed.

Step 2. Open the Form Maker Lite component in the Components menu. The component should open and display. A list of pre-built forms will display.

Step 3. Click the green New button in the component's top menu.

Step 4. For the **[O]** Form Title, enter **Form Maker One** (Figure 26-10).

Step 5. Execute a **[P]** Save action.

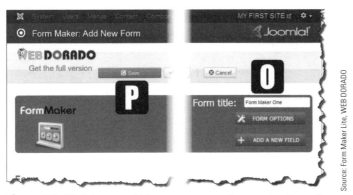

Figure 26-10 *It is a good idea to execute a Save action immediately after entering form values.*

Step 6. Go back to the Admin Control Panel by clicking the Joomla! logo in the top left corner of the screen.

Step 7. Re-open the Form Maker Lite component. Verify the Form Maker One form displays on the list; it should be the last item.

Step 8. Click on the form name, or tick the box next to the name and click Edit in the component's top menu.

Step 9. Open the **[Q]** Form Options using the link to the right of the screen. This opens the Options tab for the form. Notice how the component fires up an automatic save action during parameter section changes (Figure 26-11).

Figure 26-11 *The Form Options for this component sets the parameters for publishing, email, and actions after form submission.*

Step 10. Make sure the Published parameter is set to Yes. The Theme Preview does not work in the Lite version of this component.

Step 11. Open the Email Options tab.

Step 12. Enter the administrator's email address. You can use your regular email address to receive submissions, although this can be set to any email.

Step 13. Enter **admin@anydomain.com** in the Email From field, or any other email address. It does not need to be a real, working email address. A Do-Not-Reply@... email address is typical for forms.

Step 14. Enter **ADMIN** for the from name.

Step 15. Make sure the Send E-mail parameter under the Email Options tab is set to Yes.

Notice the **%all%** in the message test area. This indicates that all of the from fields will be email. In the paid version of this component, the "All Fields List" is accessible for creating customized forms to be received by the administrator or the user who sent it.

Step 16. Execute a Save action.

If you want a copy of the form to go to the sender, complete that section's information.

Step 17. Open the Actions after Submissions tab.

Step 18. Select Custom Text in the Action type drop-down.

Step 19. Enter **Thanks for submitting the form** in the text box.

Step 20. Execute a Save & Close action.

Step 21. Open the **[R]** Add a New Field manager using the link to the right of the screen (Figure 26-12). This opens the Options tab for the form.

Figure 26-12 *The Add a New Field function is where the form elements are actually selected and configured.*

Step 22. Click the **[S]** Text Input icon in the left menu, top-right (Figure 26-13).

Step 23. Select the **[T]** Name field type. The **[U]** form element will display on the right side of the screen. The field label (Name) can be edited in the left of the parameters area. The names of the individual fields can be edited by clicking on the field name in the right panel.

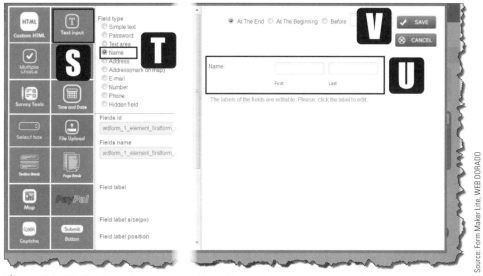

Figure 26-13 *The form elements are all configurable on one screen in this component.*

Step 24. Execute a **[V]** Save action using the blue button to the right of the screen.

Step 25. Re-open the Add a New Field manager (Figure 26-12).

Step 26. Select the **[W]** Single Choice option in the left menu (Figure 26-14).

Figure 26-14 *Some form elements must be modified in the left parameter window.*

Step 27. At the bottom of the left parameter area, change the **[X]** options for the radio buttons to the following:

> I am a male.
>
> I am a female.

Step 28. Execute a **[Z]** Save action using the blue button to the right of the screen. The form should display with both form elements. The icons next to the elements allow the fields to be moved up or down. You can also make other changes to the individual elements.

Step 29. Re-open the **[R]** Add a New Field manager (Figure 26-12).

Step 30. Select the **[Y]** Submit button at the bottom of the left menu, which brings up the **[Z]** Submit and Reset buttons (Figure 26-15).

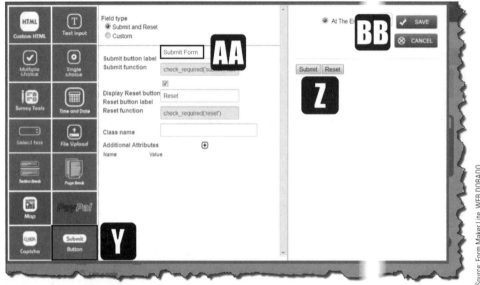

Source: Form Maker Lite, WEB DORADO

Figure 26-15 *Form buttons can have a text label other than Submit, which allows forms to be customized based on the form's intended use.*

Step 31. Change the **[AA]** Submit text to **Submit Form**.

Step 32. Execute a **[BB]** Save action using the blue button to the right of the screen.

You should now see three form elements.

Step 33. Execute a Save & Close action for the component.

Step 34. At the bottom of the list, find the form and notice the code to the far right of the screen.

Step 35. Click in the grey box and use the Copy command on your keyboard to copy the text. As the alternative to using Copy/Paste, you can manually type the same text into the text area.

Step 36. Return to the Admin Control Panel.

Step 37. Click the Add New Article link in the left menu.

Step 38. Enter **FML Form Sample** into the article's Title field.

Step 39.   Paste the copied text from Step 35 into the article text area. The **{loadform maker 11}** text can also be manually entered rather than copy/paste (the sequential number of the form depends upon how many forms were created).

WHAT ARE THE BRACES { AND } FOR?

The typographic braces { } are used to enclose code in Joomla! 3 articles or modules that call some sort of action caused by a plug-in. In this case, it is **loadformmaker** and then the ID number of the form. Any plug-ins that require entries like this will usually have a sample of the syntax shown in the plug-in manager.

Step 40.   In the right column, assign this article to the Uncategorized category.

Step 41.   Execute a Save & Close action.

Step 42.   Return to the Admin Control Panel.

Step 43.   Open the Menu Manager under Structure in the Admin Left Menu.

Step 44.   Open My First Menu.

Step 45.   Click the green New button to create a new menu link item.

Step 46.   Give the link the **Form Maker Lite** menu title.

Step 47.   For the menu item type, select Articles > Single Article in the pop-up window.

Step 48.   In the Select Article parameter, click the grey Select button.

Step 49.   In the pop-up window, filter the articles by selecting Uncategorized in the Select Category drop-down.

Step 50.   Select FML Form Sample from among the results.

Step 51.   Execute a Save & Close action. The new menu link item should appear at the bottom of the list, making it the last item that will display in the menu.

Step 52.   Go to the website front-end and refresh the browser window.

Step 53.   Click on the Form Maker Lite menu link item.

Nothing showing, other than the code entered into the article? This is correct, because the "Content - Load Form Maker" plug-in has not yet been set to Enabled.

Step 54.   Go to the Extensions > Plugins and select the Disabled status in the top filter, in the left part of the screen.

Step 55.   Find "Content - Load Form Maker" and click the red X in its Status column. The plug-in will no longer display on the Disabled screen. It is now enabled, and will trigger the display of the form in the article when the menu item is clicked.

> **PLUG-INS GET TRIGGERED**
>
> For plug-ins to work, they must be "triggered" into action. The plug-in inserts the code when the menu link item is clicked (the trigger). If you perform a function and the plug-in doesn't fire, always double-check to make sure it is set to enabled.

Step 56. Go back to the front-end of the website and refresh the browser window.

Step 57. Complete the form and execute the Submit action.

Step 58. The green "success" message should display.

Step 59. Check the inbox for the email address designated for the administrator to receive it. You should receive the email with the form information results.

Different Components, Different Methods

The two form extensions installed in this chapter require dramatically different methods to achieve the same result. A form was created, published, and executed, and then the results were received. One was connected directly to a menu link item, the other was embedded into an article, which was accessed the same way. Two ways of doing the same thing. This is not atypical of how things work with Joomla! 3's extensions, especially those that allow creation/inclusion of forms on the website.

Determining which form extension to use on a website actually requires that you download the ones you're interested in, and then create sample forms by executing all the steps involved for the particular extension.

Of course, there is a wide range of additional form parameters that you can configure, way too many to cover in a single chapter in this book. After using the form extensions for a while, you will get a better understanding of the mechanics involved and how to customize forms. This could include both actions of the form elements along with the visual appearance of the forms, fill-in text fields, and their colorization.

Forms can be fun to work with and create, so mastering the extension you install will make it "productive fun" for your or your clients' websites.

Keeping Forms Secure

One of the big issues with forms is keeping them secure. Hackers and spammers often exploit online forms to flood websites (and their users) with emails selling some sort of bogus products of one type or another. When your website gets hammered with thousands of these form submissions, they are no fun to deal with.

Keeping Hackers Away from Your Forms

Fortunately, a programmer a while back came up with a way of making sure that forms are being filled out by humans rather than by robots. In general, the term used is *captcha*, which is actually a brand name that has been loosely used in the same way the brand name Xerox is used to describe copy machines.

Basically, captcha involves adding a form element that requires the user to re-enter some information that's shown on the screen. This could be numbers, a couple of words, or even images that you must repeat to prove that you are human.

The words you see on the screen that you must type into a box are actually graphics, and robots cannot see or read them. They are not actual words, and human interaction is therefore required to validate the form.

Using Captcha

Captcha is a form element that the administrator adds. The following exercise explains how to add a captcha element to a form.

EXERCISE 26-3: ADDING A CAPTCHA ELEMENT

Objective: This exercise will show you how to add a captcha element to the example form you created in Exercise 26-2.

Step 1. Log in to the Admin backend of the website and open the Form Maker Lite component.

Step 2. Open the form entitled Form Maker One.

Step 3. Click the Add a New Field button to the right of the screen (Figure 26-12).

Step 4. At the lower left of the window, click the **[CC]** Captcha icon (Figure 26-16).

Step 5. The **[DD]** Captcha parameter screen and sample should display. Notice the different settings for the element. The display shown is simple captcha, but the "letters/words" version of it is called Recaptcha, and cannot be displayed in this view, because the words are generated on the fly on the website front-end when the form is opened.

Step 6. Execute an **[EE]** Save action. The **[FF]** Captcha field should show up on the form view, next to the Submit/Reset buttons (Figure 26-17).

Figure 26-16 *Simple* **[DD]** *captcha elements have easy-to-read (for humans) words. To robots and spiders, they are images, which they cannot read.*

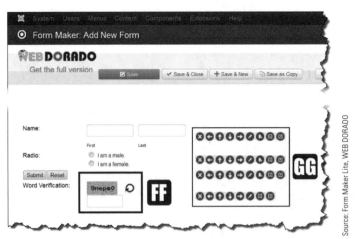

Figure 26-17 *The* **[GG]** *icon rows to the right of the form elements allow the administrator to move and rearrange the form elements.*

Step 7. Execute a Save & Close action for the component.

Step 8. Go to the website front-end. Click the Home button to regenerate the website display.

Step 9. Click the Form Maker Lite menu link item in My First Menu on the right.

The form should now display with the captcha code verification field.

Chapter 27

Using Fonts with Joomla! 3

Learning Objectives

What's included in this chapter:

◆ Fundamentals of using fonts on a Joomla! 3 website.

◆ Why it's best to avoid using font replacement.

◆ Extensions that add font capabilities.

◆ Fundamentals of using CSS.

◆ Issues with using fonts on websites.

◆ How to use the HD Gfonts plug-in extension.

◆ How to use the Phoca Font component.

◆ Why it's best to avoid using too many fonts.

◆ Other ways to include additional fonts.

About Font Use

Let's face it, using the same limited collection of fonts is boring. On top of that, we have all seen websites that have clean, good looking typefaces on their websites and wonder how to get that look.

Fonts are "typefaces" and the two terms are often used interchangeably. Fonts is the term used with template CSS files and with extensions. Sure, there are differences in the actual technical use of the terms, but for the purposes here, "fonts" is the best term.

One way to add fonts to a Joomla! 3 website is to hard-code Google Fonts. This is probably one of the best and easiest ways to use the font repositories that are built into Joomla! 3. However, unless you can work with CSS code and files, and know what you are doing, adding Google Fonts manually isn't a good idea.

As you have seen in other chapters in this book, when there is a "hard way" of doing things, there is often an "easy way" somewhere in the Joomla! 3 extensions library. Using Google Fonts is no exception.

The two extensions discussed in this chapter show you how to best use non-standard fonts on a Joomla! 3 website.

Avoiding Font Replacement

A few years ago, when the major web browser companies could not agree on font implementation, some programmers figured out an alternative to using fonts on a website. This process was loosely called *font replacement*.

Font replacement involves taking the font identified on the system and changing it to an image. The *image* of the font is then displayed on the browser. The individual characters are converted to individual images and displayed as graphics.

The only problem was the excessive consumption of resources to pull it off. There was no way that the body text could be replaced by font images. Imagine a website with 10 million characters being converted to images. It took too much time.

However, font replacement could be used with success for smaller pieces of text, such as with headings. This worked pretty well, but still gobbled up resources and bandwidth and wasn't a real solution.

Google Fonts and some other systems solved the problem by providing a method where non-restricted fonts can be included and downloaded with the pages. That is the process being described in the exercises in this chapter.

It is strongly suggested that you not use font replacement on any of your Joomla! 3 websites. There are easier and better ways to implement fonts.

Understanding CSS for the Novice

Before you get started using font extensions, it's important to understand how fonts are designated and managed. This is done via Cascading Style Sheets (CSS), which consists of coding that tells websites using style sheets how to use fonts and display content.

Joomla! 3 doesn't have an exclusive on use of CSS, fonts, and the like for content display. Every website in the world uses some variation of these to display and manage its visual aspects.

The secret to it all lies with the browser used to view websites. Each browser is programmed to interpret certain CSS "tags" for content, and relate the tags with the values designated in the CSS style sheet.

Website text is controlled by CSS, which uses some standardized coding. Here are three of the CSS identifiers that are typically used:

<body>—Controls the physical layout of the "body" of the web page.

<p>—The general text designator in CSS parlance, and is typically any text that is not otherwise classified. Sometimes called body text.

<h1> through <h6>—These are text headings, with <h1> usually being the largest, and <h6> the smallest. It is rare to see websites that use any heading over <h3>, although some ecommerce websites use all six levels.

What is interesting in the use of CSS is that fonts or a font family can be assigned to each CSS tag globally, or as an override on specific tags.

There are a number of tags associated with fonts. I suggest you look up CSS and fonts to get a better understanding of how the tags are coded. There are many well-written books devoted strictly to CSS. If you want to learn how to code CSS, by all means, further your education through books or online research.

Every web page has a coded page that displays the content. In the case of Joomla! 3, it is the index.php page for the respective template. Keep in mind that more than one template can be used on a website. The index.php page has one or more associated "cascading style sheets" that are designated and attached.

When the web page opens in a browser window, there is an attached style sheet. The content is coded to use style tags and the style sheet tells the web browser how to display the content. It's that simple—yea, right! It is easily explained, but not quite that easy to implement.

WANT TO LEARN MORE?

The companion website to this book, located at **joomla3bootcamp.com**, has an extensive list of learning resources and reference locations, some of which deal with CSS. If you want to learn more about coding CSS style sheets, visit the suggested resources listed on the website.

Understanding the Font Issue

The big issue with fonts is that by their inherent nature, a web browser can only display the fonts that reside on the computer on which the browser operates. That's a serious limitation.

The biggest and most comprehensive font library in the world is offered by Adobe Systems. The fonts are not free. The font library is quite expensive, well out of the range of most web folks. However, it is within the range of those designers that create print layouts such as brochures, magazines, and the like, where a multitude of high-quality fonts must be used for the best result. So, you are thinking, why can't I use those on my website? Well, one of the license provisions of those fonts is they cannot be downloaded to any other computer or shared. That is the stumbling block.

The high-quality Adobe fonts cannot be simply attached to a web page and downloaded to every computer in the world.

To meet the needs of website designers, Adobe has created a method by which their fonts can be used on a website. They have set up a use method, not free of course, and with many limitations. Find out more about Adobe's font use at **https://typekit.com/plans**. If you want to spend the money for the annual fee, by all means do so.

There are variations and workarounds for all these font issues, and several of the major browser manufacturers tried to work out a common ground for font use on their respective browsers, but they didn't like sharing, and the effort was abandoned.

After that effort, along came Google and its financial horsepower. They created the Google Fonts Library, which is comprised of a collection of high-quality, open source, free fonts that can be used and shared any which way.

This leads you back to the purpose of this chapter: using Google Fonts on a Joomla! 3 website. This is the easiest way to use fonts on your Joomla! 3 websites.

Using the Hyde-Design HD Gfonts Extension

Fortunately for Joomla! 3 administrators, these is a small web developer shop called Hyde-Design that has approached this problem with a nice, easy-to-use solution called HD Gfonts.

The extension is available via the JED, but it is marked as being only version 2.5 compatible. However, this is one of those plug-ins that "plays well" with versions 2.5 and 3.x. There is a limitation with the extension, in that it can control only four fonts, at least at first look. You can use it creatively to control more than that.

Enough introduction, let's put this extension to work on your website.

This is an extension. Extensions are obtained via the JED, so go there and download the HD Gfonts extension (search for "fonts" to find it). When the results page displays, scroll down the list until you see the extension (Figure 27-1).

Figure 27-1 *Although this extension is marked for Joomla! 2.5, it is compatible with version 3.x, so you can download and install it successfully.*

IT MAY NOT WORK

The HD Gfonts extension does work in most Joomla! 3.2.x installations. However, if you encounter any difficulties with the initial install, abandon it and do not use the extension. Certain webserver platforms and configurations don't allow version 2.5 extensions to work with Joomla! 3. Hyde-Design is planning to release a Joomla! 3.2.x version in the near future, so check back for that version.

Before you panic about compatibility, this extension will install into a Joomla! 3.x website. Not special actions are needed. Simply download the extension and install it via the "Upload Package File" technique, something you have been doing in almost every chapter in this book.

This extension is one of those "free" ones that functions perfectly. Yup, a great extension that the folks at Hyde-Design have generously shared with the Joomla! user's community. Thanks guys!

This extension is a plug-in, which means that it must be enabled and configured. While most plug-ins do not need to have any parameters set, this one has all of the settings within the plug-in manager.

LEARN FIRST, APPLY SECOND

At this point in your experience and learning about Joomla! 3, fonts have not been a primary consideration. Master the use of Joomla! 3 as an administrator, and wait until you reach a higher level of skill and knowledge about the program, CSS style sheets, and similar topics before you get into font replacement in templates. Getting into advanced administration too early isn't a good idea, so learn first, apply second. You can always go back and implement font inclusion at any time.

Putting Font Extensions Into Action

In this exercise, you use the HD Gfonts extension to modify a few of the CSS tags. The point is to illustrate how the extension can be used to modify existing CSS, by creating a CSS override code that takes control. The override CSS code is used instead of the default code for the same CSS element.

EXERCISE 27-1: USING THE HD GFONTS PLUG-IN

Objective: This exercise enables the HD Gfonts plug-in, and explains the different configurations that can be created using the four parameter areas of the extension.

Step 1. If you're not already there, log in to the backend of the website as the super user administrator.

Step 2. Open the plug-in manager via the Extension Manager > Plugin Manager menu.

Step 3. In the Filter drop-down on the left, select **[A]** Disabled. This will enable you to view all plug-ins that are not active.

Step 4. In the resulting list, click on the plug-in called **[B]** System - HD Gfonts to open it (Figure 27-2).

Figure 27-2 *The extension installs in the disabled state, so it must be enabled to use. All of the parameter settings are located in the plug-in.*

Step 5. Change the **[C]** status to Enabled. The **[D]** selector will turn green (Figure 27-3).

Step 6. Execute a **[E]** Save action.

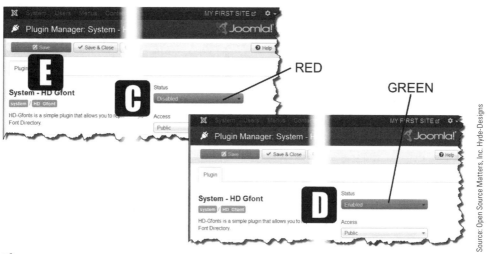

Figure 27-3 *When any extension changes from* **[C]** *Disabled (Red), the toggled item will turn* **[D]** *green.*

Step 7. View the screen (Figure 27-4). There are **[F]** four identical areas where you can set parameters to use Google Fonts. Scroll down the screen to view the other three.

Step 8. In the first **[G]** Class box, enter these values, in lowercase: **h1, h2, h3, h4, h5, h6**.

Using lowercase will force the program to match how the tags are coded in the CSS for the template. CSS tags are generally entered as lowercase letters/numbers.

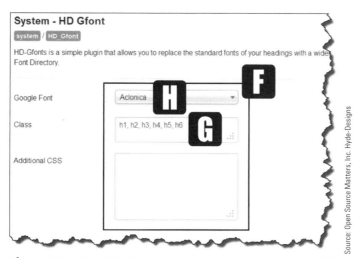

Figure 27-4 *The* **[G]** *Class text box is where you specify the CSS tag that will use the new font. The list of available* **[H]** *Google Fonts appears in the drop-down.*

CSS CODE IS CASE SENSITIVE

Generally, CSS code is written in lowercase. The "tag" can be any case, but the parameter elements must all be lowercase. If your CSS isn't working, make sure you check the use of case. If you use mixed case in the CSS, the same mixed case must be used on the web page templates. The best rule to follow is to use all lowercase letters.

Step 9. Open a new browser window and go to http://www.google.com/fonts to view the font library.

Step 10. In the Filters area on the left, select Sans Serif and click OK.

Step 11. Scroll down and view the Aclonica font. This one will be used because it is easy to visually identify. On your "live" website, you can use any font that is listed in the HD Gfonts plug-in drop-down list. Aclonica is on the list.

Step 12. Go back to the plug-in and select the **[H]** Aclonica font in the drop-down list for the "h" tags you just entered.

Step 13. Execute a Save action.

Step 14. Go to the website front-end and refresh the screen. Are the headings of articles, which are typically <h1>, in the Aclonica font? The font is somewhat "artsy" looking.

Step 15. Go back to the plug-in and change the font selection in the plug-in to Droid Sans.

Step 16. Execute a Save action.

Step 17. Go to the website front-end and refresh the screen. The headings should now be different, displaying in Droid Sans, which is a clean-looking sans serif font.

Step 18. Repeat these steps, selecting different Google Fonts, and view the front-end to see different fonts being displayed as <h1> headings.

Step 19. Change the font to **[I]** Exo, which is where you will leave the headings font assignment (Figure 27-5).

Step 20. In the **[J]** Additional CSS box, enter **color: red;** (this code must be typed in exactly as shown, ending in a semicolon). All CSS tag elements must end in a semicolon and be on separate lines.

Step 21. Execute a Save action.

Step 22. Go to the website front-end and refresh the screen. The headings should now be red.

Step 23. Go back to the plug-in and remove the code from the Additional CSS box.

Step 24. Execute a Save & Close action. The headings shown on the front-end should now be black again.

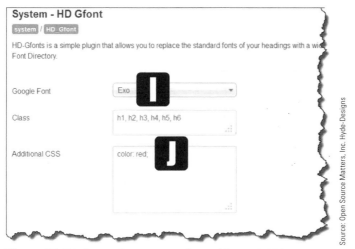

Figure 27-5 *When a class is entered, or additional CSS is specified, the settings in the plug-in "override" those in the CSS style sheet for the template.*

This is how Google Fonts are included in a Joomla! 3 website using the HD Gfonts extension.

There are more advanced features that can be employed with CSS tags and attributes and once you have a better understanding of CSS, you can add the features.

Another Extension in Action

By this time, you should realize that there is always more than one way to do things in Joomla! 3. This is true of adding fonts to a Joomla! website.

EXERCISE 27-2: USING THE PHOCA FONT COMPONENT

Objective: This exercise explains some of the uses of the Phoca Font component, and demonstrates the different configurations that can be created using the parameter settings for the component. Phoca Font requires that you download a component, a system plug-in, and a few fonts.

Use these steps to get the extension file:

Step 1.   Go to this website http://www.phoca.cz/phocafont.

Step 2.   Click the Components link in the website's top menu and select Phoca Font in the right column. This will open the Phoca Font Component web page.

Step 3.   Scroll down the page and open the Download link item.

Step 4.   Notice there are component extension files for different versions of Joomla! Download the com_phocafont_v3.0.0.zip file.

Step 5. Go back to the Components link and click on the Phoca Font plug-in in the right column, which will open the Phoca Font plug-in web page.

Step 6. Scroll down the page and open the Phoca Font Plug-in Download link item.

Step 7. Notice there are plug-in extension files for different versions of Joomla! Download the plg_system_phocafont_v3.0.1.zip file.

Step 8. Go back to the Components link and click on Phoca Font - Fonts in the right column, which will open the Phoca Font - Fonts web page.

Step 9. Scroll down the page and open the Download link item.

Step 10. This web page will open and have three separate font files to download. Download all three files. There is no need to download the fourth font on the list or the foreign language font (at the bottom of the list).

Step 11. Install the component via the Admin Backend Extension Installer using the Upload Package File. The files will reside on your computer after the download.

Step 12. Install the plug-in that was downloaded.

Step 13. Install all four of the font component files that were downloaded.

Step 14. Open the Components menu and verify that the Phoca Font component is on the list.

Step 15. Open the Extensions > Plugin Manager.

Step 16. Scroll down and find the Phoca Font plug-in and enable it, or verify that it is enabled using the Status selector at the right of the screen.

PHOCA AND GOOGLE FONTS

After the component is installed and the plug-in is enabled, Google Fonts can be added to the list of available fonts and used. You can use the entire Google Font Library in a simple, easy-to-implement manager.

If you have open source fonts, they can be converted to be compatible with the extension. This topic is discussed on the **joomla3bootcamp.com** website.

Follow these steps to add a Google Font:

Step 1. Open the Phoca Font Components **[K]** control panel (Figure 27-6).

Figure 27-6 *Unlike HD Gfonts, which is a plug-in, Phoca Font is a component and is accessed via the top* **[K]** *Components menu.*

Step 2. Open the fonts for the component. The icon is in the upper left of the screen.

Step 3. Click the green New button.

Step 4. In the **[L]** Title box, type the name of a Google Font you want to use. Type **Fauna One** if you do not have a Google Font name at hand. You can get the font names at http://www.google.com/fonts/ (Figure 27-7).

Figure 27-7 *Google Fonts are added to this extension when you enter the name of the font, which is obtained from the* **googlefonts.com** *website.*

Step 5. Observe the **[M]** Format field, which displays externalfonttype for Google Fonts. If you open one of the other fonts—the ones that were installed—you will see a different format. If you use installed fonts, make sure you change this information.

Step 6. Execute a Save & Close action.

At this point, the three Phoca Fonts were installed, and one Google Font was identified to be used on the website. The next step is to assign the fonts to CSS tags.

To ensure that you don't experience the "two bobcats in a burlap bag" effect, the HD Gfonts plug-in should be disabled. If you recall, the plug-in was used in Exercise 27-1 with the <h1> tag. Two font manager plug-ins cannot control the same CSS tag, so the HD Gfonts plug-in needs to be disabled.

To disable the font plug-in:

Step 1. Open the Extensions > Plugin Manager.

Step 2. Scroll down to where the System plug-ins are located and find System - HD Gfonts. Disable it by clicking the green checkmark next to the name.

To assign a font to a CSS tag:

Step 1. Go back to the Phoca Font control panel.

Step 2. Open the component's Options via the button at the top right of the screen.

There are three default font manager sections where you can identify CSS tags, adjust the font sizes, and add CSS code. The default font is designated in the component's Fonts area, by selecting the star in the Default column on the screen. Any installed or designated font can be designated as the default, which will replace the <body> or <p> CSS tags, depending on how the style sheet tags are configured.

Step 3. In the **[N]** Default Rule - Default Font, set the Tag, ID, or Class element to a lowercase p (Figure 27-8).

Step 4. For the **[O]** Additional CSS, enter **color: blue;** (make sure you include the colon and semicolon as shown).

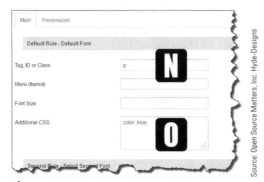

Figure 27-8 *The Default Rule - Default Font should be used for the body text* <p> *CSS tag.*

Step 5. Execute a Save action.

Step 6. Go to the website's front-end and refresh the browser window. The body text font should have changed and should be blue.

Step 7. Go back to the admin screen and remove the **[O]** Additional CSS entry from Step 4, which will return the font color to the default black.

Step 8. Execute a Save action.

Step 9. Go back to the website's front-end, refresh the browser window, and confirm the body text is again black.

Step 10. In the **[P]** Second Rule - Select Second Font section, set the Tag, ID, or Class element to a lowercase **h1,h2,h3,h4,h5,h6** (commas between each entry, but no spaces) (Figure 27-9).

Figure 27-9 *In the additional rule setting sections, the lesser used tags can be entered with different fonts if desired. If the same font, size, color, and so on is to be used for more than one CSS tag element, they can be combined as the <h> tags were.*

Step 11. Select **[Q]** Domestic Manners from the Font (Second) drop-down selector.

Step 12. Execute a Save action.

Step 13. Go to the website's front-end and refresh the browser window. The font for the article titles and module headings should have changed. The body text should be sans serif and blue. The headings should be a script face and green.

Step 14. Experiment with the other fonts and the <h> tags, and review the changes for each on the website's front-end.

Step 15. Remove the h# tags that you added in Step 10, to return the headings to their previous fonts, which is controlled by the template's CSS. If there is nothing in the Tag, ID, or Class field, the font will not be applied to anything.

Step 16. Execute a Save & Close action.

Use the extension to set the default font:

Step 1. Go back to the Phoca Font control panel.

Step 2. Open the Fonts section using the icon/button at the top left of the screen.

Any font that has been installed can be designated as the default, which is the font that is in the first parameter setting area of the component's options. The parameter area is called Default Rule - Default Font.

Step 3. The default font can be set by one of two methods (Figure 27-10):

Method 1—Check the **[R]** box next to the font name, then click the **[S]** Make Default button. The button functions as a Save action when clicked. The default font is now the one selected.

Method 2—Simply click a grey star icon in the **[T]** Default column. No other action is required. If the star turns gold, the font has been designated as the default.

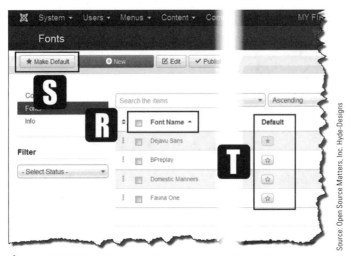

Figure 27-10 *You designate the default fonts in the Fonts management area.*

By now, you should have a pretty good idea of the basics of adding fonts to a Joomla! 3 website, and as long as developers provide the great extensions used in these exercises, CSS coding isn't necessary.

CSS coding takes a bit of technical knowledge and some studying. If you have some technical knowledge, it's a good rainy afternoon project. Just search the Internet and start reading and experimenting.

Too Many Fonts Makes Ugly Websites

Before you get too revved up about using an abundance of fonts, a word of caution.

Several things can happen if you use too many external fonts. Here are some possible results:

◆ The website can look really ugly if too many fonts are used.

◆ The website will load slowly because of the number of fonts that need to be downloaded. Remember, the fonts are not resident on the computer viewing the website.

◆ The site can break because it has too many fonts to deal with.

◆ Too many fonts can create issues for visually impaired website visitors.

It's always a good idea to limit the use of external fonts. Usually, the body text should use a common font that's resident on most computers. There is no real big need to depart from using common fonts.

The <h1> tag on Joomla! 3 websites is used for article headings, so dressing the site up with a complementary font is acceptable. If you are displaying headings for modules on web pages, that heading <h3> can be changed to improve appearance. Check your template's CSS to see what tags are being used for different heading elements.

Using Built-In Fonts

If you recall from Chapter 21, "Templates," frameworks add parameter controls to change the look and layout of the web pages. Some of the more progressive developers are including a set of parameters that allow the administrator to select/designate fonts in a manner similar to the way the HD Gfonts and the Phoca Font extensions function.

In fact, many of those templates include, as part of their primary design, certain fonts. The fonts were chosen in combination with each other to give a clean, professional appearance to the different web page layouts.

Keep the thought of using additional fonts in mind when you're shopping for templates. Check the fonts that are included with the template to make sure they meet your needs.

Summary

In this chapter, you learned:

◆ The fundamentals of using fonts on a Joomla! 3 website.

◆ Why it's best to avoid using font replacement.

◆ About extensions that add font capabilities.

◆ The fundamentals of using CSS.

◆ About issues with using fonts on websites.

◆ How to use the HD Gfonts plug-in extension.

◆ How to use the Phoca Font component.

◆ Why it's best to avoid using too many fonts.

◆ Other ways to include additional fonts.

http://docs.joomla.org

The joomla.org website has a comprehensive "Help" section consisting of documentation about using Joomla! 3.

The opening page to the "docs" section has links for Beginners, Administrators and Developers.

Take some time to view the pages that interest you and learn more about the use of Joomla! 3.

Quick Start

- Learn More About Joomla → What is the Joomla CMS, what can it do for you, and how to install it.
- Beginners → Where do I start? I am ready to use Joomla but I have no idea what to do first.
- Administrators → You are a Joomla website administrator and responsible for the day-to-day operation and maintenance of the website.
- Developers → You are a developer interested in creating a Joomla extension, module, or plugin.

Chapter 28

Website Backups

Learning Objectives

What's included in this chapter:

- ◆ Why backups are needed.
- ◆ Backups on your webserver.
- ◆ Extension for managing backups.
- ◆ What backup extensions should do.
- ◆ When to back up the website.
- ◆ Finding backup extensions in the JED.
- ◆ How to add protection to the website.
- ◆ Extensions for website security.
- ◆ Maintaining the robots.txt file.
- ◆ Maintaining the .htaccess file.
- ◆ Taking backups seriously.

Why Back Up Your Website?

Having a backup of your Joomla! 3 website is kind of like having a gold bar in a safe deposit box. Both are very valuable. You want to have a full website backup ready to reinstall if something happens to the website.

There are many reasons you should maintain backups, the most obvious being the recovery of the website in the event of some sort of calamity. In this day and age of even the most sophisticated website being "hacked," a little old Joomla! 3 website could easily fall victim to any kind of malicious attack.

If that happens, you must have a way to recover and redeploy the website.

Webhosting Backups

If you have a Joomla! 3 website hosted on either a cPanel or a Plesk Control Panel, both have the capabilities of running full backups. With WHM/cPanel, along with Plesk, you can configure the hosting environment to perform backups on a regular schedule and store the backups away from the server.

Additionally, both provide a way for you to manually perform backups. This is also good, because immediately after you make major changes to the website, it's wise to generate a full backup. Otherwise, the website will not be backed up until the next scheduled time. During the interim, all sorts of nasty things could happen, and you want to prevent that if possible.

Extensions for Website Backups

To hedge your back-up bet, it's a good idea to have another way of doing it. If you go to the JED and search for "site security," you will find a long list of possibilities. Give it a try. Go to the JED and use the Advanced Search feature. Make sure you filter the search to only find results that are Joomla! 3.2 compatible.

Did you get a lot of results? Of course you did. That's because having backups of a Joomla! 3 website is important and developers have created them for the task.

When you're selecting an extension to use for backups, you need to find one that does a complete job. So, what is a complete backup? Here are the things the backup extension should be able to do, either automatically, or via parameter settings:

Entire website files—The backup should include every file in the Joomla! 3 installation directory location; no exceptions.

Include extensions—Make sure the extension can back up the installed extensions. Again, no exceptions.

Include the database—Yes, yes, yes. The database is just as important as the rest of the website. It is where all of the content is stored. If you have a backup of the database, and cannot restore the original site files, you at least have the content.

Cron jobs—This stands for "chronological jobs," and is a fancy way of saying the backups should be performed automatically on the date/days/times specified. This would then be the automatic backup you control in addition to any backups directly on the webserver.

Storage of backups—The backup extension should have the capabilities of storing the backups on the server, as a local download, on a cloud server, or some combination of all of these options.

Restoration—The extension should be able to perform a complete restoration of the original location of the website, or another location—even on another webserver.

Easy-to-use—Both the backup function and the process of restoration should be easy to use, even by an administrator who is just starting to build websites. The extension is no good if you can't manage it.

Use tutorials—If you are a beginning Joomla! 3 administrator and don't have a handle on the lingo and what all is involved, there should be a step-by-step tutorial available for the backup extension. Check joomla3bootcamp.com for backup tutorials.

Scheduling Backups

There are several scenarios for scheduling backups:

Scenario 1, on a daily basis. If you have a very active website with content being added daily, by all means, implement a daily backup scheme.

Scenario 2, when updating the website. Before you update or make major changes to the website, be sure to start the process by manually backing up the site files, to include all of the extensions, along with a dump of the MySQL database.

Scenario 3, after the update. When you're done with the updating work, make an immediate backup to have on hand before the timed backup (Scenario 1) kicks in. A lot could happen in the ensuing hours.

Scenario 4, no automatic backups. If your server does not have automatic backups, install an extension that will perform that function. Make sure the files, extensions, and database are included in the extensions backup process.

The JED has plenty of extensions you can use for full-site backups. Every extension that performs backups is the "free" type. Download and install each and go through the process of backing up your website to see how it works. Make sure you only download and attempt to install Version 3.2-compatible extensions.

Adding Protection to Your Website

Back in the old days, when everyone lived in castles, the game plan was that if anyone broke in, you would have an army with clubs and weapons to beat the invaders off. That was okay, but you could get pretty tired doing battle on a regular basis.

So what did they do? They built a moat around the castle and installed a drawbridge. That forced invaders to first deal with the moat, and then the drawbridge, and then finally to face the crew inside with weapons. It is easier to fight off invaders if they can enter only one way (the drawbridge), because the moat stops them everywhere else.

When they really got smart, they filled the moat with oil. When the invaders tried to cross it, they lit the oil. Thus, the first "firewall" for defense.

Every webserver has a firewall, and that's well and good. But hackers can get around those in a flat ten seconds. If the website has its own firewall, the website administrator can sleep better at night.

Search the JED for "firewall" as the search term. A decent list will show up on the results screen. It is also not coincidental that some of the same developers that offer backup extensions also offer extensions that stop the invasion to begin with.

Don't immediately neglect the idea of paying a bit for a good firewall extension. The small amount you need to pay for the protection is well worth it. If you had to pay $100 for a high-quality extension, and it did its job, think about how much it would cost you in time to restore the website back to it original form. You should apply this price vs. effort evaluation to backup extensions as well. If they do their job, they are priceless to you as a website administrator.

Finding Good Security Extensions

In the JED, use the Advanced Search to search for the term "site protection." You can use the Category drop-down to make this selection. You should get 20 or so results. Notice that when you look at the list of extensions that there are both "free" and "paid" versions available.

Review the extensions to see which you want to implement on your website. If you need to pay for the one you want, remember that it will help protect the gold bar in the safe deposit box.

If you protect the website on the front-end as the primary defense against hacking, you may never need to use a backup. But don't ignore backup activity by assuming the front-end is safe.

Setting up a firewall on your website can stop many hacking attempts and save you a lot of grief.

Don't Forget the robots.txt File

The robots.txt file is located at the root level of your webserver, where the Joomla! 3 instance is installed. This is a simple little file that prevents "search robots" from accessing and adding the information to search engine results.

All of the major search engines have very sophisticated robots that are constantly cruising the Internet accessing millions of websites per hour.

A typical Joomla! 3 robots.txt file, which is automatically added during the installation process, looks like this:

```
User-agent: *
Disallow: /administrator/
Disallow: /cache/
Disallow: /cli/
Disallow: /components/
Disallow: /images/
Disallow: /includes/
Disallow: /installation/
Disallow: /language/
Disallow: /libraries/
Disallow: /logs/
Disallow: /media/
Disallow: /modules/
Disallow: /plugins/
Disallow: /templates/
Disallow: /tmp/
```

What all that means is that robots are not allowed to access certain directories within the root location where Joomla! 3 is installed. If you have added directories, you can add them to the "disallowed" list by entering the information in a similar format.

The .htaccess File

Another file that resides in the root, and is inserted during the Joomla! 3 installation process, is the .htaccess file. You may see it as htaccess.txt in the directory. If you are using a Windows-based server, leave that filename as is. If you are using a cPanel/Linux server, the filename needs to be changed to .htaccess.

This file is a bit complicated, and there is generally no need to change or modify any of the code. If you feel you need to edit the .htaccess file, search the Internet for "Joomla htaccess" to learn about this file and how the code is implemented.

There is usually no need to modify this file, but if you must, do some diligence before you do so.

> **BACK UP BEFORE**
>
> Before changing or modifying the **robots.txt** or **.htaccess** files, copy them to your local computer so you have a backup version of the original. Then perform a full backup of the entire website and the database.
>
> This updates the gold bar in the safe deposit box.

Last Bit of Advice

Don't treat backing up your website lightly. It should be one of the first things you undertake immediately after installing the program. If you know that you have a method for recovering a broken Joomla! 3 website, you can have more confidence in undertaking any administrative activities. If you "break it," you can restore the site very easily.

Backing up a website might take a little bit of time. Restoring it may also take some time. But this is a minor investment compared to rebuilding the website. Remember the old adage, "Better safe than sorry."

Summary

In this chapter, you learned:

◆ Backups are important.

◆ Hosting servers include backup features.

◆ Many backup extensions are available.

◆ How backup extensions should function.

◆ Backups are needed before and after modifications.

◆ How to find backup extensions in the JED.

◆ Websites also need security protection.

◆ How to find security extensions in the JED.

◆ The function of the robots.txt file.

◆ The function of the .htaccess file.

◆ The importance of maintaining backups.

Installing Joomla! 3 via cPanel

Learning Objectives

What's included in this appendix:

◆ Information about the tasks and steps involved in preparing a website server to accept and install a Joomla! 3 website.

◆ Instructions on how to prepare a website hosting location that operates under cPanel.

◆ Instructions on how to download the Joomla! 3 installation files from the joomla.org website to your local computer.

◆ Instructions on how to create a location directory within the server root location where Joomla! 3 will be installed.

◆ Instructions on how to upload the Joomla! 3 installer file to the newly created hosting directory.

◆ Instructions on how to extract the files from the Joomla! 3 installer file.

◆ Instructions on how to create a MySQL database for the website.

◆ Instructions on how to create and associate a user with the database.

Introduction

Now that you have secured a hosting location for your Joomla! 3 website, it is necessary to configure the server to accommodate a database-driven website. Joomla! 3 isn't the only software that can be installed on a server. Most require a database connection. The instructions in this appendix apply not only to Joomla! 3, but to other software programs as well.

The instructions in this chapter apply to a website server that is operating under a Control Panel referred to as *cPanel*, one of the more popular hosting-platform configurations used by Internet Service Providers (ISPs).

> ## USING PARALLELS PLESK?
>
> If you are using a standard Parallels Plesk for your website hosting, go to Appendix B, "Installing Joomla! 3 via the Parallels Plesk Control Panel," which will guide you through the process of getting that type of website server ready to host your Joomla! 3 website.
>
> Instructions on how to use both have been provided, as each is used extensively around the world to manage websites on leased webservers.

Getting Joomla! 3 Installed

Installing Joomla! 3 on a webserver hosting location requires several actions, such as:

Step 1. Obtain the Joomla! 3 Installation file.

Step 2. Create an installation location on a webserver.

Step 3. Upload the Joomla! 3 install file to the webserver installation location.

Step 4. Extract the actual Joomla! 3 files needed for the installation.

Step 5. Create a database for Joomla! 3.

Step 6. Create a user for the Joomla! 3 database.

Step 7. Perform the actual installation of Joomla! 3 (covered in Chapter 2, "Installing Joomla! 3").

The instructions are written with the assumption that you have never performed the tasks necessary to add a database-driven website to a hosting webserver location. Although the tasks and steps involved may seem a little daunting at first, they are actually not difficult if you follow the instructions in the exercises.

If you have experience with installing software on a webserver, you can fly right through the required steps. Just make sure that you have Joomla! 3 extracted into the **myfirstsite** folder, which is created in Exercise A-2. This location is referenced in other exercises in the chapters.

There are six exercises in this appendix that guide you through this process:

Exercise A-1—Downloading the Joomla! 3 installation files from the joomla.org website.

Exercise A-2—Creating a directory location for the Joomla! 3 website files.

Exercise A-3—Uploading the Joomla! 3 installation files to the webserver.

Exercise A-4—Extracting the files from the Joomla! 3 installation file.

Exercise A-5—Creating a MySQL database.

Exercise A-6—Assigning a user to the MySQL database.

Let's get going!

EXERCISE A-1: DOWNLOADING THE JOOMLA! 3 INSTALLATION FILES FROM THE JOOMLA.ORG WEBSITE

Objective: This exercise guides you through the Joomla! 3 installation file download from the joomla.org website to your local computer. Joomla! 3 must be installed onto a webserver. It does not operate locally on your computer like other Windows or Macintosh programs. Because Joomla! 3 is made available under the international Open Source conventions, there is no cost to download and use the program.

To obtain and download the installation files, perform the following:

Step 1. Open a web browser to joomla.org. When the website opens, find the download links located in the blue area (Figure A-1).

Step 2. Click on the orange **[A]** Download button.

Figure A-1 *The* **[A]** *Download button accesses the installer and upgrades the file packages for Joomla! 3.*

Step 3. Click the blue **[C]** Download Joomla! 3.2 button on the **[B]** Download Joomla! screen (Figure A-2).

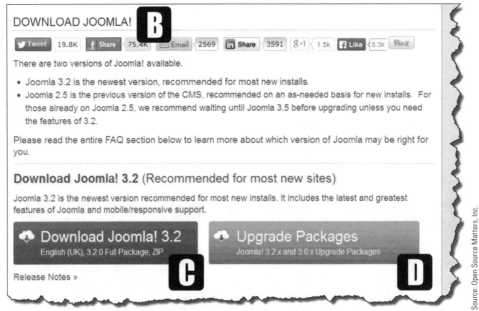

Figure A-2 *The* **[B]** *Download Joomla! screen is where you find the* **[C]** *Download Joomla! 3.2 button and the* **[D]** *Upgrade Packages button, which enable you to upgrade different versions of Joomla! to the current version.*

Step 4. Select **[E]** Save File and then click **[F]** OK to start the download. This action will download the installer file to the location on your computer (Figure A-3).

Figure A-3 *The* **[E]** *Save File option will download the installer file to your computer when you execute the* **[F]** *OK action. For screenshots in this book, the Firefox browser was used on a PC.*

IDENTIFY THE DOWNLOAD LOCATION

It is important to know where on your system the downloaded file is saved. Before starting the download, check to determine where on your system the files are saved by default. You can designate a folder on your local computer to be the default for file downloads.

After downloading the installation files, they must be uploaded to the webserver hosting location. The process involves selecting the file that was downloaded via the Browse function.

After clicking the OK button, the Joomla! 3 installation file will begin to download. This may take a while to complete, depending upon the speed of the Internet connection. If there is an anti-virus system operating on your computer, the file will be checked for viruses after being downloaded.

Once it's been downloaded, the Joomla! 3 installation files can be transferred to the webserver hosting location for your website.

USE YOUR DOMAIN NAME

On some screenshots, you will see the domain name joomla3bootcamp.com. This is the domain being used for examples, exercises, and other tutorials in this book. Substitute your domain name for joomla3bootcamp.com whenever you see it on screenshots throughout this book.

EXERCISE A-2: CREATING A DIRECTORY LOCATION FOR THE JOOMLA! 3 WEBSITE FILES

Objective: This exercise creates a directory on your webserver within the root directory into which Joomla! 3 will be installed. This location will be referred to in other exercises. The directory will not be publically viewable unless the viewer types in the exact URL location.

Exercises throughout this book refer to this location of the Joomla! 3 instance and allow you to use the book to learn Joomla! 3. You'll be using it in a development and viewing location that will not interfere with any websites created in the root directory.

To create a directory within the root directory, perform the following steps:

Step 1. Log in to cPanel using the credentials provided by the ISP providing your hosting environment. The screen, by default, opens to the main cPanel screen (Figure A-4).

Figure A-4 *The cPanel screen has been reduced to show only the actual area you will use in this exercise, which is the Files area. The* **[G]** *File Manager icon opens the location on the webserver where all files are located.*

Step 2. About one-third of the way down the screen, in the Files section, click on the icon called **[G]** File Manager. The directory tree will appear on the left side of the screen. This should open to show the folders and files to the **[H]** public_html, which is called the *root* folder of the website. If not, click on the public_html folder to open it (Figure A-5).

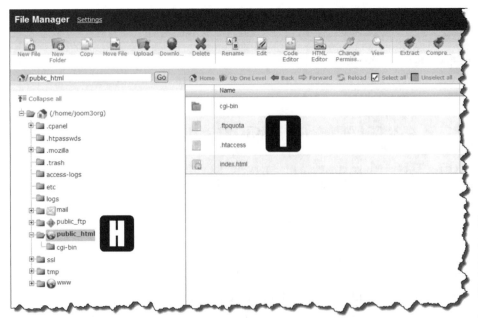

Figure A-5 *The* **[H]** *public_html folder in a cPanel is the root directory. When you open it, you may see other* **[I]** *files displayed than the ones shown here, depending on how your webserver is configured.*

Step 3. With the public_html folder open, click on the **[J]** New Folder icon in the menu bar (Figure A-6). The **[K]** current folder location is shown next to the Home icon.

Figure A-6 *The* **[J]** *New Folder icon creates folders in the* **[K]** *current location in the webserver file structure.*

Step 4. In the popup window entitled **[L]** New Folder, Enter **[M] myfirstsite** in the New Folder Name area. Leave the default /**public_html** location as is (Figure A-7). The **myfirstsite** folder will be used to host the Joomla! 3 installation on your webserver. That way, you can complete exercises and learn how to use the CMS, without enabling public access.

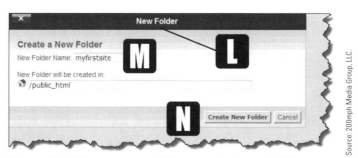

Figure A-7 *Whenever a new folder is needed, use the* **[L]** *New Folder function in cPanel and give the* **[M]** *new folder a name. Be sure to note where it will be created.*

Step 5. Execute the **[N]** Create New Folder action.

Step 6. Verify that the **[O]** myfirstsite folder was created in the root location (Figure A-8). It should be displayed in both the folder view and in the tree view on the left.

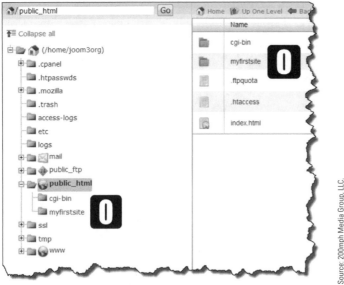

Figure A-8 *When you're in the File Manager, the folder content is shown on the left of the screen, which shows only the folders. The folder area shows both folders and files.*

EXERCISE A-3: UPLOADING THE JOOMLA! 3 INSTALLATION FILES TO THE WEBSERVER

Objective: This exercise copies the Joomla! 3 installation files from your local computer to the website server myfirstsite folder location. The installation files must reside on the webserver and then be extracted into a folder so the installation can be completed.

Perform the following steps to transfer the Joomla! 3 installation file that was downloaded previously, and copy it to the myfirstsite folder location:

Step 1. If you're not already there, go to cPanel's File Manager and open the myfirstsite folder by clicking on the name in the left tree menu, which is located within the public_html folder. When opened, the myfirstsite folder should be empty.

> **UPLOAD TO THE CORRECT LOCATION**
>
> The Upload icon is available for any folder on the webserver, so double-check to make sure that you are physically in the **myfirstsite** folder before attempting the file upload. If you are not in the **myfirstsite** folder, the file will be uploaded to the wrong location.

Step 2. Click the Upload icon in the top menu (Figure A-9). Note the location, indicating the webserver location, and that the directory is empty. This will be the destination of the Joomla! 3 installation file.

Figure A-9 *Files are uploaded via the* **[P]** *Upload function in cPanel. Make sure, whenever you are uploading a file, that you are located in the desired destination folder.*

Step 3. Click the **[Q]** Browse button, which will open a screen to your computer's file structure on your computer (Figure A-10). Find and select the Joomla! 3 ZIP file that was downloaded in Exercise A-1. The download will start immediately and a progress indicator appears in the lower-right portion of the screen. If you are using a web browser other than Firefox, the name of the button to access your computer's files might be slightly different.

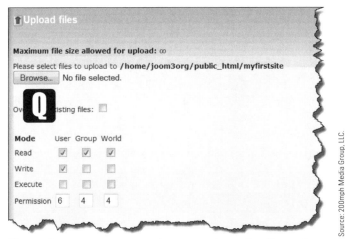

Figure A-10 *Locate the Joomla! 3 zipped installer file via the* **[Q]** *Browse button. Leave all other settings on the Upload Files screen as is.*

Step 4. When you find the file, click on its filename: Joomla_3.2.0-Stable-Full_Package .zip. The download will start immediately. No other buttons need be clicked.

When the progress indicator, at the bottom-right portion of the screen, is complete, the Joomla! 3 ZIP file should appear in the files list for the **myfirstsite** folder (Figure A-11). Close the browser tab when the upload is completed and return to the File Manager screen of cPanel.

Figure A-11 *After an upload is completed, the* **[R]** Joomla_3.2.0-Stable-Full_Package.zip *file should appear in the folder location.*

EXERCISE A-4: EXTRACTING THE FILES FROM THE JOOMLA! 3 INSTALLATION FILE

Objective: This exercise extracts the Joomla! 3 files from the compressed (ZIP) file that was uploaded in the previous exercise.

Step 1. In the **myfirstsite** folder, select the Joomla! 3 installation file by clicking on the **[S]** box icon to the left of the filename. With the file selected (shows blue), click the **[T]** Extract button in the menu bar (Figure A-12).

Figure A-12 *To extract a ZIP file, you must select the file* **[S]** *and then click the* **[T]** *Extract button.*

Step 2. The next screen (Extract) displays the **[U]** file being extracted, as well as the **[V]** folder location into which the extracted files will be written. If both of these are correct, execute the **[W]** Extract File(s) action (Figure A-13).

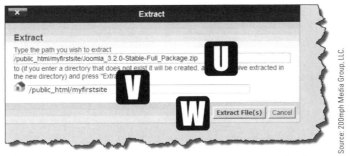

Figure A-13 *Always verify the file being extracted and the destination before executing the* **[W]** *Extract File(s) action.*

The extraction action should happen rather quickly and a popup window called Extraction Results will display showing a list of folders and files in the directory into which the file was extracted.

Step 3. Close the popup window.

Step 4. Refresh the browser window to display the file list in the folder. You do this by using the **[X]** Reload link in the menu bar (Figure A-14).

Figure A-14 *Any time you add a file and want to verify it, simply execute the* **[X]** *Reload action. It is not necessary to refresh the browser window to refresh a folder's file listing.*

After the Reload, a list of folder and files should appear within the myfirstsite folder. You can also drill down the folder/file listing in the left tree menu to verify the results of the extraction process.

EXERCISE A-5: CREATING A MYSQL DATABASE

Objective: This exercise guides you through the process of creating a MySQL database on the webserver using cPanel, to which Joomla! 3 will connect during the installation process.

Step 1. If you are not logged in to the webserver's cPanel, do so now.

Step 2. Open the **[Y]** MySQL Databases in the Databases section. When the screen opens, note in the center of the screen that there is a message in red indicating there are no databases associated with your account. If any databases are created later, they will appear on this screen (Figure A-15).

389

Figure A-15 *Any MySQL database needed for any Joomla! 3 installation is created here, by clicking the* **[Y]** *MySQL Databases icon in the Databases section of cPanel.*

Step 3. In the **[Z]** Create New Database area, enter **[AA] joom3DB** for the new database and execute the **[BB]** Create Database action (Figure A-16).

Figure A-16 *When naming a database, give the name some relevance to the website or web project you are installing. In this case,* **[AA]** joom3DB *was used.*

Step 4. When the database has been created, execute the Go Back button on the results screen and verify the **[CC]** database was created. Note that no **[DD]** users have yet been assigned. This is indicated by the fact that there is nothing listed in the Users column (Figure A-17).

Figure A-17 *Every database must have an assigned authorized user connected to it, which is required when installing Joomla! 3.*

At this point, continue the database-creation process by assigning an authorized user, following the steps in Exercise A-6.

EXERCISE A-6: ASSIGNING A USER TO THE MYSQL DATABASE

Objective: This exercise creates a user who associates with the MySQL database created in Exercise A-5. Every database must have one, or more, assigned users who are identified with the database during the Joomla! 3 installation. Each user must also have a unique password.

> **NOTE THE PREFIX**
>
> For both the database-creation and the user-assignment areas, you will see a prefix, which is typically your cPanel login username, followed by an underscore. The prefix along with the database and/or username is needed to connect Joomla! 3 to the database with the proper user. Make sure to keep this in mind when you're asked for that information during the installation process. The instructions for connecting to the database are covered in Chapter 2.

Step 1. On the MySQL Databases screen in the **[EE]** MySQL Users, Add New User area, create the user named **[FF] joom3U** and enter/confirm the **[GG]** password that is associated with that user (Figure A-18).

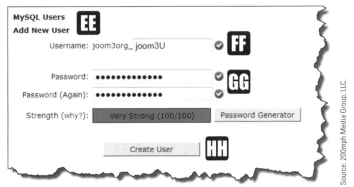

Source: 200mph Media Group, LLC.

Figure A-18 *Always make sure that the password is "very strong" when creating one for a database. Remember to write down the password if you are using the password generator to create one for you, as they are hard to remember.*

Step 2. Click **[HH]** Create User when the username and passwords have been entered.

WRITE DOWN THE PASSWORD!

If you use the password generator to create a password, be sure to write it down. You won't be able to find out what the password is if you do not record it. When you're creating a password yourself, make sure that the strength indicator shows "very strong," so that the password is more difficult to hack into.

Step 3. Go to the Add User To Database section of the screen. Confirm the **[II]** username and the **[JJ]** database name that appear in the separate drop-down lists, and then click the **[KK]** Add button to associate the user with the database (Figure A-19).

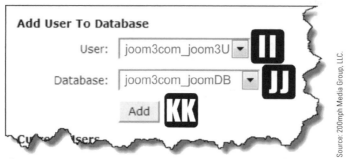

Figure A-19 *A database must always have an authorized user assigned to it. When using cPanel,* joom3com_ *(remember the underscore), was required because both databases and users require the website cPanel name as the prefix. The prefix on your webserver will be different, but do not forget to use it when installing Joomla! 3.*

Step 4. After the user/database connection action is executed, the next screen will ask for privileges or permissions for the user in regard to the database (Figure A-20). Select the check box at the top that shows **[LL]** All Privileges, and then click the **[MM]** Make Changes button.

Step 5. Execute the Go Back function after the user assignment Make Changes action.

Step 6. Verify that the joom3com_joomU user has been assigned to the joom3com_joomDB database in the Current Databases area at the center of the page. If the user appears, the connection between the two has been successful.

Now that you've set up a hosting location and created a database and an authorized user, you're ready to install Joomla! 3.

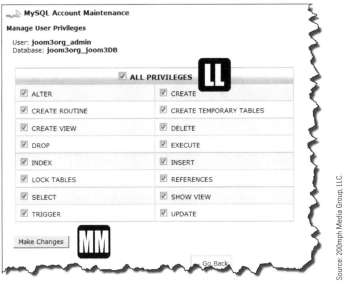

Figure A-20 *The user must be granted the correct group of privileges for the database. In this case,* **[LL]** *All Privileges were granted.*

Summary

In this appendix, you learned:

◆ How to prepare a hosting location that operates using cPanel.

◆ How to download the Joomla! 3 installation files from the joomla.org website to your local computer.

◆ How to create a location directory within the webserver root location where Joomla! 3 will be installed.

◆ How to upload the Joomla! 3 installer file to the newly created hosting directory.

◆ How to extract the files from the Joomla! 3 installer file.

◆ How to create a MySQL database for the website.

◆ How to create and associate a user with the database.

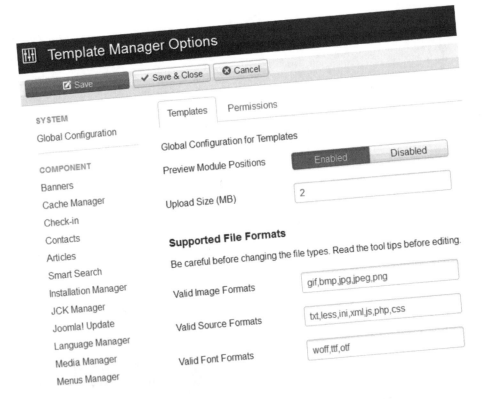

Template Manager Options

✔ Save ✔ Save & Close ✖ Cancel

Templates   Permissions

SYSTEM
Global Configuration

Global Configuration for Templates

Preview Module Positions   Enabled   Disabled

COMPONENT
Banners
Cache Manager   Upload Size (MB)   2
Check-in
Contacts
Articles   **Supported File Formats**
Smart Search   Be careful before changing the file types. Read the tool tips before editing.
Installation Manager
JCK Manager   Valid Image Formats   gif,bmp,jpg,jpeg,png
Joomla! Update
Language Manager   Valid Source Formats   txt,less,ini,xml,js,php,css
Media Manager
Menus Manager   Valid Font Formats   woff,ttf,otf

Within the Template Manager "Options,"
the types of file formats other admins or
editors may upload or use on the site
can be specified - or restricted - which
helps prevent file format errors from
affecting the display. The size of the
files may also be restricted within the
"Options" for the Template Manager.

Installing Joomla! 3 via the Parallels Plesk Control Panel

Learning Objectives

What's included in this appendix:

◆ Information about the tasks and steps involved in preparing a website server to accept and install a Joomla! 3 website.

◆ Instructions on how to prepare a website hosting location that operates under the Parallels Plesk Control Panel.

◆ Instructions on how to download the Joomla! 3 installation files from the **joomla.org** website to your local computer.

◆ Instructions on how to create a directory within the webserver root location where Joomla! 3 will be installed.

◆ Instructions on how to upload the Joomla! 3 installer file to the newly created hosting directory.

◆ Instructions on how to extract the files from the Joomla! 3 installer file.

◆ Instructions on how to create a MySQL database for the website.

◆ Instructions on how to create and associate a user with the database.

Introduction

Now that you have secured a hosting location for your Joomla! 3 website, it is necessary to configure the webserver to accommodate a database-driven website, such as Joomla! 3.

The instructions in this appendix apply to a website server that is operating under the Parallels Plesk Control Panel, one of the more popular hosting platform configurations used by Internet Service Providers (ISPs).

USING cPANEL?

If you are using a standard cPanel for your website hosting, go to Appendix A, "Installing Joomla! 3 via cPanel," which will guide you through the process of getting that type of webserver ready to host your Joomla! 3 website.

Getting Joomla! 3 Installed

Installing Joomla! 3 on a webserver hosting location requires a number of actions to be taken, including:

Action 1. Obtaining the Joomla! 3 installation file.

Action 2. Creating an installation location on a webserver.

Action 3. Uploading the Joomla! 3 install file to the webserver installation location.

Action 4. Extracting the actual Joomla! 3 files needed for the installation.

Action 5. Creating a database for Joomla! 3.

Action 6. Creating a user for the Joomla! 3 database.

Action 7. Performing the actual installation of Joomla! 3 (covered in Chapter 2, "Installing Joomla! 3").

The instructions in this appendix are written with the assumption that you have never performed the tasks necessary to add a database-driven website to a hosting webserver. And, while the tasks and steps involved may seem a little daunting at first, they are actually not difficult if you follow the instructions in the exercises.

If you have experience installing software on a webserver, you can fly right through the required steps. Just make sure that you have Joomla! 3 extracted into the myfirstsite directory that will be created in Exercise B-2. This location is referenced in other exercises in the chapters of this book.

There are six exercises in this appendix, and they guide you through the process:

Exercise B-1—Downloading the Joomla! 3 installation files from the joomla.org website.

Exercise B-2—Creating a directory location for the Joomla! 3 website files.

Exercise B-3—Uploading the Joomla! 3 installation files to the webserver.

Exercise B-4—Extracting the files from the Joomla! 3 installation file.

Exercise B-5—Creating a MySQL database.

Exercise B-6—Assigning a user to the MySQL database.

Let's get going.

EXERCISE B-1: DOWNLOADING THE JOOMLA! 3 INSTALLATION FILES FROM THE JOOMLA.ORG WEBSITE

Objective: This exercise guides you through the Joomla! 3 installation file download from the joomla.org website. Joomla! 3 must be installed onto a webserver. It does not operate locally on your computer like other Windows or Macintosh programs. Because Joomla! 3 is available under Open Source conditions, there is no cost to download and install/use the program.

To obtain and download the installation files, perform the following steps:

Step 1. Open a web browser to joomla.org. When the website opens, the download links are located in the blue area (Figure B-1).

Step 2. Click on the orange **[A]** Download button.

Source: Open Source Matters, Inc.

Figure B-1 *The* **[A]** *Download button accesses the location of the installer and upgrade file packages for Joomla! 3.*

Step 3. Click the blue **[C]** Download Joomla! 3.2 button on the **[B]** Download Joomla! screen (Figure B-2).

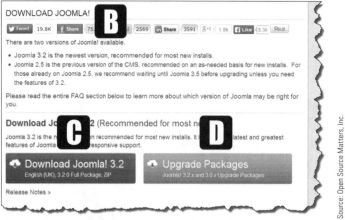

Figure B-2 *The* **[B]** *Download Joomla! screen has links to the* **[C]** *Download Joomla! 3.2 location and to the* **[D]** *Upgrade Packages, which enable you to upgrade different versions of Joomla! to the current version.*

Step 4. Select **[E]** Save File and then click **[F]** OK to start the download. This action will download the installer file to the location on your computer (Figure B-3).

Figure B-3 *The* **[E]** *Save File option will download the installer file to your computer when you execute the* **[F]** *OK action. For screenshots in this book, the Firefox browser was used on a PC.*

IDENTIFY DOWNLOAD LOCATION

It is important to know where on your system the downloaded file is being saved. Before starting the download, check to determine where on your system the files are saved by default. You can designate a directory on your local computer to be the default for file downloads.

After downloading the installation files, they must be uploaded to the webserver hosting location. The process involves selecting the file that was downloaded via a Browse function.

After clicking the OK button, the Joomla! 3 installation file begins to download. This may take several seconds or longer to complete, depending on the speed of the Internet connection. If there is an anti-virus system on your computer, the file will be checked for viruses after being downloaded.

Once completed, the Joomla! 3 installation files can be transferred to the webserver hosting location for your website.

EXERCISE B-2: CREATING A DIRECTORY LOCATION FOR THE JOOMLA! 3 WEBSITE FILES

Objective: This exercise creates a directory on your webserver within the root directory (httpdocs), into which Joomla! 3 is installed. This location is referred to in other exercises. The directory will not be publically viewable unless the viewer types in the exact URL location.

Exercises throughout this book refer to this location of the Joomla! 3 instance. This allows you to use the book to learn Joomla! 3 in a viewing location that will not interfere with any websites created in the root directory.

To create a directory within the root directory, perform the following steps:

Step 1. Log in to the website's Control Panel using the credentials provided by the ISP. The screen, by default, opens to the **[G]** Home location (Figure B-4).

Step 2. At the left side, under Home, click on **[H]** Domains. A list of domains on the webserver will display. Select the domain that will be used for the new website (Figure B-4).

Figure B-4 *In Parallels Plesk, the website location is accessible under the* **[H]** *Domains link.*

Step 3. When the screen opens, scroll down the list (if there is one) and click on the domain name under which Joomla! 3 will be installed.

Step 4. When the domain screen displays, click on the Websites & Domains tab (Figure B-5).

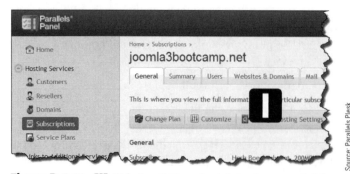

Figure B-5 *The* **[I]** *Websites & Domains tab is where most of the activity takes place relative to the administration of the website.*

Step 5. Look toward the bottom of the screen and find the **[J]** domain name. Then open the **[K]** website at httpdocs link to the right by clicking on httpdocs (Figure B-6).

Figure B-6 *Each domain has its own root directory. In Parallels Plesk, it is the* httpdocs *directory. Other webserver types may use a different name for the same location.*

Step 6. A list of the directories and files in the **root** or **httpdocs** should be displayed (Figure B-7).

Step 7. Click on the **[L]** Add New Directory icon to add a new directory to the **httpdocs** directory (Figure B-7).

Figure B-7 *When the Joomla! 3 hosting location is created, it will also display on this list.*

Step 8.   Add a new directory called **[M] myfirstsite** (Figure B-8).

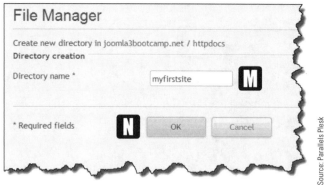

Source: Parallels Plesk

Figure B-8 *Enter* **[M]** myfirstsite *as required and click the* **[N]** *OK button. This will create the directory at the root level of the website.*

Step 9.   Click **[N]** OK to create the new directory.

Step 10.   When the process is complete, the screen will show that the directory was **[O]** successfully added and the **[P]** pathway will show the directory name. (Figure B-9).

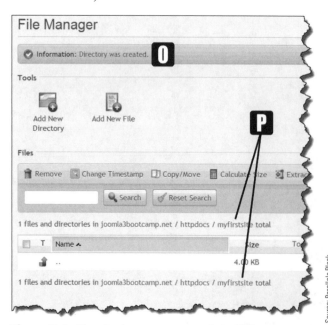

Source: Parallels Plesk

Figure B-9 *After the directory is created, the* **[O]** *message will appear, and can be confirmed as the current location by the* **[P]** *path indicators.*

Now that the hosting directory has been created, the Joomla! 3 installation file can be uploaded and extracted.

EXERCISE B-3: UPLOADING THE JOOMLA! 3 INSTALLATION FILES TO THE WEBSERVER

Objective: This exercise copies the Joomla! 3 installation files from your local computer to the website server location. The installation files must reside on the webserver and then be extracted into the **myfirstsite** directory so the actual installation can be completed.

Perform the following steps to transfer the Joomla! 3 installation file that was downloaded to your computer previously and copy it to the working directory location:

Step 1.   Go to the Control Panel and open the **myfirstsite** directory you created earlier, which is located here at Home > Subscriptions > Domain Name > Websites & Domains > File Manager (and then within the **httpdocs** directory).

Step 2.   Open the **myfirstsite** directory. Because this is a newly created directory, there should be no files listed (Figure B-10).

Step 3.   Click the **[Q]** Add New File icon above the menu bar.

Source: Parallels Plesk

Figure B-10 *The Joomla! 3 installation file is added by clicking the* **[Q]** *Add New File icon, which opens a standard Browse function screen.*

Step 4.   When the File Manager for the **myfirstsite** directory opens, click **[R]** Browse to locate the Joomla! 3 installation file that was downloaded from joomla.org. Click on it so the **[S]** filename appears next to the Browse button (Figure B-11). (The button may be named differently, depending upon which browser you are using to set up the website server.)

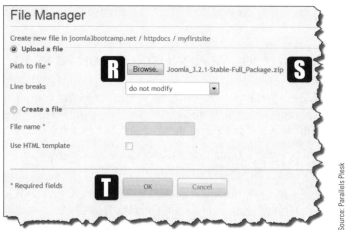

Figure B-11 *The* **[R]** *Browse button accesses your computer to locate the Joomla! 3 installer file that was downloaded. When it's selected, the* **[S]** *filename will appear next to the button.*

UPLOAD TO THE CORRECT LOCATION

The Add New File function is available for any directory on the webserver, so double check to make sure that you are physically in the **myfirstsite** directory before attempting the file upload. Note also that the default selection for the File Manager is Upload a file.

Step 5. With the file selected, click **[T]** OK to start the upload, which may take a while, depending on the speed of your Internet connection.

Step 6. When the upload is completed, the **myfirstsite** directory will display the Joomla! 3! installation filename (Figure B-12).

Figure B-12 *When the upload is completed, the screen will refresh and the* **[U]** *filename will appear as the only file in the* myfirstsite *directory.*

EXERCISE B-4: EXTRACTING THE FILES FROM THE JOOMLA! 3 INSTALLATION FILE

Objective: This exercise extracts the actual Joomla! 3 files from the compressed (ZIP) file that was uploaded in the previous exercise.

Step 1. Select the Joomla! 3 installation file by checking the **[V]** checkbox to the left of the file name (Figure B-13).

Step 2. With the file selected, click the **[W]** Extract Files button to the right of the Search area.

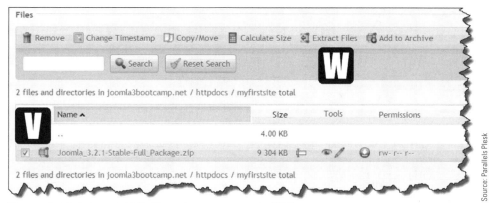

Figure B-13 *Select the* **[V]** *file and then execute the* **[W]** *Extract Files action, which will add the files into the* myfirstsite *directory.*

Step 3. The next screen identifies the **[X]** action being taken and requires a verification of the intended action. Click the **[Y]** Extract Files button to complete it (Figure B-14).

Figure B-14 *On this screen, the* **[X]** *action to be taken is verified and the* **[Y]** *Extract Files button must be clicked to execute the action.*

This action should happen rather quickly and a new screen will show a list of directories and files. Usually, **administrator** is the first directory in the list (Figure B-15). There should be more or less 25 files listed, although this number may vary with different Joomla! 3 versions.

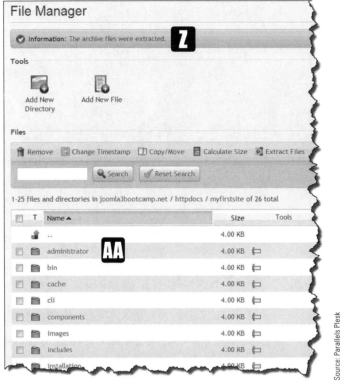

Figure B-15 *The* **[Z]** *success message will display and the directory/file list will show the* **[AA]** administrator *directory at the top.*

EXERCISE B-5: CREATING A MYSQL DATABASE

Objective: This exercise will guide you through the process of creating a MySQL database on the webserver, which will connect to Joomla! 3 during the installation process.

Step 1. If you are not logged in to the Plesk Control Panel, do so now.

Step 2. Access the Control Panel for your domain and verify that you are at the correct location on the webserver.

Step 3. Open the **[BB]** Websites & Domains tab (Figure B-16).

Step 4. Access **[CC]** Databases by clicking on the icon/name to the right of the screen. Also verify the database's domain **[DD]**.

Figure B-16 *The* **[BB]** *Websites & Domains tab opens to the* **[DD]** *domain and provides the link to create a* **[CC]** *database for the website. The domain name should be your domain.*

Step 5. Click on the **[EE]** Add New Database icon (Figure B-17).

Figure B-17 *The* **[EE]** *Add New Database action is required for each domain within the Plesk Control Panel that requires a database, including Joomla! 3.*

Step 6. On the next screen, enter **[FF] joomla3DB** into the Database Name box (Figure B-18). There will also be an option to add a prefix to the database, but you can ignore that. Just clear the box of any text and enter the database name: **joomla3DB**.

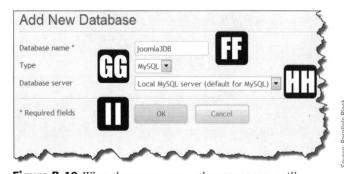

Figure B-18 *When the screen opens, the* **username_** *will appear in the Database Name box. Delete it and enter* **[FF]** *the name of the database, select the type* **[GG]** *and the database server* **[HH]** *, as well as any other parameter settings, and click the* **[II]** *OK action.*

WITH OR WITHOUT A PREFIX

You may see your domain's login username followed by an underscore in the name box. You can put any name in this box. If you keep the default, you can add the actual database name after the underscore. However, when asked for the database name during the installation process, you *must* include the full name as it appears in the box. This is also the case when you're assigning an authorized user to the database. Either way, you use the default with the name you added, or just the name **joomla3DB** by itself.

Step 7. For Type, you should select the **[GG]** MySQL option in the drop-down.

Step 8. The **[HH]** database server should be the local server. This is discussed during the actual Joomla! 3 installation when you're connecting to the database portion of the process.

Step 9. Click **[II]** OK. You should see a success screen when the process is complete (Figure B-19).

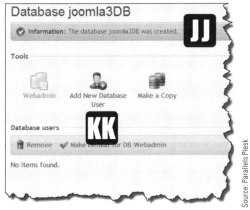

Figure B-19 *The* **[JJ]** *success message displays and the* **[KK]** *Add New Database User icon is available for use.*

At this point, continue the database-creation process by assigning an authorized user, following the steps in Exercise B-6.

EXERCISE B-6: ASSIGNING A USER TO THE MYSQL DATABASE

Objective: This exercise creates a user who is associated with the MySQL database created in Exercise B-5. Every database must have one or more assigned users who are identified with the database during the Joomla! 3 installation. The user must also have a unique password.

Step 1. Click on the **[KK]** Add New Database User icon (Figure B-19).

Step 2. In the Database Username field, enter **[LL]** joomla3U (Figure B-20).

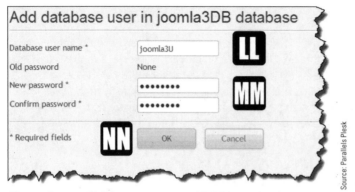

Source: Parallels Plesk

Figure B-20 *A **[LL]** username and a **[MM]** password are required to create a user who is associated with the* joomla3DB *database.*

Step 3. Enter a password into the **[MM]** New Password box and confirm it. The password should consist of upper- and lowercase letters, some numbers, and some non-alphanumeric characters, such as UserNAME2013!%&. You will need this password along with the username and database name during installation.

Step 4. Click **[NN]** OK. You'll see a success screen when the process is complete (Figure B-21).

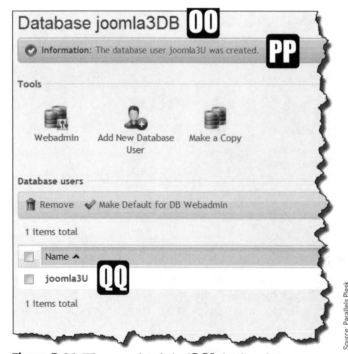

Source: Parallels Plesk

Figure B-21 *When completed, the [**OO**] database has an assigned user as indicated by the **[PP]** success message. The user is identified by **[QQ]** the name created.*

When the assigned user task is completed (Figure B-21), that means the webserver has been configured with the proper files and with the database/user to complete the installation of Joomla! 3.

You properly set up the hosting location with a directory within the website's root. You also created a database with an authorized user. Joomla! 3 is ready to be installed.

To accomplish this task, return to Chapter 2.

Summary

In this appendix, you learned:

◆ How to prepare a hosting location that operates under the Parallels Plesk Control Panel.

◆ How to download the Joomla! 3 installation files from the joomla.org website to your local computer.

◆ How to create a directory within the server root location where Joomla! 3 was installed.

◆ How to upload the Joomla! 3 installer file to the newly created hosting directory.

◆ How to extract the files from the Joomla! 3 installer file.

◆ How to create a MySQL database for the website.

◆ How to create and associate a user with the database.

**FOUND AN ERROR?
SCREENSHOT NOT RIGHT?
NEED A CORRECTION?**

At **joomla3bootcamp.com** there is a section that will list any errata in the book.

If you find somthing wrong, or any page that needs a correction, let us know. A correction will be added to the website.

There is an "Errata Submission" form system on the website to let us know if you find anything.

Index

Index

Index

Index